Symbol	Variable De
D_1	Date 1; also, start date of a coupon pe
D_2	Date 2; also, end date of a coupon pe
T	Time measured in days
T_1	Days to maturity at the beginning of the transaction; also, days in period one
T_2	Days to maturity at the end of the transaction; also, days in period two
$T_1 - T_2$	Days in the financing period
T_{im}	Days from issue to maturity
T_{sm}	Days from settlement to maturity
T_{hp}	Days in the holding period
T_n	Days from settlement to the *n*th coupon payment
T_p	Days from purchase date to maturity date
T_s	Days from sale date to maturity date
T_{ls}	Days from the last coupon date to the settlement date
T_{sn}	Days from the settlement date to the next coupon date
T_t	Terminal date
T_k	Date on which *k*th coupon is paid
$T'_k = T_t - T_k$	Reinvestment period for the *k*th coupon
A_y	Assumed number of days in a year for interest earned; also, the reinvestment period for r_{re}
A_d	Assumed number of days in a year for quoting discounts, typically equal to A_y
A_{ln}	Days in the current coupon period, i.e., days from the last-coupon to the next-coupon date (as measured by the appropriate day-count convention)
N	Number of remaining coupon payments (including the final coupon payment)
w	Number of coupon periods per year
v	The *annuity* variable, which is defined as $v = (1 + y_w)^{-1}$
t_n	$t_n = wD_n/365$
t_{sn}	Fraction of the current coupon period from settlement date to next coupon date: $t_{sn} = T_{sn}/A_{ln}$
D	Duration; also referred to as *effective duration*
D_{mac}	Macaulay duration
D_m	Modified Macaulay duration: $D_m = D_{mac}/(1 + y_w) \approx D$
D_{port}	Duration of a bond portfolio
D_j	Duration of the *j*th bond
$dolD_j$	Dollar duration of the *j*th bond
D_{sd}	Duration of the short-duration bond
D_{ld}	Duration of the long-duration bond
D_{cash}	Duration of cash
M_2	Dispersion
C_x	Convexity
V_{01}	Price value of 1 basis point
V_{32}	Yield value of 1/32
V_j	Market value of the *j*th bond held
V_{sd}	Market value of the short-duration bond
V_{ld}	Market value of the long-duration bond
x	Proportion of sale proceeds to be invested in the long-duration bond

MONEY MARKET AND BOND CALCULATIONS

MONEY MARKET AND BOND CALCULATIONS

Marcia Stigum
and
Franklin L. Robinson

Chicago • London • Singapore

Times Mirror
Higher Education Group

Library of Congress Cataloging-in-Publication Data

Stigum, Marcia L.
Money market and bond calculations / Marcia Stigum and Franklin L. Robinson.
p. cm.
Rev. ed. of: Money market calculations. c1981.
Includes index.
ISBN 1-55623-476-7
1. Investments—Mathematics. 2. Money market—Mathematics. 3. Bonds—Mathematics. I. Robinson, Franklin L. II. Stigum, Marcia L. Money market calculations. III. Title.
HG4515.3.S8 1996 95–47700
332.63'2—dc20

Printed in the United States of America
1 2 3 4 5 6 7 8 9 0 BP 2 1 0 9 8 7 6 5

Everything should be made as simple as possible, but not simpler.

Albert Einstein

PREFACE

The first edition of this book, *Money Market Calculations*, which covered a wide range of calculations, principally for the U.S. money and bond markets, was published in 1981. Since that time, fixed-income markets have evolved considerably.

Today, traders pay much more attention to duration and convexity for single issues as well as for portfolios. Also, the use of various types of floating-rate notes and of index-linked bonds has become common. Finally, due to the growing *internationalization* of money and bond markets, traders and portfolio managers now often find themselves making calculations not only for domestic securities, but for *non-domestic securities*—money market paper and sovereign bonds originating outside their native country.

Hence, in writing *Money Market and Bond Calculations,* we have added new topics and expanded our discussion of other topics as well. In particular, in Chapter 5, we focus on interest-payment conventions and on day-count fractions to set the stage for calculations covering a wider range of securities than that covered in the first version. Also, in our discussion of the bond equation, we give, using an annuity equation, a closed-form solution to the bond equation for price given yield. In addition, we have expanded our discussion of duration and convexity; also, we present closed-form solutions for the calculation of these two risk measures.

We have also added a chapter that describes various types of floating-rate notes and develops price/yield equations for each of them. We do the same for index-linked bonds.

Finally, we have added a chapter that describes the sovereign debt issued by various major countries—the United States, the United Kingdom, France, Germany, Italy, Japan, and Canada as well. In this chapter, we describe the types of securities sold, how they are issued, how they trade in the secondary market, how interest on them is taxed, and what price/yield calculations apply. In sum, we have sought, in *Money Market and Bond Calculations,* to describe and illustrate, as simply and clearly as possible, key calculations for a wide range of fixed-income securities.

This book should be extremely useful to dealers, portfolio managers, brokers, and all others whose work brings them in contact with the money and bond markets, domestic and international. In their daily work, such people constantly need to make calculations of the sort covered in this book.

To add to its usefulness and clarity, *Money Market and Bond Calculations* incorporates several features. First, all key notation used in the book is defined in Chapter 3 and is also reproduced in a table on the endpapers. Second, for money market paper, key formulae are presented, as they are developed, in a *box* to emphasize their importance. Third, all key formulae are listed by page in a table that follows the table of contents.

In the third edition of *The Money Market* (Irwin Professional Publishing, 1990), Stigum presents a comprehensive picture of the U.S. money market, of the U.S. market for governments and agencies, and of the Eurodollar market. *Money Market and Bond Calculations* is meant to complement and to be a companion to *The Money Market.* Therefore, a reader who has not read *The Money Market* may find it useful to read *part or all* of that book before reading *Money Market and Bond Calculations,* especially some of the more technical chapters such as those that deal with the standard bond equation, duration, and convexity.

For centuries, the pronoun *he* has been used by educated speakers and writers of English to mean *person;* and in thc authors' opinion, any attempt to avoid this usage leads to nothing but bad and awkward English. Hence, in this book, we frequently use *he* to denote person.

In finishing this book, we were extremely fortunate to have the assistance of Richard Gill of Eastbridge Capital, who carefully and cheerfully read over the manuscript, checked out formulas and calculations, and added a number of examples. Thanks also to Nancy Humphreys of

Citibank for patiently answering questions about current market products and providing examples. We also thank Gerald Belpaire and Samuel Aizenberg of Decision Software, Inc. for their support and assistance in checking the day-count conventions and various bond and floating-rate equations and Daniel Minerva of Eastbridge Capital, Inc. for his patient support. Needless to say, especially given the propensity of non obvious and confusing typos to rear their ugly heads in a book that contains so many equations and calculations, the authors bear full responsibility for any remaining errors.

Marcia Stigum
Tequesta, Florida
Quechee, Vermont

Franklin Robinson
New York, New York

CONTENTS

CHAPTER 1

INTRODUCTION

When the superficial characteristics of individual transactions are brushed aside, the money and bond markets reduce for all participants—issuers, salespeople, and investors—to a *numbers game*. And as in any numbers game, those who earn the most are those who best understand how to figure odds and to make other simple but important calculations.

Thus, one would expect the majority of money and bond market people to be not only comfortable with but also handy at calculating crucial figures such as the *true yield to maturity* on a short government or federal agency security, the *breakeven rate* on a reverse to maturity, the *tail* on a bill hung out on term repo, or the yield to maturity on longer-term bonds of various ilk. However, only a decade ago, many money and bond market participants had an acute aversion to numbers and refused to generalize results if doing so required that they use even elementary algebra. More recently, with the arrival on Wall Street of *rocket scientists* (*techies* who switched from nuclear physics, electrical engineering, and other high-tech disciplines to finance) and of math-literate MBAs, calculations have become for many a routine part of life on Wall Street. Yet, even today, one can still find some money market and bond market people who shy away from mathematical calculations, especially the less routine ones.

The aversion of some Wall Street (*Street* for short) people to mathematical reasoning has several easily identifiable sources. First, teachers of mathematics seem to have induced in this group, as in others, a healthy case of *terror mathematicus,* the principal symptom of which is the conviction that algebra, not to speak of calculus, is a mysterious, frightening, and difficult discipline that could not conceivably be applied by nonmathematicians to solve simple and important everyday problems.

A second source of the aversion some Street people feel toward mathematical reasoning is the sloppy notation that people who write about money and bond market relationships have chosen to use. A prime example is the following equation taken from the Security Industry Association's *Standard Securities Calculation Methods:*

$$Y = \left[\frac{\left(\frac{RV}{100} + \frac{R}{M} \right) - \left(\frac{P}{100} + \left(\frac{A}{E} \times \frac{R}{M} \right) \right)}{\frac{P}{100} + \left(\frac{A}{E} \times \frac{R}{M} \right)} \right] \times \left[\frac{M \times E}{DSR} \right]$$

To anyone who knows even a little mathematics, the algebra involved in this equation is trivial. However, figuring out what this equation means is difficult. The problem is that the authors use notation that is not mnemonic; consequently, no matter how many times one reads through the equation and the accompanying definitions of terms (omitted here), the equation continues to appear to be so much gibberish. What it in fact says is:

$$\begin{pmatrix} \text{Rate of return} \\ \text{on investment} \end{pmatrix} = \left(\frac{\text{Value at maturity} - \text{Amount invested}}{\text{Amount invested}} \right) \times \begin{pmatrix} \text{An annualizing} \\ \text{factor} \end{pmatrix}$$

This relationship is one that children learn before they leave grade school.

There is *no* reason why money market participants should be victims of *terror mathematicus* or of bad notation. Most of the relationships they need, at least for *cash-market* instruments (as opposed to *futures* and *options*), are simple enough once these relationships are put in comprehensible form, which is precisely what this book does.

One daunting—at least to the neophyte—aspect of money and bond market calculations is that there seem to be so many different instruments traded and so many different types of trades done in the markets for these instruments. There are discount instruments [Treasury bills, bankers' acceptance (BA), commercial paper], floating-rate and fixed-rate notes and bonds, and other money market instruments such as certificates of deposit (CDs), repos, reverses, and buys and sells of Fed funds and of Eurodollar time deposits as well.

Yet another complication is that many of these instruments come in more than one flavor. For example, the set of actively traded, *sovereign bonds* and notes includes not only U.S. Treasury securities but also Japanese government bonds (*JGBs*), U.K. government securities (*gilts*),

German government securities (*Bunds*), and so on. Also, within each major national capital market, there are government agency notes and bonds, and corporate notes and bonds, typically, but not always, denominated in the local currency. Finally, within the vast, unregulated, international Euromarket, there are Euronotes and Eurobonds of various ilk that may be denominated in anything from dollars to *ECUs* (*European Currency Units*).

As might be guessed, when one tosses into the collection of instruments we've listed *foreign exchange* transactions, *spot and forward,* the set of possible trades—*arbitrages* included—becomes immense.[1] In this book, we will limit our analysis to instruments traded for cash, normal, and forward settlement. The purchase of such instruments, be they fixed-rate or floating-rate, can be settled by using either cash or financing—typically repo. Generally, a seller covers a short sale either by doing a reverse or by borrowing bonds. The securities we're about to discuss come denominated in more than one currency, a fact that opens up possibilities for securities-related foreign exchange transactions, spot and forward, and for covered interest arbitrage. Fortunately, the math of all this—which is the topic of this book—is quite simple.

Futures and options are also traded in fixed-income land. In this book, we do not, for several reasons, cover these instruments. Many good books have already been written about the *Black-Scholes* (*BS*) model, which is the standard options-pricing model; also, this model cannot, unfortunately, be reduced to simple math. Finally, no one on the Street is content to use the BS model for pricing options except for simple, short-term options. For more complex and longer-term options, every dealer uses option-pricing models developed by in-house quants. Dealers regard such proprietary models as *top secret,* so one can say next to nothing, about the pros and cons of the options-pricing models used by one dealer versus those used by another.

Formerly, one could discuss, using simple math, futures trades and arbitrages that utilized futures. However, many financial futures contracts carry *imbedded options.* And, today, futures contracts are priced taking into account the value—positive or negative—of any options embedded

[1]A *forward trade* differs from a *futures trade* in that the former is not done on an organized commodities exchange whereas the latter is. In the above context, *spot* refers to trades done for *immediate settlement* as opposed to *forward settlement.*

in them. Thus, since we aren't going to talk about options pricing, we can't really talk about the pricing of most futures contracts.

ROAD MAP FOR THE READER

So as to lose no reader of this book, no matter how new to the markets, we begin Part 1 with a discussion of fundamentals. Knowledgeable readers may want to skip some of this part, but Chapter 3 should be read carefully by all, since it is there that we introduce much of the *notation* that we use throughout this book. *For the reader's convenience, we reproduce our notation on the front- and backend papers of this book.*

Chapter 5 is another chapter in this book that should be read carefully by all. There, we discuss interest-payment conventions and day-count fractions, topics that are crucial to understanding the *precise* pricing of the myriad of differing instruments we're going to discuss; for example, many bonds fall within the general category of *sovereign* bonds, but not all such bonds accrue and pay interest in the same way.

In Part 2 of this book, we develop important price/yield relationships for discount and interest-bearing money market paper. Also, for each cash instrument we discuss, we give examples of how these relationships can be used in practical and common situations to derive breakeven and other key numbers.

In Part 3, we focus first on *commonly used concepts of yield.* Second, *we develop the standard bond equation,* which is the equation most commonly used worldwide for making price/yield calculations for notes and bonds. Our discussion of the bond equation also shows how, by using an annuity equation, we can restate the relationship for price, given yield, as a closed-form solution.

In Part 4, we delve into more advanced topics regarding bonds. Specifically, we discuss *carry,* various measures of *duration, convexity,* and the ways in which the latter two measures of risk can be applied in practical arbitrage and portfolio-management situations. Also, we again use an annuity equation to derive a closed-form expression both for duration and for convexity.

Finally, in Part 5, we focus on fixed-income securities worldwide. Specifically, we discuss *covered interest arbitrage, floating-rate notes* (FRNs), and the various calculations that pertain thereto; lastly, we provide descriptions of and calculations for the *sovereign debt* issued by major countries worldwide.

The reader will find that the examples that we give in this book assume *yields ranging from low to high.* We do this for several reasons: first, interest rates vary widely over time; second, the impact of many operations we discuss (e.g., switching from yield on a discount basis to yield on a simple-interest basis) is greater the higher the level of yield assumed.

The money market is an innovative place, and those who participate in it are constantly developing new instruments, approaches, and transactions. Consequently, no book could give an equation to cover every possible situation, and this book does not purport to do so. What it does offer the careful reader is a kit of simple analytic tools that he can use to solve particular problems as they arise.

ABBREVIATIONS

To hold down verbiage, we will use several common market abbreviations throughout this book. First, we use, as does every trader on his trade tickets, M *to denote thousand,* where thousand is associated with a specific par amount for which a trade is done. Thus, if a trade of a specific long bond were done for a par amount equal to $5,000, that trade would be written up as 5M of that issue. Consistent with this practice, money market traders also use the abbreviation MM *to denote million.* Thus, 5 million par of the 3-month bill becomes 5MM of 3-month bills. In wholesale transactions in securities denominated in U.S. dollars and most other major currencies, transactions are typically in thousands or millions, and M and MM are thus the abbreviations that we'll use most often. However, when we speak about money and bond market transactions denominated in Japanese yen or Italian lire, we'll often be talking about transactions that run into the billions. In that case, we will use b *to denote billion;* thus, 2 billion yen of JGBs becomes ¥2b of JGBs.

A basis point equals 1 one-hundredth of a percentage point, that is, 0.0001. Again, following common market practice, we will use bp to denote basis points where they are associated with a specific number. Thus, 10 basis points becomes 10bp.

Traders and others in fixed-income land tend to write and to *talk* about months using abbreviations such as Feb, Aug, and Sep. To reflect this practice, we'll write such abbreviations without any following period. For example, we'll talk about bonds that mature in Feb 02 (February 2002).[2]

A MARKET OVERVIEW

One last note: Anyone desiring a complete description of the money market, U.S. and Euro, should read the third edition of *The Money Market,* by Marcia Stigum (Burr Ridge, IL: Irwin Professional Publishing, 1990). This book is written as a companion to and an extension of that book.

We have tried to make the second edition of *Money Market and Bond Calculations* a stand-alone book, but in some chapters of this book, such as those on duration and convexity, we thought it inappropriate to start with a truly elementary introduction to the concept discussed. In fact, by the time we get to Part 4, we are implicitly assuming that the reader is familiar with certain basic money and bond market concepts. Any reader who's unfamiliar with a given concept such as duration, should turn to the discussion of that concept in Stigum's *The Money Market* before she reads, in the present book, our discussion of calculations based on that concept.

THE NEXT CHAPTER

To set the stage for the many calculations we present later in this book, we give, in the next chapter, a quick rundown of the various types of *straight* (no imbedded options), fixed-income instruments traded in the money and bond markets.

---

[2]A bond market trader, in talking about these bonds, would, for example, refer to them as *the Feb ooh twos.*

PART 1

SOME FUNDAMENTALS

CHAPTER 2

THE INSTRUMENTS IN BRIEF

Here's a quick rundown of the major money and bond market instruments discussed in this book. Don't look for subtleties; we say just enough to lay the groundwork for later chapters.

DEALERS AND BROKERS

The markets for all money market instruments are made in part by brokers and dealers. *Brokers* bring buyers and sellers together for a commission. By definition, brokers never position securities. Their function is to provide a communications network that links market participants who are often numerous and geographically dispersed. Most brokering in the money and bond markets occurs between banks that are buying funds from or selling funds to each other and between dealers in money market instruments and bonds.

Dealers make markets in money market instruments and bonds by quoting—to each other, to issuers, and to investors—bid and asked prices at which they are prepared to buy and to sell. Whenever a dealer trades securities, he is acting as *principal,* that is he trades for his own account; thus, assuming positions—long and short—is an essential part of dealing. Naturally, when a dealer goes long or short, he hopes to profit: to later *sell* at a *higher* price securities he goes *long* or to later *buy* at a lower *price* securities he *shorts.*

Dealers also act as *agents* in the issuance of commercial paper and medium-term notes (MTNs), including bank deposit notes. To say that a dealer acts as an agent in the issuance of new paper means that, through his distribution network, he sells to investors for a *fee* (or commission) new paper that an issuer wants distributed. In this case, the dealer is representing the issuer rather than dealing with him as principal. Like a broker, a dealer acting strictly as agent does not position. It is, however, not unusual for a dealer to act both as agent and principal in the same market. For example, a dealer will typically act as an agent in distributing MTNs, that is, in the *new issue market* for MTNs, but as principal when, to provide market liquidity, he makes bids for and offers of outstanding MTNs. A market in which outstanding issues are traded is referred to as a *secondary market.*

U.S. TREASURY SECURITIES

To finance the U.S. national debt, the Treasury issues several types of securities. Some are nonnegotiable, for example, savings bonds sold to consumers and special issues sold to government trust funds. The bulk of the securities sold by the U.S. Treasury are, however, negotiable.

What form these securities take depends on their maturity. Those with a maturity at issue of a year or less are known as *Treasury bills, T bills* for short or just plain *bills.* T bills bear no interest. An investor in bills earns a return because bills are issued at a *discount from* face value and redeemed by the Treasury at maturity for *full* face value. The amount of the discount at which a given bill issue trades and its time to maturity together imply some specific yield that bills of that issue will pay an investor who holds them to maturity.

T bills are currently issued in 3-month, 6-month, and 1-year maturities.[1] In issuing bills, the Treasury does not set the amount of the discount. Instead, the Federal Reserve auctions off each new bill issue to investors and dealers, with the bills going to those bidders offering the highest price; that is, the lowest interest cost to the Treasury. By auctioning new bill issues, the Treasury lets current market conditions establish the yield at which each new issue is sold.

The Treasury also issues interest-bearing *notes*. These securities are issued at or very near face value and redeemed at face value. Notes have an *original maturity* (maturity at issue) of 2 to 10 years.[2] Interest on Treasury notes is paid semiannually. Notes, like bills, are sold through

---

[1] For tactical debt-management purposes, the Treasury occasionally meets gaps in its cash flow by issuing very short-term *cash management bills.*

[2] A five-year note has an *original maturity* at issue of five years. One year after issue, it has a *current maturity* of four years.

auctions held by the Federal Reserve. Thus, the coupon rate on a new Treasury note, like the rate of discount on a new T bill, is determined by the market.

In addition to notes, the Treasury issues interest-bearing *bonds* that have a maturity at issue of 30 years. The only difference between Treasury notes and bonds is that bonds are issued with a longer original maturity. Treasury bonds, like T notes, are normally sold at yield auctions.

Banks, other financial institutions, insurance companies, corporations, pension funds, and mutual funds (including money market funds) are all important investors in U.S. Treasury securities. So too are foreign central banks and other foreign institutions. The market for government securities is largely a wholesale market; and especially at the short end, multimillion dollar transactions are common. However, when interest rates get extremely high, as they did in 1974 and again in 1978 to 1982, individuals with small amounts to invest are drawn into the market.

Because of the high volume of Treasury debt outstanding, the market for bills and short-term government securities is the most active and most carefully watched sector of the U.S. money market. At the heart of this market, stands a varied collection of dealers who make the market for *governments* (market jargon for government securities) by standing ready to buy and sell huge amounts of these securities. These dealers trade actively not only with investors but also with each other. Most trades of the latter sort are carried out through brokers.

Governments offer investors several advantages. First, because they are constantly traded in the *secondary market* in large volume and at narrow spreads between the bid and asked prices, they are highly *liquid.* Second, governments are considered to be free from credit risk because it is inconceivable that the government would default on them in any situation short of destruction of the country. Third, interest income on governments is exempt from taxation by the states that comprise the United States. Because of these advantages, bills and governments normally trade at yields below those yields at which paper issued by private credits trade.

The Yield Curve

Generally, yields on governments are higher the longer their *current maturity,* that is, time left to maturity. The reason is that the longer the current maturity of a debt security, the more its price will fluctuate in response to changes in interest rates and therefore, the greater the *price risk* to which it exposes the investor. There are times, however, when the *yield curve* inverts, that is, yields on short-term securities rise above those on long-term securities. This, for example, was the case during much of the period from 1979 to 1981 and again in 1989 and mid-1995. The reason for an inverted yield curve is that market participants anticipate, correctly or incorrectly, that interest rates will fall. As a result, borrowers choose to borrow short-term while investors seek out long-term securities; the result is that supply and demand force short-term rates above long-term rates.

30-Year Bills, Alias STRIPs

In the late 1980s, the Treasury permitted the creation, out of standard T bonds, of what amounted to T bills with distant maturities. Here's the story.

The Treasury once issued, upon request, notes and bonds in bearer form. Some dealers came up with the idea of *stripping*—clipping off coupons from—bearer bonds and selling, at discounted prices, the resulting pieces. Each such piece was a *noninterest-bearing security with a fixed maturity and a fixed value at maturity*. Such securities are known generically as *zero-coupon securities* or simply as *zeros.*

Dealers could make money stripping bearer Treasuries because demand for the pieces was so great that the sum of the values of the pieces exceeded the value of the whole bond. Unfortunately, the Treasury and the Federal Reserve opposed, for various reasons (including possibilities for tax evasion), the stripping of bearer Treasuries.

To satisfy investors' desire for long-term zeros, Merrill Lynch got a bright idea: It bought Treasuries, placed them with a custodian in a special trust, and then sold to investors participations in its trust. Under the Merrill scheme, each such participation sold was a *zero-coupon security,* backed by unstripped Treasuries. Merrill named its product TIGRs. Soon, every other major dealer was offering its addition to the *zoo.* Salomon Brothers (Sali) sold CATs; Shearson Lehman Brothers, LIONs; and so on. Also, some dealers sold plain vanilla TRs (Trust Receipts).

The new zoo zeros sold extremely well to institutional investors and even to individuals. The Treasury, eyeing this success, said, "There's money to be made in stripping, let *us* earn it." So in 1985, for certain new T-bond issues, the Treasury introduced an additional feature: Any owner of such a bond—Merrill, a small dealer, or even an individual—could ask the Treasury to cut that bond into pieces, provided it was in book-entry (electronic-recordkeeping) form. Each such piece corresponds to a different payment due on the bond, and each carries its own CUSIP (ID) number.[3] On a 30-year bond, there are 61 such payments: 60 semiannual coupon payments and 1 payment of *corpus* (principal) at maturity. Stripped Treasuries created in the manner we've just described were dubbed STRIPs.

Today, on Wall Street, STRIPs are a popular item. They are actively traded by the same dealers who make markets in regular Treasury notes, bonds, and bills.

Internationalization of the Market for Treasuries

Once, when one spoke of *the* market for Treasuries, one was referring to a market that was almost exclusively domestic. The borrower was domestic and so too were most of the investors, except for a few foreign central banks. Today, that situation has changed dramatically. Non-U.S. investors have become big buyers of Treasury securities.

Not surprisingly, there are now active markets for Treasuries in Tokyo, in London, and, to a lesser extent, in certain other foreign financial centers. Today, the market for these securities has become a 24-hour international market. The dealers who make this round-the-globe market are of two sorts: big American dealers, such as Merrill and Sali, who have opened offices in major financial centers around the globe, and non-U.S. dealers who have opened offices in the United States and become a big factor in the domestic and international trading of Treasury securities.

Treasury Futures

In discussing the market for governments, we have focused on the *cash market,* that is, the market in which existing securities are traded for same- or next-day delivery. In addition, there are markets in which

[3] CUSIP is an acronym for the Committee on Uniform Securities Identification Procedures. Treasury securities, most federal credit agencies (including mortgage banks), municipal bonds, corporate stocks, and corporate bonds all have identifying CUSIP numbers. These numbers are assigned, for a fee, by Standard & Poor's.

Treasury bills, notes, and bonds are traded for *future* delivery. The futures contracts in Treasuries that are actively traded are for 3-month bills with a face value of $1MM at maturity and for notes and long bonds with a par value of $100,000.[4]

FEDERAL AGENCY SECURITIES

From time to time, Congress becomes concerned about the volume of credit that's available to various sectors of the economy and the terms on which that credit is available. Congress's usual response is to set up a federal agency to provide credit to that sector. Thus, the Federal Home Loan Bank System lends to the nation's savings and loan associations, Banks for Cooperatives make seasonal and term loans to farm cooperatives, Federal Land Banks give mortgages on farm properties, and so on.

Initially, all the federal agencies financed their activities by selling their own securities in the open market. Today, all except the largest borrow from the Treasury through an institution called the Federal Financing Bank. Those agencies still borrowing in the open market do so primarily by issuing notes and bonds. These securities (known in the market as *agencies*) bear interest, and they are issued and redeemed at face value. Instead of using the auction technique for issuing their securities, federal agencies typically look to the market to determine the best yield at which they can sell a new issue, put that yield on the issue, and then sell it through a syndicate of dealers. Some agencies also sell short-term discount paper that resembles Treasury bills.

Normally, agencies yield slightly more than Treasury securities of the same maturity for several reasons. First, agency issues are smaller than Treasury issues and are therefore less liquid. Second, while all agency issues have de facto backing from the federal government (it's inconceivable that the government would let one of them default on its obligations), the securities of only a few agencies are explicitly backed by the full faith and credit of the U.S. government. Third, interest income on some federal agency issues is subject to state taxation.

The market for agencies, while smaller than that for governments, is an active and important sector of the U.S. credit market. Agencies are

[4] MM is an abbreviation for million, one that's commonly used in the money and bond markets.

traded by the same dealers that trade U.S. governments and in much the same way.

OTHER SOVEREIGN DEBT

Every country issues its own *sovereign debt.* In this book, we will cover calculations not only for U.S. government securities but also for the securities issued by governments in major countries whose debt securities are widely bought by nondomestic investors; such countries include the United Kingdom, France, Germany, Italy, Japan, and Canada.

The types of sovereign debt securities issued by these countries varies widely. In addition to standard bills and fixed-rate notes and bonds, one also finds floating-rate notes, index-linked bonds, perpetual bonds, and so on.

FEDERAL FUNDS

In the United States, all banks and other *depository institutions* (savings and loan associations, savings banks, credit unions, and foreign bank branches) are required to keep reserves on deposit at their district Federal Reserve Bank.[5] The reserve account of a depository institution (*DI* for short) is much like an individual's checking account; the DI makes deposits into its reserve account and can transfer funds out of it. The main difference is that, while an individual can let the balance in his checking account run to zero and stay there, each DI is required by law to maintain some *minimum* average balance in its reserve account over the week—Wednesday to Wednesday. That minimum average balance is based on the total deposits of various types held by the DI during the current settlement week.

The category of DIs that holds by far the largest chunk of the total reserves that all DIs together maintain at Federal Reserve Banks is

---

[5] The Federal Reserve System, which comprises 12 district Federal Reserve Banks, is the U.S. central bank, and as such it is responsible for the implementation of domestic monetary policy. Prior to passage of the Monetary Control Act of 1980, only *member banks* in the Federal Reserve System were required to hold reserves at the Fed.

commercial banks. Funds on deposit in a bank's (or other DI's) reserve account are referred to as *Federal funds* or *Fed funds*. Any deposits a bank receives add to its supply of Fed funds, while loans made and securities purchased reduce that supply. Thus, the basic amount of money any U.S. bank can lend out or otherwise invest equals the total funds it has received from depositors minus the reserves it's required to maintain.

For some banks, this supply of available funds roughly equals the amount they choose to invest in securities plus that demanded from them by borrowers. But for most banks it does not. Specifically, because the nation's largest corporations tend to concentrate their borrowing in big money market banks in New York and other financial centers, the loans and investments these banks must fund exceed the deposits they receive. Many smaller banks, in contrast, receive more money from local depositors than they can lend locally or choose to invest otherwise. Because large banks have to meet their reserve requirements regardless of what loan demand they face and because excess reserves yield no return to smaller banks, it was natural for large banks to begin borrowing the excess funds held by smaller banks.

This borrowing is done in the *Federal funds market*. Most loans of Fed funds are overnight transactions. One reason is that the amount of excess funds a given lending bank holds varies daily and unpredictably. Some transactions in Fed funds are made directly, others through New York brokers. Despite the fact that transactions of this sort are all loans, the lending of Fed funds is referred to as a *sale* and the borrowing of Fed funds as a *purchase*. While overnight transactions dominate the Fed funds market, transactions for longer periods also occur there. Fed funds traded for longer periods are referred to as *term* Fed funds.

DIs other than domestic commercial banks also participate in the Fed funds market. Foreign banks are particularly active buyers and sellers of funds.

The rate of interest paid on overnight loans of Federal funds, which is called the *Fed funds rate,* is a key interest rate in the money market; all other short-term rates relate to the funds rate. The Fed used to closely peg the funds rate, but starting in October 1979, the Fed allowed this rate to fluctuate over a wide band; in more recent years, the Fed has gone back to pegging the Fed funds rate.

REPOS AND REVERSES

Various bank and nonbank dealers act as market makers in governments, agencies, CDs, and BAs. Because dealers, by definition, buy and sell for their own accounts, active dealers inevitably end up holding some securities. They will, moreover, buy and hold substantial positions if they believe that interest rates are likely to fall and that the value of these securities is therefore likely to rise. Speculation and risk taking are an inherent and important part of being a dealer.

While dealers have significant amounts of capital, the positions they take are often a large multiple of that amount. As a result, dealers have to borrow to finance their positions. Using the securities they own as collateral, they can and do borrow from banks at the dealer loan rate. For the bulk of their financing, however, they resort to a cheaper alternative, entering into *repurchase agreements* (*repos,* for short) with investors.

Much repo financing done by dealers is on an overnight basis. It works as follows: The dealer finds a corporation, money fund, or other investor who has funds to invest overnight. He sells this investor, say, $10MM of securities for roughly $10MM, which is paid in Federal funds to his bank by the investor's bank against delivery of the securities sold. At the same time, the dealer agrees to repurchase these securities the next day at a slightly higher price. Thus, the buyer of the securities is in effect making the dealer a one-day loan secured by the obligations sold to him. The difference between the purchase and sale prices on the repo transaction is the interest the investor earns on his loan. Alternatively, the purchase and sale prices in a repo transaction may be identical; in that case, the dealer pays the investor an explicit rate of interest.

Often, a dealer will take a speculative position that he intends to hold for some time. He might then do a repo for 30 days or longer. Such agreements are known as *term* repos.

From the point of view of investors, overnight loans in the repo market offer several attractive features. First, by rolling overnight repos, investors can keep surplus funds invested without losing liquidity or incurring price risk. Second, because repo transactions are secured by top-quality paper, investors expose themselves to little or no credit risk.

The overnight repo rate generally is less than the Fed funds rate. The reason is that the many nonbank investors who have funds to invest overnight or very short term and who do not want to incur any price risk, have nowhere to go but the repo market because (with the exception of S&Ls and other DIs) they cannot participate directly in the Fed funds market. Also, lending money through a repo transaction is safer than selling Fed funds because a sale of Fed funds is an unsecured loan.

On term, as opposed to overnight, repos, investors still have the advantage of their loans being secured, but they do lose some liquidity. To compensate for that, the rate on a repo transaction is generally higher the longer the term for which funds are lent.

Banks that make dealer loans fund them by buying Fed funds, and the lending rate they charge—which is adjusted daily—is the prevailing Fed funds rate plus a ⅛ to ¼ markup. Because the overnight repo rate is lower than the Fed funds rate, dealers can finance their positions more cheaply by doing repos than by borrowing from banks.

A dealer who is bullish on the market will position large amounts of securities. If he's bearish, he will *short* the market, that is, sell securities he doesn't own. Since the dealer has to deliver any securities he sells whether he owns them or not, a dealer who shorts has to borrow securities one way or another. The most common technique today for borrowing securities is to do what's called a *reverse repo,* or simply a *reverse.* To obtain securities through a reverse, a dealer finds an investor holding the required securities; he then buys these securities from the investor under an agreement that he will resell the same securities to the investor at a fixed price on some future date. In this transaction, the dealer, besides obtaining securities, is extending a loan to the investor for which he is paid some rate of interest.

A repo and a reverse are identical transactions. What a given transaction is called depends on who initiates it; typically, if a dealer hunting money does, it's a repo; if a dealer hunting securities does, it's a reverse.

A final note: The Fed uses reverses and repos with dealers in government securities to adjust the level of bank reserves.

BONDS BORROWED

A dealer who shorts securities may also do a *bonds borrowed* trade to obtain securities to cover his short. In this case, the dealer who's short borrows securities from an institutional investor who's willing to lend securities from his portfolio; in return, for the term of the trade, the dealer generally (1) gives the lender of securities collateral equal in value to the bonds he's borrowed and (2) pays the lender a 50bp fee.[6]

To keep reverses and bonds borrowed straight, remember this: *a reverse is a swap of cash for collateral* whereas *bonds borrowed is a swap of collateral for collateral.* In recent years, repos, reverses, and securities lending have been increasingly used in international, cross-border transactions.

EURODOLLARS

Many foreign banks will accept deposits of dollars and grant the depositor an account *denominated in dollars.* So, too, will the foreign branches of U.S. banks. The practice of accepting dollar-denominated deposits outside of the United States began in Europe, so such deposits came to be known as *Eurodollars.* The practice of accepting dollar-denominated deposits later spread to Hong Kong, Singapore, the Middle East, and other centers around the globe. Consequently, today, *a Eurodollar deposit is simply a deposit denominated in dollars in a bank or bank branch outside the United States,* and the term *Eurodollar* has become a misnomer. To make things even more confusing, in December 1981, domestic and foreign banks operating in the United States, were permitted to open *international banking facilities* (*IBFs*) in the United States. Dollars deposited in IBFs are also Eurodollars.

Most Eurodollar deposits are for large sums. They are made by corporations—foreign, multinational, and domestic; foreign central banks and other official institutions; U.S. domestic banks; and wealthy individuals. With the exception of *call money,* all Eurodeposits have a fixed term, which can range from overnight to five years.[7] The bulk of Eurodollar transactions are in the range of six months and under. Banks receiving Eurodollar deposits use them to make loans denominated in dollars to foreign and domestic corporations, foreign governments and government agencies, domestic U.S. banks, and other large borrowers.

Banks that participate in the Eurodollar market actively borrow and lend Euros among themselves, just as domestic banks borrow and lend in

---

[6] A basis point equals 1/100 of 1%. A common abbreviation for basis points is *bp.* Thus, a 50bp fee should be read as a 50 basis point fee.

[7] Call money is money deposited in an interest-bearing account that can be called (withdrawn) by the depositor on a day's notice.

the Fed funds market. The major difference between the two markets is that in the market for Fed funds, most transactions are on an overnight basis, whereas in the Euromarket, interbank placements (deposits) of funds for longer periods are common.

For a domestic U.S. bank with a reserve deficiency, borrowing Eurodollars is an alternative to purchasing Fed funds. Also, for a domestic bank with excess funds, a *Europlacement* (i.e., a deposit of dollars in the Euromarket) is an alternative to the sale of Fed funds. Consequently, the rate on overnight Euros tends to closely track the Fed funds rate. It is also true that, as one goes out on the maturity scale, Euro rates continue to track U.S. rates, though less closely than in the overnight market.

Eurodollar Futures

Currently, *futures* for 3-month Eurodollar deposits are actively traded in Chicago, London, and Singapore.

FRAs

In recent years, Eurodollar futures have been joined by an over-the-counter (OTC) product known as a *forward rate agreement* (FRA, pronounced like *frog* with no *g*). Under a FRA, two parties agree to trade a specific amount of Euros for a specified period at a specified rate on a specified future date. For example, the parties might agree to trade 5MM of 3-month Euros 2 months hence at a rate of 4.50. What distinguishes a FRA from a forward trade is that when the future date specified in the FRA agreement arrives, no Eurodeposit changes hands. Instead, there is a cash settlement. A FRA thus turns out to be not a forward trade, but an OTC futures contract that permits cash settlement only, not delivery.

COMMERCIAL PAPER

While some cash-rich industrial firms participate in the bond and money markets only as lenders, other such firm must, at times, borrow to finance either current operations or expenditures on plant and equipment. One source of short-term funds available to a corporation is bank loans. Large firms with good credit ratings, however, have an alternative source of funds that is cheaper, namely, the sale of commercial paper.

Commercial paper is an unsecured promissory note issued for a specific amount and maturing on a specific day. All commercial paper is negotiable, but most paper sold to investors is held to maturity. Commercial paper is issued not only by industrial and manufacturing firms but also by finance companies. Finance companies normally sell their paper directly to investors. Industrial firms, in contrast, typically issue their paper through dealers. Over the years, bank-holding companies, municipalities, and municipal authorities have joined the ranks of commercial paper issuers.

The maximum maturity for which commercial paper may be sold is 270 days, since paper with a longer maturity must be registered with the Securities and Exchange Commission (SEC), a time-consuming and costly procedure. In practice, very little 270-day paper is sold. Most paper sold is in the range of 30 days and under.

Since commercial paper has such short maturities, the issuer rarely will have sufficient funds coming in before the paper matures to pay off his borrowing. Instead, he expects to *roll* his paper, that is, sell new paper to obtain funds to pay off his maturing paper. Naturally, the possibility exists that some sudden change in market conditions, such as when the Penn Central went belly-up (bankrupt), might make it difficult or impossible for him to sell his paper for some time. To guard against this risk, commercial paper issuers back all or a large proportion of their outstanding paper with lines of credit from banks.

The rate offered on commercial paper depends on its maturity, on how much the issuer wants to borrow, on the general level of money market rates, and on the credit rating of the issuer. Almost all commercial paper is rated with respect to credit risk by one or more of several rating services: Moody's, Standard & Poor's, and Fitch. While only top-grade credits can get ratings good enough to sell paper these days, there is still a slight risk that an issuer might go bankrupt. Because of this and because of lesser liquidity, yields on commercial paper are higher than those on Treasury obligations of similar maturity.

Over the years, one pronounced change that has occurred in the domestic commercial-paper market is that an increasing number of foreign entities, sovereigns, government agencies, banks, and corporates have taken to selling commercial paper in the U.S. money market. Some do so to raise dollars; others swap the dollars they get into their native currency.

In recent years, the growth in commercial paper outstanding has outstripped that of any other money market security with the result that the commercial-paper market is now bigger than the Treasury-bill market.

So long as banks were regarded as top-quality credits and made loans at tight spreads off Euro interbank rates, there was little or no opportunity for the growth in London of a market in Euro commercial paper. However, in recent years, conditions have changed. Banks are out of favor with investors; sovereigns, corporates, and others are in favor. Consequently, the spread has gone out of a lot of Eurobank lending, and a viable market in *Euro commercial paper* finally seems to be developing. Borrowers in this market cover the lot: They include sovereigns, government agencies, top corporate credits, and lower-quality corporate credits; they are domiciled anywhere from Iceland to Amman, but principally in Europe and the United States.

INTEREST-RATE SWAPS

The rate that a borrower must pay depends on his credit, whether he wants to borrow fixed-rate or floating-rate money, and on the term for which he wants to borrow. Generally, if a would-be borrower is a particularly good credit, he will find not only that he is able to borrow more cheaply than other borrowers can but also that the advantage he enjoys over other borrowers in the rate he gets will be greatest when he borrows at a *fixed rate* for three to five years or longer. To reap the maximum benefit from his privileged access to the capital market, that's how a good credit should borrow. In contrast, a lesser credit will find that, when he borrows medium- to longer-term funds, his poor rating will penalize him least if he borrows at a *variable rate*.

Often, a top credit, say, a J. P. Morgan to pick a bank name, will find that its comparative advantage lies in borrowing medium-term, fixed-rate money, whereas what it really wants to borrow is variable-rate money. Meanwhile somewhere, some single B corporate will be saying, "The penalty I have to pay for borrowing medium term at a fixed rate is awfully high, but fixed-rate money is what I really need." This sets the stage, realized a few prescient dealers in the early 1980s, for a *liability swap*. The triple-A credit borrows medium term at a fixed rate; the single-B credit borrows medium term at a variable rate; and then in effect, they *swap liabilities*—more precisely they swap, on negotiated terms, the future interest-rate payments each contracts to pay.

Surprisingly, such a swap is *not a zero-sum game*. Far from it, the situation is a perfect example of the gains that can be realized from specialization along lines of comparative advantage (recall that David Ricardo based his famous argument for free trade on differences in national comparative advantage, and the argument for free trade still stands today on that same ground). Triple A and single B can together reduce their joint costs of borrowing by each borrowing in the market when they get the best terms; then, using a swap, they can divvy up the savings they have realized *and* each ends up with the type of liability wanted in the first place.

All this may sound a touch esoteric and theoretical, but it's the basis in a nutshell of a business that grew during the 1980s from a zero base into one where outstandings are now measured in the hundreds of billions.

The swap we've just described, fixed for floating, is known as a *coupon swap*. A natural variation of this swap is to a *cross-currency swap*. Depending on who a borrower is, what currency he wants to borrow, and whether he wants to pay fixed or floating, it may be cheaper for him to do one sort of borrowing in one currency and then, via a swap or swaps, end up with a different borrowing in a different currency. For example, a borrower wanting to borrow dollars at a floating rate might find that his cheapest alternative is to borrow fixed-rate Swissy, swap it into fixed-rate dollars, and then do a fixed-to-floating coupon swap. The possibilities are endless and exist thanks to all sorts of market anomalies: differences in the terms at which corporates may borrow in different markets (e.g., Spain lacks a corporate bond market), differences in the way credits are perceived in different markets (e.g., to a German lender, Lufthansa is *the* national flag carrier, not just another credit), national differences in accounting practices or in tax policies, and so on.

As the swap market grew, swap terms became standardized. Today, swaps are quoted at Treasuries plus, with the understanding that the Treasuries-plus rate is the fixed rate for a swap against *LIBOR*, the *London Interbank Offered Rate* for Eurodollar deposits (there are many LIBORs—1-month LIBOR, 3-month LIBOR, and so on). Those terms would leave a borrower in the commercial paper market who wanted to pay fixed, as a number of paper issuers do, with a spread risk: the spread of the LIBOR to the commercial paper rate. To eliminate that risk, the commercial paper issuer would first swap floating to floating—the commercial paper rate to LIBOR—and then he'd swap floating to fixed—LIBOR to Treasuries plus.

A borrower, unless he happens to also be, say, a bank dealer in swaps, lacks the resources to follow all of the ins and outs of and the opportunities in the swap market. So swaps are a big business for dealers who concoct sometimes complex swaps. Every big swap dealer—both bank and nonbank dealers are active in this business—runs a hedged swap book. Banks also use unhedged swaps as a tool of gap management.

The swap business began with the swapping of liabilities. Then, some entrepreneurial type recalled that what's good for the goose is good for the gander, and *asset swaps* were born. In the past, an investor who held a fixed-rate, Canadian dollar bond and who said, "Hey, what I'd really like to be in at this moment is Aussi-dollar, floating-rate paper," would figure that to make the switch he'd have to sell his Canadian bonds, do a foreign exchange transaction, and buy Aussi paper. His friendly corporate finance swap advisor—bank or nonbank—now tells him otherwise: With a swap or two, he can get from the asset he has to a *synthetic* version of the asset he desires; and when the play he wants to make has run its course, he can return to his initial position simply by reversing the swaps he's put on. Today, asset swaps are a rapidly expanding part of the swap business.

OPTIONS

Over the years, another innovation in the money market has been the introduction of trading in *options,* rights to buy or to sell at a fixed price over a preset period, certain money market securities and futures contracts for such securities. Options, like futures, are actively traded by hedgers, speculators, and arbitrageurs.

The most actively exchange-traded options are options on futures contracts. There are also over-the-counter (OTC) options traded on cash governments.

The area in which dealers stand to make the biggest profit is in selling proprietary products. A dealer might, for example, sell a borrower a *cap* on the rate he must pay over time on a variable-rate loan priced at a spread to LIBOR. Such a cap is simply a series of options: on each rate-reset date, the cap gives the borrower the right to pay either the cap rate or the formula, loan-agreement rate, whichever is lower. A *floor* in contrast is a series of options that promises a receiver of a variable rate the right to receive either the floor rate or the formula variable rate, whichever is higher. A *collar* is a cap *cum* floor that holds a rate within a given range.

In selling an option product, a dealer assumes a risk for which he naturally charges a fee. Since the risk is often large, so too is the fee. One way a borrower might use a collar would be to reduce the net fee he pays for buying a cap by collecting a fee for selling a floor.

Dealers trade option products in a *book* in which they generally seek to maintain a hedged position. Because of their peculiar nature, an option—except when a dealer is lucky enough to have one option position that's the mirror image of another—is far more difficult to hedge than is a straight security. A testimony to the difficulty of both pricing and hedging options, particularly options on complex products, is the fact that more than one big house has taken a major bath in its options book.

The most recent option product to become faddish is a *swaption,* which is an option on an interest-rate swap.

CERTIFICATES OF DEPOSIT AND DEPOSIT NOTES

The maximum rate banks may pay on savings deposits and time deposits (a time deposit is a deposit with a fixed maturity) used to be set by the Fed through *Regulation Q*. Essentially, what Reg Q did was to make it impossible for banks and other depository institutions (that were each subject to their own versions of Reg Q) to compete with each other for small deposits by offering depositors higher interest rates.[8] One exception to Reg Q was that, on large deposits of $100,000 or more, banks used to be able to pay any rate they chose so long as the deposit had a minimum maturity of 14 days. This exception led, so to speak, to the invention in 1961 of negotiable certificates of deposit.

There are many corporations and other large investors that have hundreds of thousands, even millions, of dollars they could invest in bank time deposits. Few do so, however, because they would lose liquidity by making a deposit with a fixed maturity. The illiquidity of time deposits and their consequent lack of appeal to investors led banks, which

---

[8] The rates banks and thrifts may pay depositors were gradually deregulated under the Monetary Control Act (MCA) of 1980. Also the Banking Act of 1982 permitted depository institutions to begin offering unregulated rates on Super-NOW and money market deposit accounts.

were free to bid high rates for large deposits, to begin to offer big investors *negotiable certificates of deposit, CDs* for short.

CDs are normally sold in $1MM units. They are issued at face value and typically pay interest at maturity. CDs can have any maturity longer than 14 days, and some 5- and even 7-year CDs have been sold (these pay interest semiannually). Most CDs, however, have an *original maturity* of 1 to 6 months.

Years ago, CDs issued by money center banks were a top money market instrument; and well over 100 billion of them were issued by money center and other large banks. Today, thanks to a variety of factors that include the weakening of bank credits, the rise of the interest-rate swap market, deregulation of the rates that banks may pay on deposits, changes in reserve requirements, and the creation of the deposit-note market, U.S. money center banks issue few wholesale CDs in the domestic market.

Today, when large banks want to buy term deposits wholesale, they turn typically to the *deposit note* market. In this market, banks sell notes that are designed to resemble and to trade in the secondary market like a corporate note or bond, but which are in fact a bank deposit. Original maturities on deposit notes range from 18 months out to five years. The lower cutoff is 18 months because, on a deposit of this length or longer, reserve requirements drop to zero. Deposit notes pay a fixed rate, but what banks want today is floating-rate money; so, when they sell deposit notes, they usually do an interest-rate swap, fixed for floating, and end up in the best of all possible worlds: with no reserve requirements and with floating-rate debt that does not have to be constantly rolled as did short-term CDs.

Bank notes are a variant on deposit notes. A bank selling a bank note claims that the money garnered is *not* a deposit and that it therefore does not have to pay FDIC insurance premiums on it, a point that the FDIC has disputed. The deposit and bank note markets are a part of the medium-term note market described below.

The old standard variety of 1-, 3-, and 6-month wholesale CDs are still issued by some regional banks and thrifts that are good credits. Currently, however, the CD market is but a glimmer of its past glory. "Today," said one banker in jest, "CD is an acronym for Certificate of Death."

Banks used to sell a lot of their CDs directly to investors. Sometimes, however, banks paid dealers a small fee to sell their new

CDs. These same dealers made an active secondary market in bank CDs. Today, banks issue deposit notes through dealers who, depending on the situation, may act as agents or principals. These dealers also make a secondary market in deposit notes.

Bank paper, whatever form it takes, always trades at a spread above Treasuries of the same maturity. Investors regard bank paper as carrying some credit risk, which Treasuries do not; also, investors regard bank paper as being significantly less liquid than Treasuries; hence, investors demand some extra yield for buying bank paper rather than Treasuries.

In the spring of 1982, a futures market for three-month CDs was launched in Chicago. For various reasons, including differences in the credit ratings of the top banks whose paper could be delivered by sellers of the contract, the CD contract died.

Eurodollar CDs

A Eurodollar time deposit, like a domestic time deposit, is an illiquid asset. Since some investors in Eurodollars wanted liquidity, banks in London that accepted such deposits began to issue *Eurodollar CDs*. These resemble domestic CDs except that, instead of being the liability of a domestic bank, they are the liability of the London branch of a U.S. bank, of a British bank, or of some other foreign bank with a branch in London.

Many of the Eurodollar CDs issued in London are purchased by other banks operating in the Euromarket. A large proportion of the remainder are sold to U.S. corporations and other U.S. institutional investors. Many Euro CDs are issued through dealers and brokers who also make a secondary market in these securities.

For the investor, a key advantage of buying Euro CDs is that they offer a higher return than do domestic CDs. The offsetting disadvantages are that Euro CDs are less liquid and carry—at least in the eyes of some U.S. investors—a slight extra risk because they are issued outside the United States.

The Eurodollar CD market is, today, more active than the market for domestic, wholesale CDs, but less active than it was in the past. One change from the past is that, whereas quality-conscious American investors used to want only top-10 American names, today they are more willing to buy foreign-name paper.

Yankee CDs

Non-U.S. banks issue dollar-denominated CDs not only in the Euromarket but also in the U.S. market through branches established there. CDs of the latter sort are frequently referred to as *Yankee CDs;* the name is taken from Yankee bonds, which are bonds issued in the U.S. market by foreign borrowers.

Yankee, as opposed to domestic, CDs expose the investor to the extra (if only in perception) risk of a foreign name; they are also less liquid than domestic CDs. Consequently, Yankees trade at yields close to those on Euro CDs. The major buyers of Yankee CDs are corporations that are yield buyers and that "fund to dates" (i.e., invest in short-term securities that mature on the date they will need funds).

Today, the market in Yankee CDs is, like that in domestic CDs, far smaller than it once was. To the extent that Yankee banks need term deposits of dollars, they find, for many of the same reasons that domestic banks do, that the best place to buy them is in the deposit note market.

BANKERS' ACCEPTANCES

Bankers' acceptances (*BAs*) are an unknown instrument outside the confines of the money market. Moreover, explaining them isn't easy because they arise in various ways out of a variety of transactions. The best approach is to use an example.

Suppose a U.S. importer wants to buy shoes in Brazil and pay for them four months later after she has had time to sell them in the United States. One approach would be for the importer to borrow from his bank; however, short-term rates may be lower in the open market. If they are, and if the importer is too small to go into the open market on her own, then she can go the bankers' acceptance route.

In that case, he has her bank write a letter of credit for the amount of the sale and sends this letter to the Brazilian exporter. Upon export of the shoes, the Brazilian firm, using this letter of credit, draws a time draft on the importer's U.S. bank and discounts this draft at its local bank, thereby obtaining immediate payment for its goods. The Brazilian bank, in turn, sends the time draft to the importer's U.S. bank, which then stamps "accepted" on the draft (i.e., the bank guarantees payment on the draft and thereby creates an *acceptance*). Once this is done, the draft becomes an irrevocable primary obligation of the accepting bank. At this point, if the Brazilian bank did not want cash immediately, the U.S. bank would return the draft to that bank, which would hold it as an investment and then present it to the U.S. bank for payment at maturity. If, on the other hand, the Brazilian bank wanted cash immediately, the U.S. bank would pay it and then either hold the acceptance itself or sell it to an investor. Regardless of who ends up holding the acceptance, it is the importer's responsibility to provide its U.S. bank with sufficient funds to pay off the acceptance at maturity. If the importer fails to do so, the bank is still responsible for making payment at maturity.

Our example illustrates how an acceptance can arise out of a U.S. import transaction. Acceptances also arise in connection with U.S. export sales, trade between third countries (e.g., Japanese imports of oil from the Middle East), the domestic shipment of goods, and domestic or foreign storage of readily marketable staples. Currently, most BAs arise out of foreign trade; they may be in manufactured goods but more typically are in bulk commodities, such as cocoa, cotton, coffee, and crude oil. Because of the complex nature of acceptance operations, only large banks with well-staffed foreign departments act as accepting banks.

Bankers' acceptances closely resemble commercial paper in form. They are short-term, noninterest-bearing notes sold at a discount and redeemed by the accepting bank at maturity for full face value. The major difference is that payment on commercial paper is guaranteed only by the issuing company. In contrast, bankers' acceptances, in addition to carrying the issuer's pledge to pay, are backed by the underlying goods being financed and carry the guarantee of the accepting bank. Consequently, bankers' acceptances are less risky than commercial paper and thus sell at slightly lower yields.

The big banks through which bankers' acceptances are originated generally keep some portion of the acceptances they create as investments. The rest are sold to investors through dealers or directly by the bank itself. Major investors in BAs are other banks, foreign central banks, money market funds, corporations, and other domestic and foreign institutional investors. BAs have liquidity because dealers in these securities make an active secondary market in those that are eligible for purchase by the Fed.

The United Kingdom has an active BA market where they are called *trade bills*.

MEDIUM-TERM NOTES

Medium-term notes (*MTNs*) began really as an extension of the commercial paper market to longer maturities. Basically, the issuer files, if it's not a bank—bank securities are exempt—a shelf registration with the SEC; it then posts rates for different maturities and sells its paper off the shelf through a dealer or group of dealers. MTNs are interest-bearing, not discount, securities; and they pay on a corporate-bond basis.

Initially, maturities of MTNs ranged from nine months out to several years; the paper really was medium term. Then, as both investors and issuers became comfortable with the MTN market, maturities of new MTNs sold began to lengthen; MTN maturities now run out, in a few instances, as far as 30, even 40 years. Also, over time, all sorts of bells and whistles have been added to MTNs: some are all callable, some have put features, some are collateralized, some are floating rate, and so on. Gradually, MTNs have encroached on the turf of the traditional bond market. That raises the question of what differences, if any, there are today between MTNs and corporate bonds.

The answer is that corporate bonds differ from MTNs in that they are underwritten. If an issuer wants a goodly chunk of money, at least 100MM in a single maturity, on a given date at a given rate, it makes sense and is cost effective for him to go to the expense and trouble of doing an underwritten deal. If, alternatively, the issuer wants to raise money continuously in different maturities, he's better off selling MTNs. Finance companies are big issuers of MTNs. Because of their large and varied financing needs, it suits finance companies to continuously offer their paper in different maturities and to continuously receive inflows of moneys in different maturities.

MTNs were the success story of the 1980s. During this period, outstandings of MTNs in the United States went from literally zero to over 70 billion, and they are still growing at an explosive pace. Naturally, dealers tried to transplant the MTN market to the Euromarket. Their efforts succeeded, but the Euro MTN market is still a far smaller market than is the U.S. MTN market.

MUNICIPAL NOTES

Debt securities issued by state and local governments and their authorities are referred to as *municipal securities*. Such securities can be divided into two broad categories: bonds issued to finance capital projects and short-term notes sold in anticipation of the receipt of other funds, such as taxes or proceeds from a bond issue.

Municipal notes, which are an important U.S. money market instrument, are issued with maturities ranging from a month to a year or more. They bear interest, and minimum denominations are highly variable ranging anywhere from $5,000 to $5MM.

Most muni notes are general obligation securities; that is, payment of principal and interest is secured by the issuer's pledge of its full faith, credit, and taxing power. This sounds impressive, but as the spectacle of New York City and later Orange County, California, tottering on the brink of bankruptcy brought home to all, it is possible that a municipality might default on its securities. Thus, the investors in evaluating the credit risk associated with publicly offered muni notes rely on ratings provided principally by Moody's and by Standard & Poor's.

The major attraction of municipal notes to a U.S. investor is that interest income on them is exempt or at least partially exempt from federal taxation and usually also from any income taxes levied within the state in which they are issued. The value of this tax exemption is greater the higher the investor's tax bracket, and the muni market thus attracts highly taxed investors, such as cash-rich corporations and wealthy individuals, and tax-free mutual funds designed to appeal to high-tax-bracket investors.

Large muni-note issues are sold to investors by dealers who obtain the securities either through negotiation with the issuer or through competitive bidding. The same dealers also make a secondary market in muni notes.

The yield a municipality must pay to issue notes depends on its credit rating, the length of time for which it borrows, and the general level of short-term rates. It used to be that a good credit risk could normally borrow at a rate well below the yield on governments of equivalent maturity because of the value to the investor of the tax exemption on municipal securities. Over the years, numerous complex changes and proposed changes in the federal tax code have lessened the value of the tax exemption attached to municipal securities. As a result, muni securities have, at times, actually traded at rates above Treasuries, which is precisely where they would trade were it not for the tax advantages they offer. Because of the ever-changing federal tax code and the consequent changing nature of the spread of Treasury to muni yields, some municipal bodies have begun, in recent times, to issue fully taxable securities and even to tap the Euromarket for money. Today, the muni market is an innovative place, and some muni issuers have even experimented with issuing zero-coupon securities.

MONEY AND BOND MARKET CALCULATIONS WORLDWIDE

Initially, we will focus our discussion of fixed-income calculations on U.S. paper. However, we also discuss how calculations used for U.S. money market paper and Treasury securities must, in some cases, be modified country to country, principally because of differences that exist, country to country, in the types of securities issued (e.g., index-linked bonds) and in the interest-payment conventions and day-count fractions used in calculating accrued interest on specific securities in specific countries.

THE NEXT CHAPTER

The next chapter serves as a preface to our discussion in later chapters of fixed-income calculations. In this preface, we introduce several mathematical operators, and we describe and list the *notation* we'll use throughout this book. Some readers may choose to skip the early sections of Chapter 3, but to save time, every reader should note carefully the description we give Chapter 3 of our notation.

CHAPTER 3

NOTATION: CONVENTIONS USED IN THIS BOOK

Before we broach the broad topic of developing money market and bond market calculations we take, in this chapter, an all-important first step: We develop a *notation* that's economical, consistent, and mnemonic (easy to remember). Specifically, this notation is designed to make the equations we'll develop later both easy to grasp and to manipulate.

DENOTING VARIABLES

In developing our notation, we break with several frequently used industry practices; here's an example: Most of the publications that have been widely circulated in the dealer community and that deal tangentially or primarily with money and bond market calculations make frequent use of multiletter symbols, such as DSM and RV, to denote individual variables. This practice can be faulted on several counts.

A mathematical purist, as opposed to a computer programmer, would regard such notation as sloppy and awkward. Since the subset of all money market participants who are mathematical purists probably has zero members, this objection seems minor. Mathematical purists have, however, good reason for insisting that all variables in a relationship be represented by a single family, composed of Helen, Peter, and Marcia. The computer programmer would undoubtedly denote Helen Hanson as HH, Peter Hanson as PH, and Marcia Hanson as MH. The mathematician, on the other hand, would observe that the important identifying characteristic of this group (*set*) of individuals, is that they are all Hansons; and to identify individuals in the set, he would use subscripts as follows: H_h for Helen Hanson, H_p for Peter Hanson, and H_m for

Marcia Hanson. If you understand how surnames and given names are used, you understand all you need to know about subscripts.

Here's a simple example. In the notation we present below,

$$\begin{aligned} y &= \text{simple yield} \\ y_{365} &= \text{simple yield on a 365–day–year basis} \\ y_{360} &= \text{simple yield on a 360–day–year basis} \end{aligned}$$

Asterisks: Another ID for Variables

Many of the problems we'll tackle in later chapters involve solving for a *true* yield, a *breakeven* yield, or a *breakeven* price. In every case, we affixed these variables with an *asterisk.* Like a subscript, an asterisk does *not* denote a mathematical operation. Think of an asterisk simply as an add-on to a symbol that denotes a particular variable—the purpose of the asterisk being to identify a particular characteristic of that variable. As noted, we could use H_m to denote *a* Marcia Hanson. Further, we could use H_m^* to denote *the* Marcia Hanson, whose middle name is Lee, among all Marcia Hansons.

To illustrate, in our notation,

$$\begin{aligned} r &= \text{rate} \\ r_{rp} &= \text{repurchase (rp) rate} \\ r_{rp}^* &= \text{breakeven repurchase (rp) rate} \end{aligned}$$

PARENTHESES AND BRACKETS

For the nonmathematical reader, a few words should be said about parentheses and brackets. An expression such as

$$a(b + x)$$

simply means that a is multiplied by the sum of two numbers, b and x, inside the parentheses.

If two expressions in parentheses are placed next to each other, that means that the one is multiplied by the other; for example,

$$(a - y)(b + x)$$

means that the difference between a and y is multiplied by the sum of b and x.

Sometimes, a multiterm expression, such as

$$\left[\frac{ay+b(x+c)}{b}\right]$$

is placed in brackets when it is to be multiplied or otherwise operated on by another term. Brackets, like parentheses, indicate that whatever is inside them forms a single term in the equation. In an algebraic expression, there is *no* difference in use or meaning between parentheses and brackets. It is simply a matter of style to substitute brackets for oversized parentheses when an expression gets to a certain size or when parentheses are used within the expression.

THE SUMMATION SIGN, Σ

In certain calculations, especially the calculation of the price of a bond, we are required to sum a number of terms with the result that we could easily end up with an unwieldy expression. Fortunately, there's a shorthand device we can use to avoid this problem.

This device is the *summation sign,* Σ. Let

$$n = \text{some indefinite positive number}$$

Then, Σ, which is a *mathematical operator,* is defined as follows:

$$\sum_{k=1}^{n} x_k = x_1 + x_2 + x_3 + \cdots + x_n$$

In this expression, the *ellipsis* (the three consecutive dots) represent *ordered, omitted* terms.

While Σ is a simple operator, it may appear confusing to those who encounter it for the first time. To dispel any possible confusion, we present two examples:[1]

$$\sum_{k=1}^{4} x^k = x + x^2 + x^3 + x^4$$

and

$$\sum_{k=1}^{2} \frac{a}{(1+x)^k} = \frac{a}{1+x} + \frac{a}{(1+x)^2}$$

ITALICS

In mathematics, it is standard practice to *italicize variables, but not functions.* Thus, one writes the statement, variable y equals a function of variable x as follows:

$$y = \mathrm{f}(x)$$

In this expression, the variables, y and x, are italicized, but the letter f, denoting a function, is not.

In the next chapter, we use PV and FV to denote present value and future value, respectively. Like Σ, PV and FV are *mathematical operators or functions;* that is, like a plus or minus sign, they instruct one what to do with certain variables. Thus, PV and FV do not violate the rule we assert below that we will abjure using multiletter symbols—that rule applies only to variables.

A LIST OF THE NOTATION USED IN THIS BOOK

Table 3–1 presents the major notation we will use throughout this book. In looking over this table, bear in mind that we have tried, in constructing our notation, to adhere to certain rules and practices in order to make

---

[1] With respect to these examples, note that

$$x^1 = x$$

Also, the variable n equals 4 in the first expression, 2 in the second expression.

(1) our notation consistent and easy to remember, and (2) our equations easy to follow and easy to manipulate. These rules and practices are as follows:

1. We have tried to keep our notation *mnemonic*. For example, in our notation,

$$F = \textit{face} \text{ value of a security}$$
$$P = \textit{clean} \text{ price of a bond}$$

2. We have adopted the standard practice of using *lower case letters* to represent *rates* and other *ratios*. Thus, in our notation,

$$c = \text{coupon rate}$$
$$d = \text{discount rate}$$

3. Also, in our notation, rates are always expressed in *decimal form*. For example, in our notation, a coupon rate of 10% and a discount rate of 3.35% are written respectively as follows:

$$c = 0.1000$$
$$d = 0.0335$$

4. We apply subscripts to certain symbols to denote specific values of the variables represented by these symbols. For example, in our notation,

$$d_p = \text{purchase rate of discount on discount securities}$$
$$d_s = \text{sale rate of discount on discount securities}$$

5. Often in later chapters, we will be solving for a *true* or for *breakeven* yield or price. We affix such variables with an *asterisk*. For example, in our notation,

$$r^*_{rp} = \text{breakeven repurchase } (rp) \text{ rate}$$

6. We reserve *upper case letters* for *whole numbers*. In our notation, for example,

$$C = \text{dollar amount of a coupon payment}$$
$$F = \text{face value of a security}$$
$$D_p = \text{dollar amount of a discount at purchase}$$
$$T_{sm} = \text{days } (\textit{time}) \text{ from settlement to maturity}$$

7. We have tried to abjure the use of multiletter symbols for a single *variable*. However, we do use *AI* to denote *accrued interest*. This common usage is hard to avoid; but it should lead to no

confusion, since on *no* occasion do we either multiply AI by another variable or multiply A by I.

The symbols listed in Table 3–1 are about all of the notation we will need in this volume. In special situations where an additional symbol is needed or the meaning of a symbol is slightly changed, we will clearly indicate this when the relevant equation is stated. Otherwise, we will consistently use the notation presented in Table 3–1. For easy reference, this table is repeated on *the end papers*.

TABLE 3–1
Notation Used in This Book (All Rates Are in Decimal Form)

Symbol	*Variable Denoted*
y	Simple yield: the annual rate at which interest accrues
n	Compounding periods during one year
y_c	Effective yield with compounding on a money market instrument; also, current yield on a bond
y^*	Breakeven yield
y_{360}	Simple yield (360-day basis); also referred to as *money market yield*
y_{365}	Simple yield (365-day basis)
y_{be}	Bond equivalent yield
y_{tm}	Yield to maturity; also, internal rate of return; also, stated yield to maturity for a bond on a quote sheet
y_{hp}	Holding-period yield
y_w	Yield-to-maturity divided by the number of coupon periods per year: $y_w = y_{tm}/w$
y_s	Simple yield on a bond
r	Rate
r_{re}	Reinvestment rate; the rate at which all coupons on a bond are assumed to be reinvested
r_{rp}	Repurchase (*rp*) rate; also known as the repo rate
r_t	Term repo rate
r_{rv}	Reverse (*rv*) rate; also known as the resale (*rs*) rate, reverse repurchase rate, or simply reverse rate.
r^*	Breakeven rate
r^*_{rp}	Breakeven repo (*rp*) rate
r^*_{rv}	Breakeven reverse (*rv*) rate
r_{wh}	Rate of withholding tax
d	Rate of discount on a T bill or other discount security

TABLE 3–1 (*Continued*)

Symbol	*Variable Denoted*
d_1	Rate of discount at the beginning of a transaction
d_2	Rate of discount at the end of a transaction
d^*	Breakeven sale rate on a bill *tail*
d_p	Rate at which a discount security is bought
d_s	Rate at which a discount security is sold
c	Coupon rate
I	Dollar amount invested
D_p	Dollar amount of discount on a discount security
F	Face value of a security; also, for a bond, nominal value against which coupon interest is calculated; typically, $F = 100$
cF	Annual coupon on a note or bond in denomination currency
C	Periodic coupon payment, $C = cF/w$
C_n	Next coupon payment; value reflects long or short first or last coupon periods
R	Redemption value, which is the principal amount to be paid by the issuer or borrower at maturity; typically, $R = 100$
P	Price of a bond excluding accrued interest; referred to as *clean* price or *flat* price
AI	Accrued interest from last coupon-payment date to settlement date (as measured by the appropriate day-count convention)
B	Price of a bond including accrued interest, referred to as the *dirty* price of a bond: $B = P + AI$
B_h	Dirty price of a bond for a 1 basis point *decrease* in yield
B_l	Dirty price of a bond for a 1 basis point *increase* in yield
K	Number of dropped coupons
C_k	*k*th *periodic* coupon payment
D_1	Date 1; also, start date of a coupon period
D_2	Date 2; also, end date of a coupon period
T	Time measured in days
T_1	Days to maturity at the beginning of the transaction; also, days in period one
T_2	Days to maturity at the end of the transaction; also, days in period two
$T_1 - T_2$	Days in the financing period
T_{im}	Days from issue to maturity
T_{sm}	Days from settlement to maturity
T_{hp}	Days in the holding period
T_n	Days from settlement to the *n*th coupon payment

TABLE 3–1 (*Continued*)

Symbol	*Variable Denoted*
T_p	Days from purchase date to maturity date
T_s	Days from sale date to maturity date
T_{ls}	Days from the last coupon date to the settlement date
T_{sn}	Days from the settlement date to the next coupon date
T_t	Terminal date
T_k	Date on which *k*th coupon is paid
$T'_k = T_t - T_k$	Reinvestment period for the *k*th coupon
A_y	Assumed number of days in a year for interest earned; also, the reinvestment period for r_{re}
A_d	Assumed number of days in a year for quoting discounts, typically equal to A_y
A_{ln}	Days in the current coupon period, i.e., days from the last-coupon to the next-coupon date (as measured by the appropriate day-count convention)
N	Number of remaining coupon payments (including the final coupon payment)
w	Number of coupon periods per year
v	The *annuity* variable, which is defined as $v = (1 + y_w)^{-1}$
t_n	$t_n = wD_n/365$
t_{sn}	Fraction of the current coupon period from settlement date to next coupon date: $t_{sn} = T_{sn}/A_{ln}$
D	Duration; also referred to as *effective duration*
D_{mac}	Macaulay duration
D_m	Modified Macaulay duration: $D_m = D_{mac}/(1 + y_w) \approx D$
D_{port}	Duration of a bond portfolio
D_j	Duration of the *j*th bond
$dolD_j$	Dollar duration of the *j*th bond
D_{sd}	Duration of the short-duration bond
D_{ld}	Duration of the long-duration bond
D_{cash}	Duration of cash
M_2	Dispersion
C_x	Convexity
V_{01}	Price value of 1 basis point
V_{32}	Yield value of 1/32

TABLE 3–1 (*Concluded*)

Symbol	*Variable Denoted*
V_j	Market value of the *j*th bond held
V_{sd}	Market value of the short-duration bond
V_{ld}	Market value of the long-duration bond
x	Proportion of sale proceeds to be invested in the long-duration bond

THE NEXT CHAPTER

In the next chapter, we examine concepts of yield, which turn out to be numerous, varied, and often not well understood. Also, we introduce two key concepts: present value and future value.

CHAPTER 4

CONCEPTS OF YIELD

One of the first and most distressing lessons a money market neophyte learns is that yields on different money and bond market instruments are rarely quoted on the same basis and are therefore rarely directly comparable. The principal reasons are:

1. Some instruments are sold on a discount basis; others bear interest.
2. Yields on some instruments are quoted on the basis of a 365-day year; yields on others are quoted on the basis of a 360-day year.
3. For different securities, different rules apply as to how interest shall accrue.
4. Different instruments offer different opportunities for compounding the return earned.
5. A security may mature on a nonbusiness day with the result that the holding period is longer than the period during which the securities are assumed to be held in the yield calculation.
6. For a given type of security, the rules as to how interest shall accrue on that security often differ country to country. Also, Euromarket notes and bonds may follow yet other rules.

In this chapter, we define and develop formulas to calculate various measures of yield: yield on a *simple-interest basis* (which we define as *simple yield*), yield on a *discount basis,* and *compound yield*—the last over various time periods and for various frequencies of compounding.

SIMPLE YIELD

We begin with the most basic concept of yield, *simple interest.*

A 1-Year Loan

Consider an investor who invests (lends) *principal* equal to \$1,000 for 1 year and who receives at the end of that year his \$1,000 of principal plus \$80 of interest. On a *simple-interest* basis (i.e., *no compounding*), the yield he earns is calculated as follows:

$$\begin{pmatrix}\text{Simple}\\ \text{yield}\end{pmatrix}=\frac{\begin{pmatrix}\text{Principal invested plus interest}\\ \text{received at the end of one year}\end{pmatrix}-(\text{Principal invested})}{(\text{Principal invested})}$$

Let

$$y = \text{simple interest}$$

Then, plugging the numbers in our example into this equation, we get:

$$\begin{aligned}y &= \frac{\$1,080-\$1,000}{\$1,000}\\ &= 0.08 \text{ or } 8\%\end{aligned}$$

That is, our investor earns a simple yield, y, of 8%.[1]

A Loan for Less Than One Year

Suppose now that the borrower in our example needs \$1,000 for only half a year and that he offers the investor \$40 of interest for this period. If our investor were able to make the same deal (invest \$1,000 and earn \$40) during the second half of the year, he would earn \$80 of interest over the whole year, so the annual simple yield that she is being offered is 8%.

We can *annualize simple yield* earned on any investment that pays

---

[1] We write expressions such as, *0.08 or 8%,* to make our equations more compact. Actually, the correct calculation in the case at hand is:

$$0.08\ (10\%) = 8\%$$

In our examples, we use a *wide range of interest rates:* some high, some low. One reason is that rate levels vary a lot over time. A second reason is that the impact of certain subtle yield calculations, such as taking compounding into account, is far more pronounced at high-rate levels than at low-rate levels.

interest at maturity and is outstanding for less than a year as follows: We substitute the actual interest paid into the preceding expression for calculating the yield on a 1-year investment; we then divide the resulting expression by the *fraction of the year* for which the investment is made. Doing so gives us:

$$\begin{pmatrix}\text{Annual}\\\text{simple}\\\text{yield}\end{pmatrix} = \left[\frac{\begin{pmatrix}\text{Principal invested plus}\\\text{interest paid at maturity}\end{pmatrix} - \begin{pmatrix}\text{Principal}\\\text{invested}\end{pmatrix}}{\text{Principal invested}}\right] \div \begin{pmatrix}\text{Fraction of}\\\text{the year the}\\\text{investment}\\\text{is outstanding}\end{pmatrix}$$

Inserting the numbers in our second example into this equation, we get

$$\frac{\$1{,}040 - \$1{,}000}{\$1{,}000} \div \frac{1}{2} = 0.08 \text{ or } 8\%$$

That is, over *half* the year, our investor earns, as we concluded, an *annualized yield* of 8%.

To simplify our example, we used a half-year loan. Obviously, no such thing exists in real life because half a year is 182.5 days, and money and bond market investments are never outstanding for half a day nor do they pay a yield on a half-day basis. Therefore, to be precise, *the annualizing factor should be stated in terms of days.* Let

$$T = \text{days } (\textit{time}) \text{ the investment is outstanding}$$

Then, for a security on which T is less than 365,

$$\begin{pmatrix}\text{Annual}\\\text{simple}\\\text{yield}\end{pmatrix} = \left[\frac{\begin{pmatrix}\text{Principal invested plus}\\\text{interest paid at maturity}\end{pmatrix} - \begin{pmatrix}\text{Principal}\\\text{invested}\end{pmatrix}}{\text{Principal invested}}\right] \div \frac{T}{365}$$

Example. Suppose that a borrower offers to pay our investor $10 of interest for a 45-day loan of $1,000. Using the formula above, we can easily calculate that the borrower is offering to pay our investor an annualized simple yield of 8.11%.

$$\left[\frac{(\$1{,}000 + \$10) - (\$1{,}000)}{\$1{,}000}\right] \div \frac{45}{365} = 0.0811 \text{ or } 8.11\%$$

DISCOUNT SECURITIES

Many U.S. money market securities—T bills, federal agency discount paper, bankers' acceptances, and commercial paper—are sold on a *discount basis. Such securities pay no interest; instead, they are sold at a discount from face value, and they are redeemed at maturity for full face value.* Someone investing in such a security earns a return because *he receives more for his discount security at maturity than he paid for it at issue or at purchase.*

Converting a Rate of Discount to an Equivalent Simple Yield: 365-Day Basis

It's easy to convert a rate stated on a discount basis to an equivalent rate stated on a simple-interest basis.[2] When we do so, we discover something interesting: The rate of discount offered on discount paper always *understates* the simple yield earned by an investor in such paper.

Here's an example. Suppose an investor buys $1MM of 6-month *U.S. Treasury bills* at an 8% rate of discount. The dollar amount of the discount he receives at purchase will be *roughly:* 0.08(1/2)$1MM. We say roughly for two reasons:

1. The 6-month bill normally matures in precisely 26 weeks or 182 days.
2. On *all* discount securities, the discount is figured as if the year had 360 days.

Thus, the discount at which our investor buys his $1MM of bills is calculated as follows:

$$\begin{pmatrix} \textit{Discount on \$1MM} \\ \textit{of 6-month bills} \end{pmatrix} = 0.08(\$1{,}000{,}000)\frac{182}{360} = \$40{,}444.44$$

Subtracting this number from $1MM, we find that our investor must pay $959,555.56 to purchase his bills:

$$\$1{,}000{,}000 - \$40{,}444.44 = \$959{,}555.56$$

If we now insert the face value of the bills, the price paid for them,

[2] We develop the requisite formula in Chapter 6.

and the days the bills are outstanding into a variation of the formula on page 2,

$$\begin{pmatrix}\text{Annual}\\ \text{simple}\\ \text{yield}\end{pmatrix} = \left[\frac{\begin{pmatrix}\text{Face value}\\ \text{at maturity}\end{pmatrix} - \begin{pmatrix}\text{Principal}\\ \text{invested}\end{pmatrix}}{\text{Principal invested}}\right] \div \frac{T}{365}$$

we find that the simple yield earned by our investor, assuming a 365-day year, is:

$$\frac{\$1,000,000 - \$959,555.56}{\$959,555.56} \div \frac{182}{365} = 0.0845 \text{ or } 8.45\%$$

This *rate,* 8.45%, is substantially *more than* the 8% *rate of discount* at which our investor bought his 6-month bills. Specifically,[3]

$$8.453\% - 8.000\% = 0.453\% \text{ or } 45.3\text{bp}$$

Converting a Rate of Discount to an Equivalent Simple Yield: 360-Day Year

Our conversion of a discount rate to a simple yield was based on a 365-day year. Since the yields quoted on most U.S. money market instruments are based on a *360-day year,* it makes sense to ask: What simple yield, based on a 360-day year, would our investor earn on his bills? Substituting 360 for 365 in our annualizing factor, we find the answer to be as follows:

$$\frac{\$1,000,000 - \$959,555.56}{\$959,555.56} \div \frac{182}{360} = 0.08337 \text{ or } 8.337\%$$

Calculating the simple yield earned by our investor on a 6-month bill offered at an 8% rate of discount on the basis of a 360-day year, instead of a 365-day year, gives us a *smaller* number. Specifically,

$$8.453\% - 8.337\% = 0.116\% \text{ or } 11.6\text{bp}$$

The reason is that 182 days is a *larger* fraction of a 360-day year than it is of a 365-day year.

---

[3] Recall that *bp* is the abbreviation for *basis points.* As noted, a *basis point,* also called an *01* by the Street, is 1/100 of 1%. Thus,

$$45\text{bp} = 0.0045 \text{ or } 0.45\%.$$

Here, we've illustrated how a discount security works; and equally important, we've shown that *a rate of discount and a simple yield are not directly comparable.* This makes sense, since the rate of discount is actually an alternative form for the *price* of the discount security, whereas simple yield is the rate of return on the discount security. In Chapters 6 and 8, we'll cover discount securities in greater depth.

MONEY MARKET YIELD

Because so many U.S. money market instruments pay interest based on a 360-day year, *a simple yield quoted on the basis of a 360-day year has come to be known as money market yield.* This new measure of yield raises an interesting question: Would an investor who's offered a simple yield be better off if offered a money market rate or a rate based on a 365-day year?

The answer is straightforward. Suppose that our investor puts $1MM of principal into paper that pays a simple yield of 8%. If he's being paid a money market rate, he'll get his $80,000 of interest plus $1MM of principal at the end of 360 days. But, if he's being paid simple interest based on a 365-day year, he has to wait longer, 365 days to be precise. Moral: *In simple-interest land, an investor is better off if he gets paid a money market yield than if he gets paid a yield based on a 365-day year.*

Simple Yield: 360-Day-Year versus 365-Day-Year Basis

To calculate the simple yield that an investor being paid a money market yield earns on the basis of a 365-day year, we need only divide by the appropriate annualizing factor. For example, the 8.337% simple yield that we calculated in the above example was quoted *on the basis of a 360-day year;* we can convert it to a simple yield quoted *on the basis of a 365-day year* as follows:

$$0.08337 \div \frac{360}{365} = 0.08453 \text{ or } 8.453\%$$

Obviously, to do the reverse conversion, to go from a 365-day yield to a 360-day rate, one simply inverts the annualizing factor.

The conversion of a money market yield [quoted on a 360-day basis] to a simple yield quoted on a 365-day basis is something that anyone working with money market numbers must frequently do. *The easiest way to make this calculation is to think not of dividing by 360/365, but of multiplying by 365/360.* The reason is that one can always remember the proper operation by reasoning as follows:

> It's worth *more* to the investor to get his interest in 360 days than in 365 days. Therefore, if one converts a simple yield from a 360-day basis to a 365-day basis, the figure for yield earned must get *bigger.* If that's so, then the proper term by which to multiply the 360-day rate must be 365/360 (which is *greater than* 1) rather than 360/365 (which is *less than* 1).

This observation, as demonstrated above, is hardly profound, but for people who have trouble memorizing formulas, such tricks save time and money.

A final important point: In annualizing any dollar return earned on an investment over *less than one year,* it is easier to remember to *multiply* by 365/T than to divide by T/365. The reason is that multiplying by 365 obviously *raises* the yield earned which is precisely what intuition suggests is required. It's for this reason that the formulas in the box on page 50 are written as they are.[4]

A Leap Year

In a leap year, such as 1996, the number of days is 366. Thus, we're tempted to say that, during a leap year, 366 must be substituted for 365 in all of our yield equations, but that simplistic rule is *incorrect.* In Chapter 5, we will delve into the day-count conventions according to which interest accrues on different sorts of fixed-income securites. Here we note that, if a security accrues interest according to the ACT/ACT payment convention, that is, if it accrues interest on the basis *of actual days in the investment period divided by actual days in the year,* then in deciding whether to use 365 or 366 as days in the year, we must ask the following question: Does the period from the *settlement date* (the date on which the investment begins) to one year from that date include a leap day? If so, then use 366 in place of 365 for actual days in the year.[5]

---

[4]An alternative way to think of *annualizing a simple yield earned over a fraction of a year* is as follows: Divide the amount of interest earned over T days to get *daily* interest earned; then, multiply daily interest earned by the assumed number of days in the year to annualize simple yield. This approach to annualizing a simple yield earned over a fraction of a year leads, of course, to the same calculation we made above. We mention this second approach simply because it may seem, to some readers, intuitively more obvious.

[5]As we'll note in Chapter 5, interest may accrue on a given security according to any one of a number of different day-count conventions. Generally, one particular day-count convention will prevail for a given type of security. For example, on the U.S. commercial paper, interest accrues according to the ACT/360 day-count convention; but on U.S. Treasury notes and bonds, interest accrues according to the ACT/ACT day-count convention.

Examples. (1) To calculate annualized simple yield on an investment that settles on 1/31/96, and ends on 9/30/96, use *366* as actual days in the year. (2) To calculate annualized simple yield on an investment that settles on 3/31/96, and ends on 9/30/96, use *365* as actual days in the year.

Calculating Simple Yield Earned

Let

$$y = \text{simple yield}$$

$$T = \text{days investment is outstanding}$$

$$y_{365} = \text{simple yield on a 365-day-year basis}$$

$$y_{360} = \text{simple yield on a 360-day-year basis}$$

Then:

Case I: The instrument pays simple interest, and its yield, calculated on a 365-day-year basis, is given by:

$$y_{365} = \left[\frac{\begin{pmatrix}\text{Principal plus interest} \\ \text{paid at maturity}\end{pmatrix} - \begin{pmatrix}\text{Principal} \\ \text{invested}\end{pmatrix}}{\text{Principal invested}} \right] \frac{365}{T}$$

Case II: The investment is a discount security; and its simple yield, calculated on a 365-day-year basis, is given by:

$$y_{365} = \left[\frac{\begin{pmatrix}\text{Face value at} \\ \text{maturity}\end{pmatrix} - \begin{pmatrix}\text{Principal} \\ \text{invested}\end{pmatrix}}{\text{Principal invested}} \right] \frac{365}{T}$$

Case III: Converting from one basis to another:

$$y_{360} = y_{365}\left(\frac{360}{365}\right)$$

and

$$y_{365} = y_{360}\left(\frac{365}{360}\right)$$

COMPOUND INTEREST

The next wrinkle to which we turn is the *compounding* of interest. This is a concept that should be familiar to everyone, since all banks and thrifts offer compound interest to any depositor who opens an interest-bearing account with them.

Compounding Interest over a 1-Year Period

We begin our discussion by exploring the impact of compounding on the *effective yield* earned by an investor over a *1-year period.* To illustrate, suppose that our investor places $1,000 in a savings-account-type security that pays interest semiannually and permits the reinvestment of interest. If the rate offered is again 8%, our investor will receive $40 of interest at the end of the first half-year:

$$0.08(\$1{,}000)(1/2) = \$40.00$$

If, moreover, he adds that $40 to his principal invested, he will receive $41.60 of interest at the end of the second half-year:

$$0.08(\$1{,}040)(1/2) = \$41.60$$

Since

$$\$40.00 + \$41.60 = \$81.60$$

semiannual compounding clearly raises the *effective* yield the investor receives from 8.00% to 8.16%; that is, by 16bp. The actual calculation is as follows:

$$\frac{\$1{,}081.60 - \$1{,}000}{\$1{,}000}\left(\frac{365}{365}\right) = 0.816 \text{ or } 8.16\%$$

As Table 4–1 shows, the amount by which compounding raises the effective yield earned by an investor over a year depends on how high the simple yield offered is and on how often compounding occurs. Thus, we need a general formula to calculate the effective yield that an investor earns over a year when compounding is possible. Let

n = *the number of times during the year compounding occurs*

y = *the simple yield offered*

y_e = *the effective yield earned over a year with compounding n*

TABLE 4–1
The Effect of Compounding a Simple Yield on the Effective Yield Earned over One Year

y Simple Yield (%)	*n* Times during the Year that Compounding Occurs	y_c Effective Yield with Compounding (%)	$y_c - y$ (%)	$y_c - y$ Basis Points (bp)
4.00%	2	4.0400%	0.0400%	4.00
4.00	4	4.0604	0.0604	6.04
4.00	Daily	4.0808	0.0808	8.08
4.00	Continuous	4.0811	0.0811	8.11
8.00	2	8.1600	0.1600	16.00
8.00	4	8.2432	0.2432	24.32
8.00	Daily	8.3278	0.3278	32.78
8.00	Continuous	8.3287	0.3287	32.87
12.00	2	12.3600	0.3600	36.00
12.00	4	12.5509	0.5509	55.09
12.00	Daily	12.7475	0.7475	74.75
12.00	Continuous	12.7497%	0.7497	74.97

The formula for y_c is as follows:[6]

$$y_c = \left(1 + \frac{y}{n}\right)^n - 1$$

For reasons discussed in later chapters, compounding must be taken into account to make different rates directly comparable. Therefore, the reader should commit to memory the formula for y_c. Like all key formulas on money market securities, this formula has been displayed in a *box* for emphasis and easy reference.

With daily compounding, as occurs on some savings accounts, *n* equals 365. With daily compounding on money market transactions, such as overnight sales of Fed funds or repo money, *n* equals the actual number of business days in the year, a number that ranges from 240 to 260

[6] In the following section, we show how this general result can be suggested by simple induction.

Converting a Simple Yield to the Equivalent Effective Yield When Compounding Occurs *n* Times over a 1-Year Period*

$$y_c = \left(1 + \frac{y}{n}\right)^n - 1$$

*A formula for making this calculation when the investment period is *less than 1 year* is developed in the next box.

depending on the number of holidays in the market in which the investor is dealing.

An Intuitive Argument Suggesting the Formula for y_c

The formula for y_c can be suggested *by induction* as follows. Let

I = dollar amount (principal) invested

y = simple yield paid

With semiannual compounding, the amount the investor will have at the end of 1 year equals principal *plus* the interest paid at the end of the first half-year plus the interest (including interest on interest) paid at the end of the second half-year. In symbols, this amount can be represented as follows:

$$\left(I + \frac{y}{2} I\right) + \frac{y}{2}\left(I + \frac{y}{2} I\right)$$

which reduces to

$$I\left(1 + \frac{y}{2}\right)^2$$

With compounding 3 times 1 year, the amount the investor will have at the end of the year equals principal plus three interest payments. This amount represented in symbols is:

$$\left(I + \frac{y}{3} I\right) + \frac{y}{3}\left(I + \frac{y}{3} I\right) + \frac{y}{3}\left[\left(I + \frac{y}{3} I\right) + \frac{y}{3}\left(I + \frac{y}{3} I\right)\right]$$

This expression reduces to:

$$I\left(l+\frac{y}{3}\right)^{3}$$

As the emerging pattern correctly suggests, with compounding n times a year, the amount the investor will have at the end of 1 year is

$$I\left(1+\frac{y}{n}\right)^{n}$$

Thus, the *effective yield,* y_c, at which the investor earns interest over 1 year when compounding is taken into account is

$$y_c = \left[\frac{I\left(1+\frac{y}{n}\right)^{n} - I}{I}\right]$$

which reduces to

$$y_c = \left(1+\frac{y}{n}\right)^{n} - 1$$

the formula given above.

Instantaneous (Nondiscrete) Compounding

In the real world of finance, daily compounding of interest is neither typical nor unusual. At the consumer level, some banks and thrifts offer their customers daily compounding on interest-bearing deposits. At the wholesale level, dealers frequently finance securities they've positioned with overnight repo, which means that the effective financing rate they pay is the overnight repo rate compounded on a daily, or almost daily, basis.[7]

As Table 4–1 shows, the difference between the effective yield earned and the simple yield quoted, increases as the frequency of compounding increases. Naturally, finance theorists asked: What would happen to effective yield if the frequency of compounding, *n,* were not some

[7] We add the qualifier, *or almost daily,* because repos can be either initiated or rolled not 365 days a year, but only on the roughly 255 *business days* that occur during a typical year.

discrete number, such as 2 (semiannual compounding), 4 (quarterly compounding), or 365 (daily compounding), but were instead *infinity* (i.e., *continuous* or *instantaneous compounding*)? Stated more precisely, finance theorists asked: What value would y_c obtain, if the *length* of the compounding period were allowed to go to *zero* (i.e., if n were to approach infinity)? The answer is

$$y_c = e^{yt}$$

Look back at Table 4–1, the last line of each section of which gives effective yield when compounding is continuous. As the numbers in each section of this table suggest, effective yield always increases as n is increased, but *as n becomes larger, the impact on effective yield of further increases in the frequency of compounding diminishes.* Thus, the increase in effective yield that's obtained by going from daily to instantaneous compounding is small compared to the increase that's obtained by going from, say, annual payment of interest to semiannual compounding. If, for a given level of y, we plotted the relationship between y_c and n, we'd find that, as n increases from 1 to infinity (this corresponds to going from no compounding to continuous compounding), y_c would approach asymptotically the value it assumes when compounding is continuous.

Compounding When the Investment Period Is Less Than One Year

Above, we calculated the effective rate, y_c, that an investor would earn with compounding, on funds invested for a full year. Frequently, however, investors place funds for periods shorter than a full year.

To convert a simple yield to the correct annual effective yield when *the investment period is known to be less than 1 year,* one must first calculate the compound yield that the investor in fact earns over his investment period and then annualize that rate. Let

n = compounding periods *during 1 year*

n' = compounding periods *during the investment period*

T = days in the investment period

Then, if T is less than 365,

$$y_c = \left[\left(1+\frac{y}{n}\right)^{n'} - 1\right]\frac{365}{T}$$

Example. Consider an investor who has funds to invest for 90 days and who makes a series of 30-day investments, each at 6%. Assuming that the investor *reinvests* at 6% the interest he receives on each of the first two of the three 30-day investments he makes, the effective annual rate of return he will earn is:

$$y_c = \left[\left(1 + \frac{0.06}{365/30}\right)^3 - 1\right]\frac{365}{90}$$
$$= 0.0603 \text{ or } 6.03\%$$

Had T in the above example been 365, then our investor would have been able to roll his 30-day investment (*in theory at least*) 12.17 times, and the effective yield he would have earned over the 365-day period would have been 6.17%. In other words, had he had funds to invest over a full year, as opposed to 90 days, our investor would have been able to pick an extra 14bp of effective yield.

Calculating Effective Yield, y_c, When the Investment Period Is Less Than One Year

Let

y = simple yield
y_c = effective yield with compounding
n = compounding periods *during* 1 *year*
n' = compounding periods *during the investment period*
T = days in the investment period

Then,

$$y_c = \left[\left(1 + \frac{y}{n}\right)^{n'} - 1\right]\frac{365}{T}$$

As our example suggests, the difference between a simple yield and the corresponding effective yield increases not only the more times compounding occurs but also the longer the investment period is. A telling illustration of this point, which is easy to overlook but obvious once noted, is given by the figures in Table 4–2.

TABLE 4–2
Effective Yield Earned When an 8% Yield Is Compounded Daily over Investment Periods of Varying Lengths

Investment Period (Days)	*Effective Yield (%)*
1	8.0000%
30	8.0255
60	8.0519
90	8.0785
182	8.1608
365*	8.3278

*An institutional investor, even if he rolls overnight funds, cannot get compounding 365 times during a year because compounding occurs only on business days. A few investors take this into account in compounding overnight rates.

The example presented above correctly suggests a crucial point: Since it is always worth something to the investor to get yield dollars sooner than later, *comparisons between the yields on securities of differing maturity should always be made on the basis of the appropriate effective rates (values of y_c) at which they are offered when opportunities for compounding are taken into account.* Also, in making such comparisons, the length of the investment period should be taken into account if it is known to be less than one year.

Curve Interpolation

Market participants often set rates for various periods in such a manner as to guarantee that the rate for a given period (e.g., a coupon period) is realized for any given subperiod. This practice is called *curve interpolation.*

To do curve interpolation, one takes two annual rates, adjusts them for the respective periods over which they will be applied, and then sets their implied daily compounded rates equal to each other. At this point, one can solve for one rate in terms of the other. The equation is as follows:

$$\left[1+r_1\left(\frac{t_1}{360}\right)\right]^{360/t_1}=\left[1+r_2\left(\frac{t_2}{360}\right)\right]^{360/t_2}$$

where

r_1 = interest rate for period 1

r_2 = interest rate for period 2

t_1 = number of days in period 1

t_2 = number of days in period 2

We can determine the second-period rate in terms of the first-period rate by solving the above equation for r_2 as follows:

$$r_2=\left\{\left[1+r_1\left(\frac{t_1}{360}\right)\right]^{t_2/t_1}-1\right\}\frac{360}{t_2}$$

PRESENT VALUE AND FUTURE VALUE

When calculations are made in fixed-income land, two crucial questions constantly arise:

1. What's the dollar value *today* of an investment that promises a defined stream of *future* payments?
2. What's the dollar value *at a future date* of an investment made *today* that promises a defined stream of future payments?

Question one calls for calculating the present value of an investment; question two for calculating its future value.

Present Value

Present value is one of those concepts most people struggle to learn in school and promptly forget because they can think of nothing better to do with it. For money market people, however, present value is a key concept; in particular, it's fundamental for calculating the price/yield relationship on *term* CDs and on notes and bonds. To illustrate the concept of present value, let

I = principal invested

y = simple yield available on a 1-year investment

Then, by solving the expression,

$$I + yI = \$1$$

for I, we can determine that the *present value* (denoted by PV) of \$1 to be received 1 year hence is given by

$$\text{PV} = \frac{\$1}{1+y}$$

This expression renders several things obvious. First, present value equals the *discounted value* of a future sum. Second, the rate at which this future sum is discounted is y. Third, the higher y is, the smaller is the present value of the future sum.

Example. Suppose $y = 7\%$. Then, the present value of \$1 to be received 1 year hence is

$$\text{PV} = \frac{\$1}{1+0.07} = \$0.9346$$

Note also that there's nothing magic about one year. We could just as well have calculated the present value of \$1 to be received 30, 60, or however many days hence provided we know what day-year basis we want to use so that we can calculate an appropriate annualizing factor.

Thus, if we are using a 360-day-year basis, the present value of \$1 to be received T days hence is given by

$$\text{PV} = \frac{\$1}{\left[1+y\dfrac{T}{360}\right]}$$

Example. Let T = 45. Then on a 360-day basis, the present value of \$1, again at, $y = 7\%$ is given by

$$\text{PV} = \frac{\$1}{\left[1+0.07\left(\dfrac{45}{360}\right)\right]} = \$0.9913$$

Future Value

Basically, the present value of money to be received in the future is the amount that a rational person, who knows the yield, y, at which he could invest money from today to that future date, would pay for that future sum.

An alternative way to get from the present to the future is to think in terms of *future value* (denoted by FV). Suppose that a borrower offers to pay a lender a simple yield, y, for *one, 360-day year.* We can easily calculate the principal, I, that the lender would have to invest to obtain a given future value, say FV = \$1, at the end of 1 year. To do so, we solve the formula,

$$\text{FV} = \$1 = (1 + y)\,I$$

for I, which gives us

$$I = \frac{\$1}{1+y}$$

Comparing this formula to the formula we gave above for present value, we see that present value and future value are simply flip sides of the same calculation. Put precisely, *the principal one must invest today to obtain a given future value exactly equals the present value today of that amount.*

Example. Our formula for future value tells us that, at a simple yield of 7%, the amount, I, one would have to invest, over a 365-day year, in order to have \$1 at the end of one year is:

$$I = \frac{\$1}{1+0.07} = \$0.9346$$

Note this amount exactly equals the number we calculated above for the *present value* to an investor of \$1 to be received one year hence if the investor can earn a yield of 7%.

YIELD TO MATURITY

In later chapters, we will consider a specific type of fixed-income securities, namely *notes and bonds that pay interest periodically* and may mature some number of years—2 years, 20 years, 30 years, whatever—

hence. In the marketplace, prices (so and so many dollars per $100 of face value) are bid and asked for such securities. Also, for each such security, a number is quoted for the *yield to maturity* that an investor would earn if he bought that security and held it to maturity.

We won't fully describe how to calculate yield to maturity on a note or bond until we get to Part 3. However, we can give here a short-form, *indirect* definition of this key concept of yield.

When a note or bond trades at a given price, its yield to maturity is the rate at which all the future dollar flows that that security will throw off must be discounted back to the present in order that the sum of these discounted values equal the *dirty price* (price *plus any accrued interest*) asked for the security. In other words, *the price asked for a security equals its present value when all of the dollar flows it will throw off are discounted back to the present at a rate equal to the security's yield to maturity.*

NOMINAL YIELD AND REAL RATE OF RETURN

Our discussion of different concepts of yield naturally leads to yet another topic: the crucial distinction between *nominal yield* and *real yield* (the latter's more often referred to as the *real rate of return*).

To illustrate, consider an investor who buys a note that promises to pay him principal plus 5% interest at the end of one year. The promised 5% is the *nominal rate* our investor will receive. However, what's more important to him is the *real rate of return* he'll receive; this rate is the *nominal rate minus the rate of inflation.*

Our investor's real rate of return measures how the *purchasing power* of the dollars he puts up *grows* (or *falls* as the case may be) over his investment period. If our investor gets a 1-year nominal rate of 5% and the annual rate of inflation is 0%, then at the end of one year, the purchasing power of the dollars he's invested will have grown by 5% and his real rate of return will be 5%; alternatively, if the rate of inflation is 10%, our investor's real rate of return will be −5%

Clearly, a rational investor ought to focus on real, not nominal rates of return. In fact, what he really ought to focus on is *real, after-tax rates of return.* Calculating the impact of taxes on yields is a topic we'll touch on in later chapters.

One final thought: Even if there's no uncertainty with respect to the nominal yield that a given investment will pay over a given period, an investor can only estimate what real, after-tax yield he might earn on that investment over that period. The reason is that, absent a reliable crystal ball, the best an investor can do is to estimate what, if any, changes will occur over his investment period in the rate of inflation and in tax legislation—two variables over which he exercises *no* control.

THE NEXT CHAPTER

In the next chapter, we focus on how interest accrues on an interest-bearing security. The topic sounds simple, but in fact methods of interest accrual differ widely from instrument to instrument (e.g., in the United States, from muni bonds to Treasury bonds) and, for a given instrument, from country to country (e.g., from U.S. Treasuries to other sovereign debt). Consequently, to talk about interest accrual, we must first delve into the esoteria of interest-payment conventions and day-count fractions.

CHAPTER 5

INTEREST-PAYMENT CONVENTIONS AND DAY-COUNT FRACTIONS

From our discussion of yield in Chapter 4, it's clear that fixed-income paper comes in two forms: discount paper and interest-bearing paper.

When a borrower issues *interest-bearing paper,* he promises to pay some percentage rate of return to the buyer of his paper. That rate is referred to as the *coupon rate.* For example, on a given day, a bank might offer 3-month CDs with a 3.05% coupon while the U.S. Treasury is issuing 10-year notes with a 6¼% coupon.

In this chapter, we describe *how interest accrues on an interest-bearing security.* Specifically, we answer the following general question:

> If an investor holds, from date D_1 to date D_2 a given interest-bearing security with a known coupon, how much interest will he have earned (i.e., how much interest will have accrued on his investment) over this period?

Unfortunately, this deceptively simple-sounding question may be answered in *several* ways. For a *given* security, which answer is correct depends on which of several *interest-payment conventions* the issuer of the security has chosen to use. Thus, in this chapter, we must delve into interest-payment conventions; and as we do so, we'll explain precisely how interest accrues on different types of interest-bearing paper.

THE DAY-COUNT FRACTION

In determining how much interest will accrue on a given security between two dates, D_1 and D_2, step one is to identify the interest-payment convention that the security incorporates. Step two is to answer the following basic questions:

1. How many interest-accrual days exist between the two dates, D_1 and D_2?
2. How many days exist in the current coupon period?

Each interest-payment convention contains rules for counting each of these *two* numbers.

To calculate accrued interest on a given coupon security over a given period, we need to construct an appropriate *day-count fraction.* The *number* of *interest-accrual days,* counted according to the interest-payment convention used, is the *numerator* of this fraction. The *number of days in the current coupon period,* also counted according to the interest-payment convention used, is the *denominator* of this fraction. Thus, the expression for a day-count fraction is as follows:

$$\begin{pmatrix}\text{Day-count}\\ \text{fraction}\end{pmatrix} = \left(\frac{\begin{array}{c}\text{Number of interest-accrual days,}\\ \text{according to the}\\ \text{interest-payment convention used}\end{array}}{\begin{array}{c}\text{Days in the relevant coupon period,}\\ \text{according to the}\\ \text{interest-payment convention used}\end{array}}\right)$$

For a money market instrument, the denominator of the day-count fraction, which equals days in the *relevant coupon period,* is the days-in-the-year basis, typically 360 or 365, on which that instrument is quoted. In the United States, rates on money market instruments are, for example, quoted on the basis of a 360-day year. Because of the way we've defined *relevant coupon period,* the application of a specific interest-payment convention will differ depending on whether the security is a note, a bond, or a money market instrument.

INTEREST-PAYMENT CONVENTIONS BASED ON ACTUAL ACCRUAL DAYS

Among the various interest-payment conventions that have been devised to determine interest-accrual and coupon-period days, several take interest-accrual days to equal the *actual* (exact) number of *calendar* days during the interest-accrual period. The principal differences among such conventions lie in how each accounts for leap days.

ACT/ACT

The simplest and most logical way to deal with interest accrual on *notes and bonds* is the interest-payment convention called *ACT/ACT.*[1] According to *the ACT/ACT interest-payment convention,* the day-count fraction is as follows:

$$\begin{pmatrix}\text{ACT/ACT}\\ \text{day-count}\\ \text{fraction}\end{pmatrix} = \left(\frac{\text{Actual days held}}{\text{Actual days in the coupon period}}\right)$$

Under the ACT/ACT convention, counting the number of days in *the numerator of the day-count fraction* is straightforward. For example, the ACT/ACT numerator would be 31 days for a bond held through the month of January (i.e., from January 1 through January 31) but in a nonleap year, it would be only 28 days for a bond held through the month of February (i.e., from February 1 through February 28).

According to the ACT/ACT convention, *the denominator of the day-count fraction always equals the number of calendar days in the coupon period.* For example, if interest is paid *semiannually,* then the denominator of the day-count fraction equals the actual number of days in the relevant half-year coupon period. Alternatively, if interest is paid *annually,* then the denominator of the day-count fraction equals the actual number of days, 365 or 366, in the relevant 1-year coupon period.

The denominator in the ACT/ACT day-count fraction for each coupon period always equals the actual number of days between the preceding and the subsequent coupon dates. Because 365 is not evenly divisible by two, *for any semiannual-pay, ACT/ACT security, the actual number of days in a given coupon period must, in a nonleap year, differ from the actual number of days in the subsequent coupon period.* On such a security, the actual number of days in a particular 6-month coupon period can vary from 181 to 184 days.

Example. Consider the 10-year note issued by the U.S. Treasury on November 15, 1991. This issue, which carries a coupon of 7½% matures on November 15, 2001, and is known as the 7½s of 11/01, has two

[1] The ACT/ACT day-count convention (pronounced *aak/aak,* as in kids imitating gunfire) is not used for money market instruments.

coupon dates: May 15 and November 15. There were *182 days* in the first coupon period, November 15, 1991, to May 15, 1992, and *184 days* in the subsequent coupon period, May 15, 1992, to November 15, 1992.[2] Thus, for the 7½s of 11/01, the day-count fraction for a 30-day holding period during its *first* coupon period, was 30/182, whereas the day-count fraction for a 30-day holding period during its *second* coupon period, was 30/184. Because the first coupon period included the *leap day,* February 29, 1992, the sum of the *actual days* in first two coupon periods of the 7½s of 11/01 was *366,* not *365.*

The ACT/ACT payment convention is the most straightforward of the various payment conventions in wide use. The necessary offset to this advantage is that interest typically accrues on an ACT/ACT security *at slightly different rates in successive coupon periods.* The reason, as noted, is that the actual number of days in two successive coupon periods always differs, and consequently, so too do the day-count fractions used in determining how much interest accrues per day in successive coupon periods.[3]

ACT/365

ACT/365, a simple variant of the ACT/ACT day-count convention, differs from ACT/ACT in that the *denominator* of the ACT/365 day-count fraction always equals 365 days, even in leap years. Thus, under ACT/365, the day-count fraction 366/365 is possible.

---

[2] Since the *last* day of a given coupon period is the *first* day of the subsequent period, this day cannot be an accrual day in *both* periods. The U.S. Treasury stipulates that the *first* day of a coupon period is *not* an accrual day, but that the *last* day is.

[3] Note some authors confuse this point: They seem to imply that, if, say, the current coupon period of an ACT/ACT bond comprises 183 days, the proper way to calculate accrued interest in the current coupon period on a semiannual-pay bond is to proceed as if the *denominator* of the day-count fraction were 2 × 183 in *two consecutive* coupon periods (i.e., as if the year base were 366 days). Although this approach gives the correct figure for accrued interest in the current coupon period, it can cause problems when calculating the appropriate fraction of a coupon period for the purpose of discounting future cash flows. Those who fall into error tend to think of the calculation of accrued interest as follows:

$$AI = \frac{c \times \text{actual days}}{2 \times \text{days in the current coupon period}}$$

This method makes the term, (2 × the length of the current coupon period), appear to be a significant constant, whereas it's actually a number that changes from one coupon period to the next.

Example. Under the ACT/365 payment convention, the day-count fraction for the period December 2, 1991, to March 5, 1992, is 94/365 or 0.258.

Any ACT/365 bond that pays periodic interest will, in general, accrue interest at a rate such that interest accrued over a full coupon period will not equal the periodic coupon payment. *Thus, for an ACT/365 issue, day-count fractions and interest accruals over a full coupon period need not generate the actual coupon payment for the period.* This counterintuitive result, which reflects the fact that 365 is not evenly divisible by 2, 4, or 12, is a possible source of confusion and erroneous calculations. The reader should therefore think it through carefully; to help, we provide the following example.[4]

Example. Under the ACT/365 payment convention, the day-count fraction for a semiannual pay bond over the full coupon period, November 15, 1991, to May 15, 1992, is 182/365 or 0.499. Since the day-count fraction for the full coupon period equals 0.499, not 0.500, and since the semiannual coupon payment must equal exactly one-half the annual payment, *this example demonstrates that the interest accrued on a given ACT/365 security over a given coupon period need not equal the actual coupon payment due at the end of that period.* This anomalous result cannot occur for an ACT/ACT security paying a regular coupon.

ACT/365—Japanese

Another variant of the 365-day-year payment convention is *ACT/365—Japanese.* This payment convention is used by the Japanese government to calculate accrued interest on *Japanese Government Bonds* (*JGBs*). Under ACT/365—Japanese, *leap days are always ignored.*

ACT/365—Japanese, like ACT/365, assumes that all years comprise exactly 365 days. Thus, the only difference between ACT/365—Japanese and ACT/365 lies in the *numerator* of the day-count fraction; and this difference exists only in a leap year.

---

[4] Note also the examples provided later in Table 5–6.

ACT/365 ISDA

A third variant of the ACT/365 payment convention, one defined by the *International Swap Dealers Association* (*ISDA*), is *ACT/365 ISDA*.[5] This payment convention, like ACT/365, takes the number of days in a *non-leap year* to be 365. However, ACT/365 ISDA does adjust the calculation of accrued interest for coupon periods that include a leap day.

The *rule* for adjusting for a leap day, as defined by *ISDA,* is as follows:[6]

> [If ACT/365 ISDA] is specified, the actual number of days in the Calculation Period or Compounding Period in respect of which payment is being made divided by 365 (or, if any portion of that Calculation Period or Compounding Period falls in a leap year, the sum of (A) the actual number of days in that portion of the Calculation Period or Compounding Period falling in a leap year divided by 366 and (B) the actual number of days in that portion of the Calculation Period or Compounding Period falling in a nonleap year divided by 365) . . .

Under ACT/365 ISDA, the day-count fraction for a coupon period that includes days that fall within a leap year is the *sum* of two calculations—steps A and B defined in the above quote from the ISDA manual. In step A, the *numerator* is set equal to the actual number of days in the coupon period that fall within the leap year and the *denominator* is set equal to 366. In step B, the *numerator* is set equal to the actual number of days in the coupon period that *do not* fall within the leap year and the *denominator* is set equal to 365. The day-count fraction equals the *sum* of the fractions obtained in steps A and B.

Under ACT/365 ISDA, the day-count fraction for a coupon period that does not include days falling within a leap year is calculated precisely the same way as is the ACT/365 day-count fraction.

For a coupon period that includes a leap day, the ACT/365 ISDA day-count fraction is:

---

[5] This convention is sometimes referred to as ACTUAL/ACTUAL, but most people try to avoid doing so because of the possible confusion between ACT/365 ISDA and the ACT/ACT payment-convention used by the U.S. Treasury.

[6] ISDA, *1991 ISDA Definitions* (New York: International Swap Dealers Association, 1991), pp. 10–11.

$$\begin{pmatrix}\text{ACT/365 ISDA}\\ \text{day-count fraction}\end{pmatrix} = \frac{\begin{pmatrix}\text{Interest-accrual days}\\ \text{falling within}\\ \text{the leap year}\end{pmatrix}}{366} + \frac{\begin{pmatrix}\text{Interest-accrual days}\\ \text{not falling within}\\ \text{the leap year}\end{pmatrix}}{365}$$

ACT/360

The ACT/360 payment convention is a simple variant of ACT/365. Under ACT/360, the *numerator* is, as usual, taken to be the *actual* number of days between two dates, *but* the *denominator* is always taken to be exactly 360 days. The ACT/360 payment convention is important because it is the interest-payment convention used for *money market instruments* in most major capital markets worldwide; the principal exceptions are the United Kingdom and Canada.

Under ACT/360, as under ACT/365, the annual coupon rate is used in calculating accrued interest.

INTEREST-PAYMENT CONVENTIONS BASED ON A 30-DAY MONTH

Interest-payment conventions based on actual accrual days are difficult to implement without calculators or computers. Hence, prior to the advent of calculators, people developed several interest-payment conventions that could be implemented easily by hand. All such conventions are based on the assumption that each month comprises exactly 30 days and that a year comprises exactly 360 days.

The 30/360 Day-Count Convention

Under the 30/360 day-count convention, each coupon period comprises an equal number of days; also, under 30/360, as under ACT/ACT, interest always accrues at a rate such that a full period's accrued interest equals exactly the coupon payment for that period.

Several variants of the 30/360 day-count convention are used by issuers worldwide. To identify each such variant, we will append to 30/360 the name of the organization that defines a particular variant of 30/360. The several variants of 30/360 differ only in how the *numerator* of the day-count fraction is defined, including how the last day of February is to be treated. In *all* variants of 30/360, the *denominator* of the day-count fraction is taken to be 360. In presenting examples of U.S. securities that pay according to the 30/360 day-count convention, we will use the 30/360 day-count convention as defined by the *Public Securities Association* (*PSA*). Also, in our examples, we will avoid bonds having a coupon date that falls on the last day of February.

In implementing the 30/360 day-count, the standard practice is to define D_1 and D_2, the start and end dates respectively, as follows:

$$D_1 = (\text{month}_1,\ \text{day}_1,\ \text{year}_1)$$

$$D_2 = (\text{month}_2,\ \text{day}_2,\ \text{year}_2)$$

In all cases, the numerator of the day-count fraction (i.e., the number of interest-accrual days) is defined by the following expression:

$$\begin{pmatrix}\text{Interest-accrual}\\ \text{days}\end{pmatrix} = 360\left(year_2 - year_1\right) + 30\left(month_2 - month_1\right) + \left(day_2 - day_1\right)$$

Thus, the standard 30/360 day-count fraction is:

$$\begin{pmatrix}\text{30/360}\\ \text{day-count}\\ \text{fraction}\end{pmatrix} = \left(\frac{\text{Interest-accrual days}}{360}\right)$$

30/360 ISDA

The 30/360 ISDA interest-payment convention is a variant of the 30/360 day-count convention described above. Although we append the ISDA designation, this is probably the *standard* definition of the 30/360 day-count convention. The PSA and SIA variants are simple extensions of the ISDA definition. The 30/360 ISDA rule for calculating the number of interest-accrual days is as follows:[7]

$$\text{If } (day_1 = 31),\ \text{then set } day_1^* = 30$$

$$\text{otherwise, set } day_1^* = day_1.$$

$$\text{If } \left([day_2 = 31] \text{ and } [day_1^* = 30]\right),\ \text{then set } day_2^* = 30$$

$$\text{otherwise, set } day_2^* = day_2.$$

---

[7] Ibid.

Now substitute day_1^* for day_1 and day_2^* for day_2 in the standard 30/360 equation for number of accrued days.

30/360 PSA

The *Public Securities Association* (*PSA*) rule for determining the *numerator* of the 30/360 day-count fraction differs from the ISDA rule only when the D_1 is the *last day of February;* in this case, under the PSA convention, day_1 is *always* changed to 30. Thus, the PSA rule for calculating the numerator of the 30/360 day-count fraction is:[8]

$$\text{If } \left([day_1 = 31] \text{ or } [day_1 = \text{ last day of February}]\right), \text{ then set } day_1^* = 30$$
$$\text{otherwise, set } day_1^* = day_1.$$
$$\text{If } \left(\left[day_2 = 31\right] \text{ and } \left[day_1^* = 30\right]\right), \text{ then set } day_2^* = 30$$
$$\text{otherwise, set } day_2^* = day_2.$$

Now substitute day_1^* for day_1 and day_2^* for day_2 in the standard 30/360 equation for number of accrual days.

30/360 SIA

The *Securities Industry Association* (*SIA*) rule for determining the *numerator* of the 30/360 day-count fraction is a combination of the ISDA and PSA rules. The SIA and ISDA rules will generate the same day-count fraction except in the case of bonds that pay coupons on the *last day of February.* In that *special case,* the SIA and PSA formulas will generate the same day-count fraction.

The SIA rule is as follows:[9]

---

[8] PSA, *PSA Uniform Practices* (New York: Public Securities Association, 1990), p. SF–17.

[9] John J. Lynch, Jr., and Jan H. Mayle. *Standard Securities Calculation Methods: Fixed Income Securities Formulas* (New York: Securities Industry Association, 1986), pp. 13–19.

$$\text{If}\left(\left[day_1 = 31\right] \text{ or } \left[\begin{array}{c}\left[\begin{array}{c} day_1 = \text{ last day of} \\ \text{February}\end{array}\right] \\ \text{and} \\ \left[\begin{array}{c}\text{the bond pays a} \\ \text{coupon on the} \\ \text{last day of February}\end{array}\right]\end{array}\right]\right), \text{ then set } day_1^* = 30;$$

$$\text{otherwise, set } day_1^* = day_1.$$

$$\text{If } \left(\left[day_2 = 31\right] \text{ and } \left[day_1^* = 30\right]\right), \text{ then set } day_2^* = 30$$

$$\text{otherwise, set } day_2^* = day_2.$$

Now substitute day_1^* for day_1 and day_2^* for day_2 in the standard 30/360 equation for number of accrued days.

30E/360

The *30E/360 payment convention,* which is a variant of 30/360 ISDA, is used primarily in Europe; hence, the *E* in the name of this convention. In the United States, 30E/360 is sometimes used for interest rate swaps.

The 30E/360 payment convention differs from the 30/360 ISDA payment convention whenever the *second* date is 31. In the 30E/360 formulation, the *second* date is *always* set equal to 30. Thus, the 30E/360 rule for counting interest-accrual days is as follows:

$$\text{If } (day_1 = 31), \text{ then set } day_1^* = 30$$

$$\text{otherwise, set } day_1^* = day_1.$$

$$\text{If } (day_2 = 31), \text{ then set } day_2^* = 30$$

$$\text{otherwise, set } day_2^* = day_2.$$

Now substitute day_1^* for day_1 and day_2^* for day_2 in the standard 30/360 equation for number of accrued days.

February and the 30/360 Day Count

The several variants of the 30/360 interest-payment convention differ in their treatment of the last day of February. Further, the number of interest-accrual days will typically jump by one, two, or three days as the end date for the period goes from February 27 to March 1. Despite the adjustments that the PSA and SIA rules make, this problem can still arise, since those adjustments apply only to the *first* date, *not* to the *second* date.

This indeterminacy we've just noted is particularly troublesome when a bond pays a coupon on the *last day* of February; and, for this reason, issuers are usually advised not to issue a bond that pays a coupon on that day.

Examples of 30/360 Day-Count Conventions

To clarify further our explanation of the various formulations of the 30/360 interest-payment convention, we present in Table 5–1 a number of examples taken from the SIA manual.[10]

TABLE 5–1
Examples of 30/360 Day Counts under Alternative Interest-Payment Conventions[11]

		Day Counts, Start Date to End Date, under Alternative 30/360 Interest-Payment Conventions			
Start Date	*End Date*	*Actual Days*	*30/360 ISDA*	*30/360 PSA*	*30E/360*
Jan-01-86	Feb-01-86	31	30	30	30
Jan-01-86	Jan-01-86	365	360	360	360
Jan-15-86	Feb-01-86	17	16	16	16
Feb-01-86	Mar-01-86	28	30	30	30
Feb-15-86	Apr-01-86	45	46	46	46
Mar-15-86	Jun-15-86	92	90	90	90
Mar-31-86	Apr-01-86	1	1	1	1
Mar-31-86	Apr-30-86	30	30	30	30
Mar-31-86	Dec-31-86	275	270	270	270
Jul-15-86	Sep-15-86	62	60	60	60
Aug-21-86	Apr-11-87	233	230	230	230
Nov-01-86	Mar-01-87	120	120	120	120
Dec-15-86	Dec-30-86	15	15	15	15
Dec-15-86	Dec-31-86	16	16	16	15
Dec-31-86	Feb-01-87	32	31	31	31
Feb-01-88	Mar-01-88	29	30	30	30

[10] Ibid., p.19

[11] No column for SIA results is shown, since the SIA result always equals, depending on whether the bond pays interest on the last of February, either the ISDA result or the PSA result. See the definition of the SIA 30/360 day-count convention.

Examples of 30/360 Day-Counts Involving the Last Day of February

To clarify further our explanation of the variants of the 30/360 interest-payment convention, we present in Table 5–2 a number of examples involving the last day of February.[12]

TABLE 5–2
Examples of 30/360 Day-Counts that Involve the Last Day of February[13]

		Day Counts, Start Date to End Date, under Alternative 30/360 Interest-Payment Conventions			
Start Date	*End Date*	*Actual Days*	*30/360 ISDA*	*30/360 PSA*	*30E/360*
Aug-30-91	Aug-31-91	1	0	0	0
Aug-31-91	Sep-01-91	2	1	1	1
Aug-30-91	Feb-27-92	181	177	177	177
Aug-30-91	Feb-28-92	182	178	178	178
Aug-30-91	Feb-29-92	183	179	179	179
Aug-30-91	Mar-01-92	184	181	181	181
Aug-30-91	Aug-29-92	365	359	359	359
Aug-30-91	Aug-30-92	366	360	360	360
Aug-30-91	Aug-31-92	367	360	360	360
Aug-30-91	Sep-01-92	368	361	361	361
Aug-31-91	Sep-01-91	1	1	1	1
Aug-31-91	Sep-02-91	2	2	2	2
Aug-31-91	Feb-27-92	180	177	177	177
Aug-31-91	Feb-28-92	181	178	178	178
Aug-31-91	Feb-29-92	182	179	179	179
Aug-31-91	Mar-01-92	183	181	181	181
Aug-31-91	Aug-29-92	364	359	359	359
Aug-31-91	Aug-30-92	365	360	360	360
Aug-31-91	Aug-31-92	366	360	360	360
Aug-31-91`	Sep-01-92	367	361	361	361
Jan-15-92	Feb-28-92	44	43	43	43
Jan-15-92	Feb-29-92	45	44	44	44
Jan-15-92	Mar-01-92	46	46	46	46
Jan-15-93	Feb-27-93	43	42	42	42
Jan-15-93	Feb-28-93	44	43	43	43
Jan-15-93	Mar-01-93	45	46	46	46

[12] John J. Lynch, Jr., and Jan. H. Mayle. *Standard Securities Calculation Methods: Fixed Income Securities Formulas* (New York: Securities Industry Association, 1986), p. 19.

[13] Ibid.

TABLE 5–2 (*Concluded*)

Start Date	*End Date*	*Actual Days*	*30/360 ISDA*	*30/360 PSA*	*30E/360*
Feb-28-92	Feb-27-92	−1	−1	−1	−1
Feb-28-92	Feb-28-92	0	0	0	0
Feb-29-92	Feb-29-92	1	1	1	1
Feb-28-92	Mar-01-92	2	3	3	3
Feb-28-92	Mar-02-92	3	4	4	4
Feb-28-92	Aug-27-92	181	179	179	179
Feb-28-92	Aug-28-92	182	180	180	180
Feb-28-92	Aug-29-92	183	181	181	181
Feb-28-92	Aug-30-92	184	182	182	182
Feb-28-92	Aug-31-92	185	183	183	182
Feb-28-92	Sep-01-92	186	183	183	183
Feb-28-92	Sep-02-92	187	184	184	184
Feb-28-92	Feb-27-93	365	359	359	359
Feb-28-92	Feb-28-93	366	360	360	360
Feb-28-92	Mar-01-93	367	363	363	363
Feb-28-92	Mar-02-03	368	364	364	364
Feb-28-92	Mar-03-93	369	365	365	365
Feb-29-92	Feb-29-92	0	0	−1	0
Feb-29-92	Mar-01-92	1	2	1	2
Feb-29-92	Mar-02-92	2	3	2	3
Feb-29-92	Aug-27-92	180	178	177	178
Feb-29-92	Aug-28-92	181	179	178	179
Feb-29-92	Aug-29-92	182	180	179	180
Feb-29-92	Aug-30-92	183	181	180	181
Feb-29-92	Aug-31-92	184	182	180	181
Feb-29-92	Sep-01-92	185	182	181	182
Feb-29-92	Sep-02-92	186	183	182	183
Feb-29-92	Feb-27-93	364	358	357	358
Feb-29-92	Feb-28-93	365	359	358	359
Feb-29-92	Mar-01-93	366	362	361	362
Feb-29-92	Mar-02-93	367	363	362	363
Feb-29-92	Mar-03-93	368	364	363	364
Feb-28-93	Feb-27-93	−1	−1	−1	−1
Feb-28-93	Feb-28-93	0	0	−2	0
Feb-28-93	Mar-01-93	1	3	1	3
Feb-28-93	Mar-02-93	2	4	2	4
Feb-28-93	Aug-27-93	180	179	177	179
Feb-28-93	Aug-28-93	181	180	178	180
Feb-28-93	Aug-29-93	182	181	179	181
Feb-28-93	Aug-30-93	183	182	180	182
Feb-28-93	Aug-31-93	184	183	180	182
Feb-28-93	Sep-01-93	185	183	181	183
Feb-28-93	Sep-02-93	186	184	182	184
Feb-28-93	Feb-27-94	364	359	357	359
Feb-28-93	Feb-28-94	365	360	358	360

ACCRUED INTEREST

Interest accrues on a coupon-bearing instrument during a coupon period at the rate specified by its interest-payment convention. Also, whenever a coupon-bearing security is traded, the amount that the seller receives from the buyer is the clean price of the security *plus* accrued interest. Specifically, if the holder of a coupon-bearing security sells that security during a coupon period, the buyer will pay the seller, on the date the trade settles, all interest that has accrued on that paper from the prior coupon payment date up to, but not including, the settlement date. On a coupon-payment date, the issuer will make the required coupon payment to the (registered) owner of the security. Thus, an investor holding a coupon-bearing security (even when the holding period constitutes only a fraction of a coupon period) always receives the proper coupon interest due him.

For any coupon-bearing security, accrued interest, *AI,* equals the day-count fraction times the coupon rate for the relevant coupon period times the face amount of the security. The formula is:

$$AI = \begin{pmatrix}\text{Day-count}\\ \text{fraction}\end{pmatrix}\begin{pmatrix}\text{Coupon rate for the}\\ \text{relevant coupon period}\end{pmatrix}(\text{Face amount})$$

Example: Calculating *AI* on a U.S. Treasury Note

All U.S. Treasury notes and bonds pay interest semiannually according to the ACT/ACT payment convention. A U.S. Treasury note might, for example, pay half of its annual coupon on February 15, the other half six months later on August 15.

To illustrate the calculation of accrued interest on an ACT/ACT security, consider again the 10-year note that was issued by the U.S. Treasury on November 15, 1991. This issue, which carries a coupon of 7½% and matures on November 15, 2001, has two coupon dates, May 15 and November 15. The actual number of days in the first coupon period of this issue (November 15, 1991 to May 15, 1992) was 182 days, whereas the actual number of days in the second coupon period (May 15, 1992 to November 15, 1992) was 184 days.

To figure the accrued interest for any 30-day holding period during the first coupon period on a $10MM face amount of the 7½s of 11/01, would multiply the appropriate day-count fraction (30/182), times the coupon divided by 2 times the face amount.[14] Doing so we get:

$$AI = \left[\left(\frac{30}{182}\right)\left(\frac{0.075}{2}\right)\right](\$10\text{MM})$$
$$= \$61,813.19$$

To calculate accrued interest, for any 30-day holding period during the second coupon period, on a $10MM face amount of the 7½s of 11/01, we would again multiply the appropriate day-count fraction (30/184) times the coupon times the face amount.[15] Doing so we get:

$$AI = \left[\left(\frac{30}{184}\right)\left(\frac{0.075}{2}\right)\right](\$10\text{MM})$$
$$= \$61,141.30$$

The discrepancy between the two numbers we got for accrued interest on the 7½s of 11/01 over a 30-day holding period in each of two consecutive coupon periods was to be expected. On an ACT/ACT-pay security, interest accrued per day, necessarily differs from one coupon period to the next because the number of days in a coupon period cannot be 182.5 (i.e., precisely one-half a year).[16]

AN ODD FIRST COUPON PERIOD

A bond's *dated date* is the date on which interest begins to accrue. Interest will continue to accrue until the maturity date. If the bond makes periodic interest payments, these payments will be made on the coupon-payment dates. The dated date of a bond may differ from its *issue date* (i.e., the date on which the purchase of the bond by the investor from the issuer *settles*).

Typically, a bond's dated date is an *anniversary* of the bond's *first* coupon date. In this case, a bond has a *normal* first coupon period. However, coupon-bearing securities are sometimes issued with an *odd*—

---

[14] See discussion on pages 65–66 of the day-count fraction for this security in this coupon period.

[15] See discussion on pages 65–66 of the day-count fraction for this security in this coupon period.

[16] A possible exception would be if one coupon period included a leap day. In that special case, a 183-day coupon period could be followed by another 183-day coupon period.

short or long—first coupon period. The computation of the day-count fraction for an *odd* first coupon period is straightforward.[17]

Odd first periods are defined relative to *virtual* coupon dates. A virtual coupon date is defined as any anniversary of the *first coupon date* occurring *prior* to the first coupon date.

Example. Consider the the 7½s of 11/01 whose dated and issue dates are November 15, 1991, and whose first coupon date is May 15, 1992. *Virtual* coupon dates include, May 15, 1991, and November 15, 1991. The virtual coupon payment date immediately preceding the first coupon date, in this example November 15, 1991, is referred to as the *first prior virtual coupon payment date.* Likewise, May 15, 1991 is referred to as the *second* prior virtual coupon payment date.

A Short First Coupon Period

A bond has a *short* first period when the dated date is *after* the first prior virtual coupon payment date. When the *first* coupon period is *less than* a full coupon period, the numerator of the day-count fraction is the actual days, as defined above, whereas the denominator is the number of days in the *full* coupon period between prior virtual coupon payment date and the first coupon payment date. The adjustment to the numerator of the day-count fraction *reduces* the *first* coupon payment, hence the meaning of *short.*

Example. If the 7½s of 11/01 had been issued on November 18 instead of November 15, the day-count fraction for the period December 2 to March 5 would have been 94/182 or 0.516; and the day-count fraction for the full period would have been 179/182 or 0.984.

A Long First Coupon Period

A bond has a *long* first period when the dated date occurs *before* the first prior virtual coupon payment date and *after* the second prior virtual coupon payment date. When the *first* coupon period is *greater than* a full

---

[17] The following accrual methods for odd-first-coupon periods is a generalization of the U.S. Treasury method.

coupon period, the calculation of the day-count fraction for the long first coupon period equals the sum of two parts—the *regular* part of the long first coupon period and the *stub* or *short* part of the long first coupon period.

The regular part of the long first coupon period is defined by the first prior virtual coupon-payment date and the first coupon-payment date. As the regular part of the long first coupon period is a full coupon period, the calculation of the day-count fraction for it is the same as is that for any normal coupon period.

The stub or short part of the long first coupon period is defined by the second prior virtual coupon-payment date and the first prior virtual coupon-payment date. Since the dated date lies between the second and first prior virtual coupon dates, the day-count fraction for the *stub* is defined as is that for a *short* first coupon period.

Finally, the day-count fraction for a long first coupon period is the sum of the day-count fraction for the stub and regular parts of the long first coupon period.

Example. If the 7½s of 11/01 had been issued on October 18 instead of November 15, the day-count fraction for the period December 2 to March 5 would have been 94/182 or 0.516; and the day-count fraction for the entire long first coupon period would have been (28/184) + (182/182) or 1.152. During the *stub* part of the long first coupon period, interest accrues based on a 184-day coupon period; while during the *regular* part of the long first coupon period, interest accrues based on a 182-day coupon period.

BONDS THAT TRADE EX-DIVIDEND

Some issuers of notes and bonds require that their securities trade *ex-dividend.*[18] The coupon period for such securities is split into two subperiods determined by the *ex-dividend date.* During the period from

[18] The use of the term *ex-dividend* instead of accrued interest derives from the British practice of referring to bonds as *stocks.* Hence, whenever we refer here to *dividend,* we actually mean accrued interest. The market practice of trading coupon-bearing securities with accrued interest is referred to as *cum-dividend.*

the last coupon date up to but not including the ex-dividend date, the security trades with accrued interest or *cum-dividend.* Starting with the ex-dividend date, the security trades *without the coupon,* which means that the next coupon payment will be paid to the holder of record as of the ex-dividend date, *not* to the holder as of the coupon-payment date. This practice is similar to the practice prevailing in equities markets, since an equity (stock) *always* trades ex-dividend after its *record* (ex-dividend) date.

In the trading of coupon-bearing securities, market practice is that the buyer of such a security will pay the price plus accrued interest. Consequently, consistency in pricing demands that a coupon-bearing security, such as a U.K. gilt, that trades *ex-dividend* must trade, *throughout its ex-dividend period,* with *negative accrued interest.*

Example of an Issue that Trades Ex-Dividend

To illustrate just how interest payments work on a bond that trades ex-dividend, we consider the price behavior of U.K. gilts in Tables 5–3 and 5–4.

TABLE 5–3
Specifications of the Gilt Used in Our Ex-Dividend Example

Coupon	8.500%
Maturity date	Sep-01-97
Issue date	Jan-13-88
Payments per year	2
Face value (par)	$10,000
Payment convention	ACT/365
Ex-dividend rule	37 days prior to coupon date
Last coupon date	Sep-01-93
Next coupon date	Mar-01-94
Ex-dividend date	Jan-23-94

TABLE 5–4
Accrued Interest on the Gilt Described in Table 5–3 as of Selected Dates

		Accrued Interest Calculation			
		Cum-Dividend		*Ex-Dividend*	
Settlement Date	*Actual Days*	*Day-Count Fraction*	*Accrued Interest*	*Day-Count Fraction*	*Accrued Interest*
Jan-03-94	124	0.340	$288.77	0.340	$288.77
Jan-10-94	131	0.359	305.07	0.359	(305.07)
Jan-17-94	138	0.378	321.37	0.378	(321.37)
Jan-24-94	145	0.397	337.67	−0.103	(87.33)
Jan-31-94	152	0.416	353.97	−0.084	(71.03)
Feb-07-94	159	0.436	370.27	−0.064	(54.73)
Feb-14-94	166	0.455	386.58	−0.045	(38.42)
Feb-21-94	173	0.474	402.88	−0.026	(22.12)
Feb-28-94	180	0.493	419.18	−0.007	(5.82)

ACCRUED INTEREST VERSUS COUPON PAYMENTS

It's important to understand that coupon interest *accrues* according to the *interest-payment convention* specified by the issuer, whereas coupon interest is *paid* according to the *coupon-payment schedule* specified by the issuer. An example will clarify this point. See Tables 5–5 and 5–6.

In defining the ACT/ACT and ACT/365 day counts, we observed that there was a difference between interest accruals and coupon payments. Table 5–6 highlights these differences. Note that any ACT/ACT issue accrues interest at a rate such that a full coupon period's accrual equals the full coupon payment due for that period. In contrast, an

TABLE 5–5
Specifications of a Hypothetical Issue Used as a Basis for Table 5–6

Coupon	7.500%
Maturity date	Nov-15-01
Issue date	Nov-15-91
Payments per year	2
Face value (par)	$10,000

TABLE 5–6
Comparison of ACT/ACT and ACT/365 Interest Payment Conventions

Coupon Dates	*Coupon Payment*	*Actual Days*	*ACT/ACT Day-Count Fraction*	*Accrued Interest*	*ACT/365 Day-Count Fraction*	*Accrued Interest*
May-15-92	$375.00	182	1.000	$375.00	0.499	$373.97
Nov-15-92	375.00	184	1.000	375.00	0.504	378.08
May-15-93	375.00	181	1.000	375.00	0.496	371.92
Nov-15-93	375.00	184	1.000	375.00	0.504	378.08
May-15-94	375.00	181	1.000	375.00	0.496	371.92
Nov-15-94	375.00	184	1.000	375.00	0.504	378.08
May-15-95	375.00	181	1.000	375.00	0.496	371.92
Nov-15-95	375.00	184	1.000	375.00	0.504	378.08
May-15-96	375.00	182	1.000	375.00	0.499	373.97
Nov-15-96	375.00	184	1.000	375.00	0.504	378.08
May-15-97	375.00	181	1.000	375.00	0.496	371.92
Nov-15-97	375.00	184	1.000	375.00	0.504	378.08
May-15-98	375.00	181	1.000	375.00	0.496	371.92
Nov-15-98	375.00	184	1.000	375.00	0.504	378.08
May-15-99	375.00	181	1.000	375.00	0.496	371.92
Nov-15-99	375.00	184	1.000	375.00	0.504	378.08
May-15-00	375.00	182	1.000	375.00	0.499	373.97
Nov-15-00	375.00	184	1.000	375.00	0.504	378.08
May-15-01	375.00	181	1.000	375.00	0.496	371.92
Nov-15-01	375.00	184	1.000	375.00	0.504	378.08

ACT/365 issue does not accrue interest at a rate such that a full coupon period's accrual equals the full coupon payment due for that period.

COMPARING YIELDS

Calculating accrued interest correctly is not the only reason for delving into payment conventions. A second crucial reason for doing so is that dealers, investors, and others who operate in fixed-income land frequently have to compare yields. A comparison of two yields quoted on securities that pay according to the same payment conventions can be done *directly* because one is comparing an apple to an apple. However, a comparison of two yields quoted on securities that pay according to two different payment conventions cannot be done directly because in doing so one would be comparing an apple to an orange.

Situations in which this problem arises are easy to find. A Treasury bond trader who's financing his position with repo and wants to make a breakeven calculation has a problem: The yield quoted on his bonds is for a semiannual-pay, *ACT/ACT* security whereas the repo rate he must pay is quoted on an *ACT/360 day* basis; and if the trader relies primarily on overnight financing, that rate may be compounded as often as once every business day.

To make a valid comparison of yields quoted on different bases, one must first convert one yield to the basis on which the other yield is quoted. We have already done one simple yield conversion: Specifically, we converted a yield quoted on a discount basis to a simple yield quoted on a 365–day-year basis and then to a simple yield quoted on a 360-day basis. A T bill trader who wanted to do a breakeven calculation on a bill position financed with repo would, for example, want to convert the discount rate at which he acquired his bills to a simple yield on a 360-day basis in order to make that rate directly comparable to the repo rate he was paying; in addition, he'd want to determine what effective repo rate he was really paying when allowance, if any were needed, was made for compounding.

An investor who's holding notes and bonds that pay on different bases faces a similar but more complicated conversion of yields: Specifically, he needs to convert the yields to maturity on all bonds in which he considers investing to a single basis. Which basis he picks will depend on the sorts of bonds he typically buys. If he invests just in sovereign bonds, he will probably do what everyone else does: compare quotes on a U.S. Treasury equivalent basis (i.e., on an ACT/ACT basis). This practice reflects the fact that, in the world of sovereign bonds, U.S. Treasuries tend to be the dominant security, if for no other reason than the huge amount of them outstanding. In contrast, an investor who's buying a lot of munis, corporates, and Eurobonds will probably want to standardize on a 30/360 basis. For a dealer making up a quote sheet, whether he uses a 360-day or a 365-day year depends on where his dominant business lies.

THE NEXT CHAPTER

In the next chapter, we'll work out the basic calculations for *discount securities,* a family that includes Treasury bills (issued by the United States and other sovereigns), U.S. federal agency discount paper, bankers' acceptances, and most U.S. commercial paper.

PART 2

MONEY MARKET PAPER: CALCULATIONS AND APPLICATIONS

CHAPTER 6

DISCOUNT PAPER: CALCULATIONS

In Chapter 6, we develop basic formulas for calculating the amount of the discount, the price, and the yield on a *discount security.* We also show how to calculate, for a discount security, various numbers such as money market yield and the value of an 01. Later, in Chapter 8, we describe ways in which these calculations—all important and fundamental—can be used by imaginative traders and investors.

To illustrate our discussion, we need a concrete example. So, we've chosen to begin this chapter with an analysis of price/yield relationships for *U.S. Treasury bills.*

In the United States, calculations for *T bills and all other U.S.-origin discount paper* (e.g., commercial paper, federal credit agency discount paper, and bankers' acceptances) are based on an assumed *360-day year.* In the Euromarket and in most other countries, calculations for discount paper are also based on an assumed 360-day year. However, the United Kingdom and Canada are major exceptions; there, calculations for discount paper are based on an assumed *365-day year.*

When one moves from the United States to the United Kingdom or Canada, the formulas for discount securities do *not* change; what does change is just one variable, the assumed number of days in a year for quoting such securities. To allow for this difference, we restate, at the end of this chapter, all the discount-paper equations we derive in a *general form* in which *the assumed number of days in a year is treated as a variable.*[1]

---

[1] See also Chapter 20.

CALCULATING DISCOUNT AND PRICE WITH RATE OF DISCOUNT GIVEN: *U.S.* PAPER

Assume that an investor who participates in an auction of U.S. Treasury *year bills* picks up \$1MM of them at 8%. This means that the Treasury sells to the investor \$1MM of bills that mature in one year at a price approximately, but not precisely, 8% below their face value.

The "approximately, but not precisely" qualifier reflects, as suggested in Chapter 4, two factors. First, in the United States, the year bill is outstanding not for one year, but for 364 days. Second, the Treasury calculates the discount as if a year had only 360 days. So the fraction of the year for which the year bill is outstanding is 364/365, and the true *discount* an investor receives on \$1MM of year bills is calculated as follows:

$$\begin{pmatrix}\text{Discount on \$1MM of}\\ \text{the year bill bought at 8\%}\end{pmatrix} = 0.08(\$1{,}000{,}000)\frac{364}{360}$$

$$= \$80{,}888.89$$

The *price* the investor pays for \$1MM of the year bill equals *face value minus the discount,* that is,

$$\begin{pmatrix}\text{Price paid for \$1MM of}\\ \text{the year bill bought at 8\%}\end{pmatrix} = \$1{,}000{,}000.00 - \$80{,}888.89$$

$$= \$9{,}189{,}111.11$$

Generalizing from this example, we can construct formulas for calculating both the discount from face value and the price at which T bills will sell, depending on their current maturity and on the rate of discount at which they are quoted. These formulas are given in the box below.

Calculating Dollar Discount and Dollar Price with Rate of Discount Given: *U.S.* Discount Securities

Let

D_p = discount from face value in dollars

F = face value in dollars

d = rate of discount (decimal)

T_{sm} = days settlement to maturity

Then,

$$D_p = dF\frac{T_{sm}}{360}$$

and

$$P = F - D_p = F\left(1 - \frac{dT_{sm}}{360}\right)$$

Examples. To illustrate use of the formulas in the box above, let

$$d = 0.08$$
$$T_{sm} = 11$$
$$F = \$225,000$$

Then,

$$D_p = 0.08(\$225,000)\frac{11}{360}$$
$$= \$550$$

Also, since

$$P = F - D_p$$

we can calculate that

$$P = \$225,000 - \$550 = \$224,450$$

CALCULATING RATE OF DISCOUNT WITH DOLLAR DISCOUNT OR PRICE GIVEN: *U.S.* PAPER

Using the formulas derived above, it's easy to obtain an expression for d when the value of either D_p or P is given. Let's start with D_p *given.* We know that

$$D_p = dF\frac{T_{sm}}{360}$$

Solving this equation for d, we obtain d as the following function of D_p:

$$d = \frac{D_p}{F}\frac{360}{T_{sm}}$$

Alternatively, if P is *given,* we recall that

$$D_p = F - P$$

and substitute this expression for D_p into the equation,

$$d = \frac{D_p}{F}\frac{360}{T_{sm}}$$

This yields

$$d = \left(\frac{F - P}{F}\right)\frac{360}{T_{sm}}$$

This expression reduces to

$$d = \left(1 - \frac{P}{F}\right)\frac{360}{T_{sm}}$$

Calculating Rate of Discount with Dollar Discount or Price Given: *U.S.* Discount Securities

Let

D_p = discount from face value in dollars

F = face value in dollars

d = rate of discount (decimal)

T_{sm} = days from settlement to maturity

P = price

Case I: If discount in dollars given, calculate d as follows:

$$d = \frac{D_p}{F}\frac{360}{T_{sm}}$$

Case II: If price in dollars given, calculate d as follows:

$$d = \left(1 - \frac{P}{F}\right)\frac{360}{T_{sm}}$$

Examples. We can illustrate the formulas in the box on page 90 using the same numbers we used above when we solved for D_p and P when the givens were d, T_{sm}, and F. Let

$$T_{sm} = 11$$
$$D_p = \$550$$
$$F = \$225{,}000$$

Then,

$$d = \frac{\$550}{\$225{,}000}\left(\frac{360}{11}\right)$$
$$= 0.08 \text{ or } 8\%$$

Alternatively, if the calculation is made using the dollar value not for D_p, but for P, which is \$224,450, then

$$d = \left(1 - \frac{\$224{,}450}{\$225{,}000}\right)\frac{360}{11}$$
$$= 0.08 \text{ or } 8\%$$

T BILL QUOTES

Table 6–1 reproduces selected T bill quotes from *The Wall Street Journal.* These rates, which were gathered mid-afternoon on Wednesday, June 14, 1995, are for *regular* (*next-business day*) settlement on Thursday, June 15, 1995.[2]

MEASURES OF YIELD ON A T BILL

We've talked about the rate of discount offered by a T bill. Other measures of yield are also used to gauge the return offered by a T bill.

---

[2] Early in the day, U.S. T bills and other money market and government paper can, if the buyer and the seller so choose, also be traded for *cash (same-day) settlement.*

TABLE 6–1
Selected U.S. T Bill Quotes from *The Wall Street Journal*, June 14, 1995, for Settlement on June 15, 1995

Matures on, Date	*Days to Maturity*	*Bid d, (%)*	*Asked d, (%)*	*Asked Yield,* (%)*
Jun 22 '95	6	5.65%	5.55%	5.63%
Aug 03 '95	48	5.40	5.36	5.47
Sep 14 '95	90	5.44	5.42	5.59
Oct 26 '95	132	5.43	5.41	5.61
Dec 14 '95	181	5.40	5.38	5.61
May 30 '96	349	5.29	5.27	5.57

*On a *bond equivalent basis* (see discussion below).

Equivalent Simple Yield

As noted in Chapter 4, the rate at which a discount security is offered *understates* the simple yield that an investor in such a security would earn. Moreover, as the numbers in Table 6–2 show, *the discrepancy between the two rates is greater the higher the rate of discount and the longer the time to maturity.*

TABLE 6–2
Comparisons at Different Rates and Maturities between Rate of Discount and Equivalent Simple Yield on a 365–Day-Year Basis

	Equivalent 365–day-year, simple yield y (%)		
Rate of Discount, d (%)	*30-Day Maturity*	*182-Day Maturity*	*365-day Maturity*
2%	2.03%	2.05%	2.07%
4	4.07	4.14	4.23
6	6.11	6.11	6.48
8	8.17	8.45	8.82
10	10.22	10.68	11.27
12	12.29	12.95	13.84
14	14.36	15.28	16.53
16	16.44	17.65	19.35

Obviously, investors in and issuers of discount securities need a formula for converting a discount rate to a simple yield. With a few manipulations, this formula can easily be obtained. Let

$$y_{365} = \text{simple yield on a 365–day-year basis}$$

Referring to the formula on page 47, we observe that, on a discount security, this simple yield is given by

$$y_{365} = \frac{F-P}{P} \div \frac{T_{sm}}{365}$$

If we now substitute for P the expression, $F - D_p$, and simplify, we get

$$y_{365} = \left(\frac{D_p}{F-D_p}\right)\frac{365}{T_{sm}}$$

Next, we recall that

$$D_p = dF\frac{T_{sm}}{360}$$

and substitute this expression for D_p into the preceding formula. Doing so gives us

$$y_{365} = \left[\frac{dF\frac{T_{sm}}{360}}{F-dF\frac{T_{sm}}{360}}\right]\frac{365}{T_{sm}}$$

an expression that reduces to

$$y_{365} = \frac{365d}{360-dT_{sm}}$$

Bond Equivalent Yield: A Short Bill

In the money market, y_{365} is referred to as a bill's *bond equivalent or coupon equivalent yield.* This jargon derives from the fact that U.S. Treasury notes and bonds pay interest on the basis of a 365-day year.

Bond equivalent yield is an important concept. Thus, we need a symbol to denote it. Let

$$y_{be} = \text{bond equivalent yield}$$

Before we apply this concept of yield to bills, we need to distinguish between two common measures of maturity, original and current maturity. *The original maturity of any security is its time to maturity at issue.* Thus, the original maturity of a year bill is 364 days. *The current maturity of any security is its time to maturity from the current date.* Thus, the current maturity of a year bill that has been outstanding for 273 days (and is now the *current* 3-month bill) is 91 days.

For a *short* bill, that is, a bill having a *current maturity of 6 months or less* (i.e., *182 days or less*),

$$y_{be} = y_{365} = \frac{365d}{360 - dT_{sm}}$$

As noted below, determining y_{be} for a bill with a current maturity *greater than* 6 months calls for a more complex calculation.

Converting the Discount Rate on a Short Bill (182 Days or Less to Maturity) to Equivalent Bond Yield

Let

d = rate of discount (decimal)
y_{365} = equivalent simple yield for a discount security
y_{be} = bond equivalent yield for a discount security
T_{sm} = days from settlement to maturity

Then, for a discount security,

$$y_{be} = y_{365} = \frac{365d}{360 - dT_{sm}}$$

Example I. To illustrate use of the above formula, let's return to the bill example given in Chapter 4; again, we assume that

$$d = 0.08$$
$$T_{sm} = 182$$

Plugging these numbers into our equation for y_{be}, we obtain

$$y_{be} = y_{365} = \frac{365\ (0.08)}{360 - 0.08\ (182)} = 0.0845 \text{ or } 8.45\%$$

which is exactly the simple yield that we demonstrated the investor was earning (pages 46–47).

Example II. Consider the Dec 14 '95 bill quoted in Table 6–1. The *asked* rate for this bill, which had a current maturity of 181 days, was 5.38%. In the final column of Table 6–1, a yield figure, *y,* is quoted. This yield figure is the *bond equivalent yield,* that an investor who bought the Dec 14 '95 bill at its *asked rate* of discount would earn on that bill. To show this, we simply plug T_{sm} = 18 and d = 0.0538 into the equation given above for y_{be} on a discount security. Our calculation,

$$y_{be} = y_{365} = \frac{365(0.0538)}{360 - 0.0538(181)} = 0.0561 \text{ or } 5.61\%$$

which is precisely the y value given in Table 6–1 for the Dec 14 '95 bill.

Money Market Yield Revisited

As noted in Chapter 4, yields on all U.S. money market instruments—discount paper, CDs, and finance contracts—are quoted on a 360–day-year basis. Consequently, investors and others frequently find it useful, in comparing the yields available on *discount* and *interest-bearing money market instruments,* to convert the stated rate of discount at which a given piece of discount paper is trading to what's called its *money market yield,* that is, to *its simple yield calculated on 360–day-year basis.* Thus, for example, money market yield on a U.S. T bill is directly comparable to yields quoted on U.S.-origin CDs and to yields quoted for repo.

Like bond equivalent yield, money market yield is an important concept. It's also one for which we've already introduced a symbol. Specifically,

$$\begin{aligned}\text{Money market yield} &= \text{simple yield on a } 360-\text{day-year basis} \\ &= y_{360}\end{aligned}$$

to obtain a *formula* for money market yield on a U.S. discount security (i.e., y_{360}), we simply divide the expression for that security's bond equivalent yield (i.e., y_{365}) by the proper annualizing factor, 365/360. Doing so, we obtain

$$\begin{pmatrix}\text{Money market yield on} \\ \text{U.S. discount paper}\end{pmatrix} = y_{360} = \frac{365d}{360 - dT_{sm}} \div \frac{365}{360}$$

This expression reduces to

$$\begin{pmatrix}\text{Money market yield on} \\ \text{U.S. discount paper}\end{pmatrix} = y_{360} = \frac{360d}{360 - dT_{sm}}$$

Example. To illustrate use of this formula, let's look again at our example of a U.S. T bill on which $d = 0.08$ and $T_{sm} = 182$. Above, we calculated that the simple yield (365–day-year basis) on this security would be 8.45%. Now plugging $d = 0.08$ and $T_{sm} = 182$ into our equation for *money market yield,* which is really y_{360}, we obtain

$$\begin{pmatrix}\text{Money market} \\ \text{yield}\end{pmatrix} = \frac{0.08}{360 - 0.08(182)}$$
$$= 0.0834 \text{ or } 8.34\%$$

A more direct way to get this result is to use the formula,

$$y_{360} = y_{365}\left(\frac{360}{365}\right)$$

that we gave in Chapter 4 for converting a yield from a 365-day basis to a 360-day basis. We know that, for the bill in our example,

$$y_{365} = 0.0845$$

Inserting this value into the above equation for y_{360}, we obtain

$$y_{360} = 0.0845\left(\frac{360}{365}\right)$$
$$= 0.0833 \text{ or } 8.33\%$$

which is the same result we obtained above for y_{360}.

VALUE OF AN 01: *U.S.* DISCOUNT PAPER

In evaluating a given issue, trading at a given price, traders and investors are interested in various measures of the issue's *sensitivity to change.* One question they ask for *bills* and other *discount paper,* as well as for *notes, bonds, and other instruments,* is the following: *By how much would the price of a given security change if its yield were to change by an 01, that is, by 1bp?*

For *discount securities,* this calculation is easily made, since an 01 is simply a *very* small value of *d.* To illustrate, let's find the value of a 01 on \$1MM of the U.S. T bills, quoted in Table 6–1, that mature on Aug 03 '95. To do so, we substitute

$$d = 0.0001$$
$$T_{sm} = 48$$

into the equation

$$D = dF\left(\frac{T_{sm}}{360}\right)$$

to obtain[3]

$$\begin{pmatrix}\text{Value of an 01 per}\\ \text{\$1MM of face value}\end{pmatrix} = 0.0001(\$1\text{MM})\frac{48}{360}$$
$$= \$13.3333 = \$13.33$$

Value of an 01 (1bp) on a U.S. Discount Security per \$1MM Face Value

Let

$$V_{01} = \begin{pmatrix}\text{Value of an 01 per \$1MM face}\\ \text{on a U.S. discount security}\end{pmatrix}$$

Then,

$$V_{01} = 0.0001(\$1\text{MM})\frac{T_{sm}}{360}$$

which reduces to

$$V_{01} = \$0.277778T_{sm}$$

[3] On a T bill with a current maturity of six months or less, the formula we have given for the value of an 01 is indisputably correct. However, as noted below, two different quotes are typically given for a bill having a current maturity of more than six months: the rate of discount at which the bill trades and its bond equivalent yield. On such bills, the value of an 01 may be calculated as above or on a bond equivalent basis; which calculation is appropriate depends on the security or securities to which a given bill is being compared. If a bill is being compared to a short note or bond (one scheduled to pay at least one more coupon before it matures), then on such a bill, the value of an 01 should be calculated on the basis of its bond equivalent yield, not its rate of discount. The calculation of the value of 1bp on a note or bond is discussed in Chapter 13.

A useful number to remember: On a 90-day, U.S. Treasury bill having a $1MM face value,

$$\begin{aligned} V_{01} &= \$0.27778(90) \\ &= \$25.00 \end{aligned}$$

MORE T BILL QUOTES

A dealer publishing a quote sheet may—depending on available space, on the types of securities it trades, and on the interests of its audience—convert the asked rate of discount for each bill it quotes into money market yield, into bond equivalent yield, or into both.[4] Also, the dealer may provide various other statistics.

In Table 6–3, we give, based on the Feb 12 '93 quote sheet of Eastbridge Capital, Inc., a primary dealer, quotes for 13 bill issues. On Dec 09 '93, 35 bills were in fact being traded: Two were *cash management* (denoted *cm* on the quote sheet) bills; both *cm* bills (of which Table 6–3 shows only one) were in fact reopenings of existing short bills.[5] Table 6–3 also shows quotes for the *current* (i.e., most recently auctioned 3-month, 6-month, and 1-year) bills, as well as quotes for the to-be-issued (denoted *wi*) 3-month, 6-month, and 1-year bills.

Instead of quoting both a bid and an offer rate of discount for each bill, Eastbridge quotes only one rate. That rate is its estimate of where, at its cut-off time, each bill issue would in fact have traded. The advantage to this approach is that it gives the best rate for *marking to market* all positions: longs, shorts, arbitrages, and so on.[6]

The most recently auctioned 3-month, 6-month, and 1-year bills are referred to respectively as *the* 3-month bill, *the* 6-month bill, and *the 1-year* bill. When an *active* bill, say *the* 3-month bill, is replaced by a newly auctioned 3-month bill, that issue then becomes known as the *old*

---

[4] For example, *The Wall Street Journal* converts the asked rate of discount, for each bill issue it quotes, into bond equivalent yield, but *not* into money market yield (see Table 6–1).

[5] Occasionally, the Treasury issues a short *(cash management)* bill outside its regular schedule of bill issuance; the Treasury's purpose is to raise cash it needs short-term.

[6] To *mark a position to market* means to value it at current, as opposed to historical, rates or prices.

TABLE 6–3

Selected U.S. T Bill Quotes from EASTBRIDGE CAPITAL, INC., Quote Sheet, for Settlement Feb. 12, 1993*

Type	*Maturity*	*Closing Price*	*Price Change*	*Closing Yield*	*Yield Change*	*MMI Yield*	*Val 01 y_{be}*	*Val 01 Disc*	*MDur*	*No. Days*	*Issue Date*	*Orig. Issue*	*Amt. Out (M)*	*CUSIP No.*
cm	1/20/94	2.960	1.0	3.004	1.0	2.962	2.46	2.78	0.027	10	7/22/93		39,732	H56
	1/27/94	2.890	−3.0	2.934	−3.1	2.894	4.37	4.72	0.047	17	7/29/93		25,319	H64
oo	3/24/94	2.955	−2.5	3.014	−2.7	2.973	19.50	20.28	0.199	73	9/23/93		24,372	J62
o	3/31/94	2.950	−2.5	3.011	−2.6	2.969	21.36	22.22	0.218	80	9/30/93		24,833	J70
3-mo	4/7/94	3.010	−3.5	3.074	−3.7	3.032	23.23	24.17	0.237	87	4/8/93	1 yr	38,824	J88
wi	4/14/94	3.025	−300	3.091	−3.1	3.048	24.55	25.28	0.247	91	1/13/94		wi	J96
oo	6/23/94	3.104	−7.0	3.230	−7.4	3.185	43.40	45.56	0.443	164	12/23/93		13,136	L36
o	6/30/94	3.140	−6.0	3.232	−6.3	3.187	45.21	47.50	0.462	171	7/1/93	1 yr	28,447	L44
6-mo	7/7/94	3.160	−7.0	3.255	−7.4	3.210	46.99	49.44	0.480	178	1/6/94		12,623	M35
wi	7/14/94	3.180	−7.5	3.277	−7.8	3.232	48.27	50.56	0.491	182	1/13/94		wi	M43
oo	10/24/94	3.285	−8.5	3.398	−9.1	3.372	74.21	78.61	0.764	283	10/21/93	1 yr	15,875	L85
o	11/17/94	3.340	−9.0	3.462	−9.6	3.439	81.26	78.61	0.764	311	10/21/93	1 yr	16,155	L93
1 yr	12/15/94	3.355	−9.0	3.485	−9.6	3.464	88.26	86.39	0.914	339	11/18/93	1 yr	16,238	M27
wi	1/12/95	3.400	−10.5	3.539	−11.2	3.539	101.11	94.17	0.980	364	1/13/94	1 yr	16,029	P81

*In Table 6–3, the underlined issues are, respectively, the most recently auctioned 3-month, 6-month, and 1-year bills. The 3-month bill, meaning the *current* (most recently auctioned) bill, has a current maturity of 91 days only on the day it originally settles after auction. Similar comments, appropriately adjusted for original maturity, apply to the 6-month bill and to the 1-year bill.

†On a *bond equivalent basis* (see discussion below).

3-month bill; and when yet another 3-month issue is auctioned, that issue then becomes known as the *old, old* 3-month bill. In Table 6–3, *the old* and *the old, old* 3-month, 6-month, and 1-year bills are denoted in the first column by *o* and *oo* respectively. Once an old, old bill is replaced by yet another newly auctioned bill, that issue gets no special moniker unless and until it's reopened; for example, a new 6-month bill will, after passage of 3 months, be reopened and when it is, that issue will become known as the new three-month bill.

At this point, the reader should use the equations we've developed so far to check the rate conversions made in Table 6–3 except for the next-to-last one. Calculating bond equivalent yield on the 1-year bill calls for a special equation that we develop in the section below. After you've read that section, look again at Table 6–3 and calculate bond equivalent yield for the year bill quoted there.

The rate conversions given in Table 6–3 (as well as in Table 6–2) provide good benchmarks for anyone programming the equations we present for making these conversions; Table 6–3 also provides good benchmarks for anyone programming the calculation of the discount value of an 01.

The Bill Cycle: Issuance

The Treasury issues bills having *initial maturities* of 3 months, 6 months, and 1 year. All T bills are issued according to a regular cycle. A new year bill is issued on the second Wednesday of each month. A new 6-month bill is issued twice a month, and every other new 6-month bill is a *reopening* (an adding to the outstanding amount) of an old year bill that now has a *current maturity* of 182 days. A new 3-month bill is issued once a week, and one such 3-month bill is always a reopening of an old 6-month bill, which in turn was a reopening of an old year bill.

Investors typically place a high value on liquidity, and a *new* bill issue trades more *actively* and is thus more *liquid* than surrounding issues. For that reason, most quote sheets indicate, in one way or another, the *new* 3-month, the *new* 6-month, and the *new* year bill. Reopenings of a bill issue have the effect of adding to the size of that issue and thus of making each reopened issue more liquid. Also, reopenings fit nicely into the bill cycle (i.e., there's never a maturity mismatch) because a new 3-month bill actually matures in 91 days; a new 6-month bill in 182 days; and a new year bill in 364 days.

Bill quotes usually include one or more issues marked *wi.* Such an issue is trading, before it's actually issued, for *forward settlement* on its actual issue date; in Street argot, it's trading on a *when issued* basis. Normally, a new bill issue will trade *wi* from the day on which the issue is announced until the day on which it settles.

The Yield Curve

Note that yield spread column in Table 6–3 shows slope and steepness of y_c as measured by bill, 1 to 364-day maturities.

BOND EQUIVALENT YIELD: A LONG BILL

Next, we turn to the calculation of *bond equivalent yield* for a discount security having a current maturity of *more than 6 months* (i.e., of more than 182 days). This topic calls for a short preface.

In the secondary market, bids for and offerings of coupon securities are quoted not in terms of yields (as is the case for discount securities), but in terms of dollar prices. However, on every quote sheet for coupon securities, there is, for each security quoted, a number that states what that security's *yield to maturity* would be if it were purchased at its quoted *asked* or *offered* price.[7]

For present purposes, the key thing to note is that, if a Treasury bond or note with an 8% coupon were to sell at *par,* (i.e., at *a price equal to its face value*), its yield to maturity on the quote sheet would be given as 8%. However, since coupon securities, most typically, pay interest semiannually, the effective yield to the investor in that security would be something *more than* 8% when possibilities for compounding were taken into account. Specifically, using the formula developed in Chapter 4,

$$y_c = \left(1 + \frac{y}{n}\right)^n - 1$$

[7] Recall that we introduced the concept of *yield to maturity* in Chapter 4. We describe different measures of bond yield in Chapter 10 and the calculation of yield to maturity in Chapter 11.

we find that, with $y = 0.08$ and $n = 2$ (because there are two coupon periods),

$$y_c = \left(1 + \frac{0.08}{2}\right)^2 - 1$$
$$= 0.0816 \text{ or } 8.16\%$$

The lesson is clear. The yield to maturity figures on a quote sheet for semiannual-pay securities, such Treasury notes and bonds, *understate* effective yield to maturity because they ignore the fact that coupon interest is paid *semiannually;* whatever the investor may do with his coupon interest, it is worth something to him to get two semiannual payments of coupon interest rather than a single year-end payment of coupon interest.[8]

As noted, it's often useful to investors to be able to compare directly yields on T bills with yields on other Treasury notes and bonds. To this end, the Street often prepares quote sheets that *restate yields on T bills on a bond equivalent basis.*

Six Months (182 Days) or Less to Maturity

The Street's decision to restate bill yields on a bond equivalent basis creates a need to distinguish between discount securities that have 6 months to run and those that have more than 6 months to run. When a coupon security is in its last *leg* (i.e., when it will mature on its next coupon date and thus offer *no* opportunity for further *compounding*) its stated yield to maturity, y_{365}, equals 21, its simple yield on a 365-day basis. For this reason, *on T bills (and other discount paper) having a current maturity of 6 months or less, bond equivalent yield is, as noted, given by the formula:*

$$y_{be} = y_{365} = \frac{365d}{360 - dT_{sm}}$$

[8] The margin by which yield to maturity on a coupon security understates effective yield widens as the frequency with which coupon payments are made during a year rises. Thus, the understatement of effective yield is greater for a quarterly pay bond than for a semiannual-pay bond.

More Than 6 Months (182 Days) to Maturity

When a coupon security has *more than 6 months to run,* yield to maturity on the quote sheet understates, as we said above, its true yield by ignoring the opportunity for compounding. To state the yield on a *long* discount security on a comparable basis, *the same understatement must be introduced* into the calculation of that yield.

The way this is done is logical but tricky. The problem is that the simple interest yield on, say, a 9-month discount security is *too high* to be directly comparable with the yield on a coupon security of the same maturity because the coupon security will yield an interest payment before it matures, whereas the discount security will not. Let

$$y_{tm} = \text{Yield to maturity on a coupon-bearing bond}$$

That is a concept we'll talk more about in later chapters. For the present, we note simply that *calculating bond equivalent yield on a discount security is equivalent to calculating its* y_{tm}. In symbols, for a long bill,

$$y_{be} = y_{tm}$$

As noted, calculating y_{tm} for a long discount security involves adjusting downward the simple interest rate yielded by such a security. To do this, we have to calculate the rate, y_{tm}, that the investor would earn if interest were paid at the 6-month mark and if interest were paid on that interest over the discount security's remaining days to maturity.

In this case, the price, P, that would yield an investor \$1 of face value at maturity, is given by the expression

$$P+\frac{y_{tm}}{2}P+\frac{y_{tm}}{365}\left(T_{sm}-\frac{365}{2}\right)\left(1+\frac{y_{tm}}{2}\right)P=1$$

This expression for y_{tm}, can be written more simply as follows:

$$P\left(1+\frac{y_{tm}}{2}\right)\left[1+\frac{y_{tm}}{2}\left(\frac{2T_{sm}}{365}-1\right)\right]=1$$

Solving this expression for y_{tm}, we get

$$y_{tm}=y_{be}=\frac{-\dfrac{2T_{sm}}{365}+2\sqrt{\left(\dfrac{T_{sm}}{365}\right)^2-\left(\dfrac{2T_{sm}}{365}-1\right)\left(1-\dfrac{1}{P}\right)}}{\dfrac{2T_{sm}}{365}-1}$$

Solving for y_{tm}. For the interested reader, we next present the steps involved in solving for y_{tm}. Readers who prefer to take this solution on faith should skip to the numerical example presented below.

The steps in the solution for y_{tm} are as follows. The expression,

$$P\left((1+\frac{y_{tm}}{2}\right)\left[1+\frac{y_{tm}}{2}\left(\frac{2T_{sm}}{365}-1\right)\right]=1$$

is multiplied out, and the resulting equation is simplified to obtain

$$\left(\frac{2T_{sm}}{365}-1\right)y_{tm}^2+\frac{4T_{sm}}{365}y_{tm}+4\left(1-\frac{1}{P}\right)=0$$

This is a standard quadratic equation of the form,

$$ax^2 + bx + c = 0$$

which can be solved as follows:

$$x=\frac{-2b\pm\sqrt{b^2}-4ac}{2a}$$

Applying this formula to our quadratic equation in y_{tm} and simplifying terms, we get

$$y_{tm}=\frac{\frac{-2T_{sm}}{365}+2\sqrt{\left(\frac{T_{sm}}{365}\right)^2-\left(2\frac{T_{sm}}{365}-1\right)\left(1-\frac{1}{P}\right)}}{2\frac{T_{sm}}{365}-1}$$

Example. Consider a bill that has a current maturity of 358 days. Inserting this number into the formula for $y_{tm} = y_{be}$, we get

$$y_{be}=\frac{-2\frac{(358)}{365}+2\sqrt{\left(\frac{358}{365}\right)^2-\left(2\frac{358}{365}-1\right)\left(1-\frac{1}{0.0336}\right)}}{2\frac{358}{365}-1}$$

$$=0.0352 \text{ or } 3.52\%$$

The rate, 3.52% is the bill's bond equivalent yield.

Calculating Bond Equivalent Yield on a U.S. Discount Security

Let

$$d = \text{rate of discount (decimal)}$$
$$y_{be} = \text{bond equivalent yield (decimal)}$$
$$T_{sm} = \text{days from settlement to maturity}$$

Case A: The discount security has *6 months or less* (182 days or less) to run:

$$y_{be} = y_{365} = \frac{365d}{360 - dT_{sm}}$$

Case B: Security has *more than 6 months* (more than 182 days) to run:

$$y_{be} = \frac{-2\frac{T_{sm}}{365} + 2\sqrt{\left(\frac{T_{sm}}{365}\right)^2 - \left(2\frac{T_{sm}}{365} - 1\right)\left(1 - \frac{1}{P}\right)}}{2\frac{T_{sm}}{365} - 1}$$

DISCOUNT SECURITIES WORLDWIDE

As we noted at the outset of this chapter, the number of days in the year in quoting discount securities varies from country to country. To allow for this, we next restate the key formulas for discount securities derived in this chapter with the *assumed number of days in the year as a variable.*

In this book, we use both T and A, both almost always with subscripts, to represent time in days. Every T variable denotes the actual number of *days* from one point to another (e.g., T_{sm} denotes days from settlement to maturity).

In contrast, an A variable always denotes a *rule* for assigning the number of days that a year is assumed to have in calculations concerning a particular security (e.g., a Euro discount security). Typically, but not always, the value of A is 360, 365, or 366. We mention here our distinction between T variables and A variables because we introduce, in this section, A_d to denote the number of days in the year for quoting discount securities.

In the next chapter, we will talk about interest-bearing money market securities. When we calculate interest earned on such a security, the *numerator* is always a T variable, the *denominator* an A variable.

Key Formulas for Discount Securities Worldwide

Let

A_d = number of days in the year for quoting discount securities
d = rate of discount
D_p = dollar discount on a discount security
F = face value
P = price
T_{sm} = days settlement to maturity
y = simple yield
y_{tm} = yield to maturity
V_{01} = value of an 01 per \$1MM of face value of a discount security

Then,

$$D = dF\frac{T_{sm}}{A_d}$$

and

$$P = F - D_p = F\left(1 - \frac{dT_{sm}}{A_d}\right)$$

Also, the rate of discount, d, can be calculated as follows if D_p is given:

$$d = \frac{D_p}{F}\frac{A_d}{T_{sm}}$$

and as follows if P is given:

$$d = \left(1 - \frac{P}{F}\right)\frac{A_y}{T_{sm}}$$

Also, if d is given, we can calculate simple yield on a discount security as follows:

$$y = \frac{dA_d}{(A_d - dT_{sm})}$$

Next, to calculate the bond equivalent yield on a discount security given its rate of discount, we use one of two formulas:
Case A: For securities with 182 days or less to maturity:

$$y_{be} = y_{tm} = \frac{dA_y}{(A_d - dT_{sm})}$$

Case B: For securities with more than 182 days to maturity:

$$y_{be} = y_{tm} = 2\left\{\frac{-\frac{T_{sm}}{A_y} + \sqrt{\left(\frac{T_{sm}}{A_y}\right)^2 - 2\left(\frac{T_{sm}}{A_y} - 1\right)\left(1 - \frac{F}{P}\right)}}{2\left(\frac{T_{sm}}{A_y}\right) - 1}\right\}$$

We can also calculate d for a discount security, given its bond equivalent yield, d_{be}, again using one of two equations:
Case A: For securities with 182 days or less to maturity,

$$d = \frac{y_{be}A_d}{(A_y + dT_{sm})}$$

Case B: For securities with more than 182 days to maturity:

$$d = \frac{A_d\left[\frac{y_{be}^2\left(\frac{T_{sm}}{A_y} - 1\right)}{2} + y_{be}\frac{T_{sm}}{A_y}\right]}{T_{sm}\left[1 + \frac{y_{be}^2\left(\frac{T_{sm}}{A_y} - 1\right)}{2} + y_{be}\frac{T_{sm}}{A_y}\right]}$$

The value of an 01, per $1MM of face value, is given by

$$V_{01} = 0.0001(\$1\text{MM})\frac{T_{sm}}{A_d}$$

THE NEXT CHAPTER

We've developed basic calculations for money market *discount* paper. In Chapter 7, we develop similar calculations for money market interest-bearing paper. Then, in Chapters 8, and 9, we illustrate how these calculations can be applied by imaginative traders and investors.

CHAPTER 7

INTEREST-BEARING PAPER: CALCULATIONS

Interest-bearing securities have been created with the liberality of design that automakers apply to producing cars. Some pay interest at maturity, others pay periodic interest; all accrue interest, but they do so based on different interest-payment conventions.[1] Therefore, we can't *generalize* about the mathematics of interest-bearing securities. Instead, we must examine individual securities and the particular calculations applicable to them. In this chapter, we focus on *money market securities that pay interest:* first, non-negotiable instruments; then, interest-bearing paper.

NON-NEGOTIABLE INSTRUMENTS THAT PAY A FIXED RATE OF INTEREST

In the money market, a vast amount of wholesale borrowing of funds, both *secured and unsecured,* is done for short periods—the most common periods being overnight, several days, one month, three months, and six months. Such short-term borrowings include transactions done in the Federal funds market (the U.S. domestic interbank market), in the U.S. repo market, in the Euro time deposit market, and in various other interbank and repo markets worldwide.

We refer to the above category of borrowings as *instruments* because none of these borrowings result in the issuance of a security, other than a confirmation that money has passed hands between parties X and

[1] See the discussion in Chapter 5 of interest-payment conventions and associated day-count fractions.

Y on such and such terms. Also, since no securities are issued, we categorize these borrowings more generally as *non-negotiable instruments that pay interest.*

Transactions in Federal funds are referred to as *buys* and *sells,* but in fact, a sale of Fed funds amounts to one bank making a short-term, *unsecured loan* to another bank for a specified period at a specified rate. Transactions in Eurodeposits amount to the same thing except that the lender making the *unsecured deposit* may be either a bank, or a nonbank entity—for example, a large, cash-rich corporation.

Euro time deposits are *unsecured* lendings, most typically of dollars, that are made from a bank or some other entity to a bank that runs a Eurobook. Most Eurodeposits have a fixed maturity, but *call deposits* are also made; basically, call deposits are overnight deposits that roll, day to day, until terminated by either the lender or the borrower. Naturally, as market rates move, the borrower is free to change, day to day, the rate he offers for call money.

A *repurchase agreement* (*repo* for short) is, as structured in the United States, in essence a *secured* lending: The borrower is supposed to deliver to the lender of money specified *collateral* (most typically governments and agencies) having a market value equal to slightly *more than* the dollar amount lent. The *margin* between the market value of the collateral and the amount of money lent is referred to as a *haircut.* The purpose of the haircut is to provide extra safety to the lender of money—specifically, to ensure that, even in the face of small market fluctuations in the price of the collateral, the loan made by the lender of money will remain *fully collateralized.* Sometimes, repos are done in which the borrower of money holds the collateral for the repo in safekeeping for the "sole benefit" of the lender of money; such "trust me" repos amount, from the perspective of the lender of money, to *unsecured* loans.[2]

Most repos are done at a fixed rate for a fixed term, most frequently overnight. However, a repo may also be done on an *open* basis; open repos are basically overnight repos that roll, day to day, until terminated by

---

[2] Technically, a repo is structured as a *buy* and future *resale,* simultaneously arranged, of the securities that serve as collateral for the repo. Thus, it has been argued many times, in court at least, that a repo is not a *collateralized loan,* but a pair of *securities transactions.* However, an investor who lends money in a repo but fails to take delivery of his collateral would be foolish to regard the trade he has done as other than making an *unsecured* loan.

either the lender or the borrower; as market rates move, the lender is free to change, day to day, the rate he pays on an open repo.

A *reverse repurchase agreement* (*reverse* for short) is the flip side of a repo: Always, *one man's repo is another man's reverse.* Typically, a dealer is said to be doing *repo* when he borrows money against collateral to fund his securities positions; in contrast, a dealer is said to be doing a *reverse* when he takes in securities (often to cover a short) and simultaneously lends money against that collateral.

A reverse is a swap of collateral for money; a *securities borrowing* is a swap of collateral for collateral. A dealer can obtain specific securities he needs by doing either sort of swap. If his customer prefers doing securities lending, as opposed to reversing out securities, the dealer, besides giving general collateral to the lender of the specific securities he seeks, will pay that lender a *fee;* 50bp is standard, but the rate may vary. Thus, securities lending, a big business, is one more money market *instrument* that pays interest.

Calculating Interest Due

All of the instruments we're discussing pay, in the United States at least, simple interest on an ACT/*360 basis,* that is, the day-count fraction used in calculating accrued interest is (actual days)/360.[3] So calculating interest due on a sale of Fed funds, a Eurodeposit, a repo, or a securities lending is trivial. Let

$$y = \text{the simple yield quoted}$$
$$I = \text{principal invested}$$
$$F = \text{face amount of securities lent}$$
$$T_{sm} = \text{the length of the transaction in } \textit{actual} \text{ days}$$
$$y_{360} = \text{the simple yield earned on an ACT/360 basis}$$
$$AI = \text{accrued interest}$$

Then, on all of the instruments we're discussing except for a securities lending, accrued interest is calculated as follows:

[3] See Chapter 5 for a discussion of the ACT/360 interest-payment convention, a convention that applies to all U.S. money market instruments and to many other money market instruments worldwide.

$$AI = y_{360}\left(\frac{T_{sm}}{360}\right)I$$

If an investor lends securities, the accrued interest he earns is given by the following expression in which y_{360} represents the rate in basis points that he's paid on the face amount of securities he lends:

$$AI = y_{360}\,F\frac{T_{sm}}{360}$$

Example I. Suppose that 3-month Euros are quoted at 4%. When a security pays on an ACT/360 basis, three months is taken to be actual days between the start and end dates of the deposit; thus, the interest that an investor earns on a \$5MM, 3-month Eurodeposit, starting on June 1 and ending on September 1, would be calculated as follows:

$$AI = 0.04(\$5\text{MM})\frac{92}{360} = \$51{,}111.11$$

Example II. Suppose next that an institutional investor holding a Treasury issue lends for 30 days \$60MM of this issue at an ACT/360 rate of 50bps. The interest the investor earns is calculated as follows:

$$AI = 0.0050(\$60\text{MM})\frac{30}{360} = \$25{,}000$$

Calculating Yield Earned on an ACT/365 Basis

The investor in our first example is earning a 4% simple yield on an ACT/360 basis (*i.e.*, he's earning $y_{360} = 0.04$). If our investor wants to calculate what simple yield he's earning on an ACT/365 basis, he needs only multiply (recall Chapter 4) by an appropriate annualizing factor to get:

$$y_{365} = 0.04\frac{365}{360} = 0.04056 \text{ or } 4.056\%$$

Another question our investor might ask is: What *compound* yield would he earn if he were to *roll* his investment *n* times? It's easy to compound a simple yield using one of the formulas developed in Chapter 4. For example, if our investor were to roll his \$5MM, 3-month Eurodeposit four times and were always to get a rate of 4%, the compound rate of return, y_c he would earn over a 360-day year could be calculated by applying the formula:

$$y_c = \left(1 + \frac{y}{n}\right)^n - 1$$

Plugging $y = 0.04$ and $n = 4$ into this equation, we get

$$y_c = \left(1 + \frac{0.04}{4}\right)^4 - 1 = 0.0406 \text{ or } 4.06\%$$

That's a simple calculation, but remember that when an investor asks, before the fact, what compound rate of return he *might* earn over a given period, he must base his calculations on *assumptions* about what rate levels might prevail over that period. Thus, while an investor can calculate, *ex ante,* what compound rates he might earn, over a given period, under various rate and roll scenarios, it's only *ex post* that he can calculate what compound rate of return he actually did earn over that period.

NEGOTIABLE SECURITIES THAT PAY A FIXED RATE OF INTEREST

The rate of interest paid on an interest-bearing security is referred to as its *coupon.* As a rule, the coupon on a new-issue, interest-bearing security is set at the time of issue to be in line with yields prevailing in the secondary market on securities that are similar in type and maturity to the new security being issued. This practice ensures that the dollar price that the new security commands at issue will equal or be very close to its *par* (*face*) *value.*[4] At maturity, interest-bearing securities are redeemed at par.

In the remainder of this chapter, we will focus on the basics of interest-bearing, *money market securities* (i.e., on money market securities that carry a fixed coupon and have a fixed maturity). Every such security is *negotiable* but the *secondary* market is far more liquid for some than for others.

---

[4] The reason that issuers generally try to price a new issue so that it will trade, at issue, at or near par is that investors don't like to buy a new issue at a price that will require them to *accrete* a large *discount* or *amortize* a large *premium* over the life of that issue.

CERTIFICATES OF DEPOSIT: U.S. AND EURO

The *typical* wholesale, dollar-denominated, negotiable CD—U.S. or Euro—is a special breed of *interest-at-maturity* security.[5] The qualifier *wholesale* is important because the CDs we're about to discuss are almost always issued and traded in the secondary market in pieces with a face amount of $1MM.[6] Individual CD trades may, of course, be for larger amounts; but a trade of $5MM CDs would be understood, in the wholesale market, to be a trade of five $1MM pieces all carrying the same name, the same coupon, and *AI* (if any), and the same maturity date (i.e., the $5MM of CDs would be understood to be homogeneous but to be divided in pieces: *5 by 1* as they say in the trade).

Price Quotes

CDs that have an *original maturity* of one year or less pay interest only once, at maturity; such CDs are quoted according to the *simple yield* that they offer an investor. Thus, CD quotes look like bill or BA quotes (see Table 7–1). However, the rate quoted on a CD is *not directly comparable* to the rate quoted on a bill or a BA because the former is a *simple yield,* the latter a *discount rate.*[7]

TABLE 7–1
Selected CD Quotes, February 11, 1993

Certificates of Deposit: Primary Offerings by N.Y.C. Banks	*Rate (%)*
30-day	2.59%
90-day	2.64
180-day	2.75

Source: *New York Times*

[5] Exceptions are variable-rate CDs and a few intermediate-term CDs that have been floated, particularly in the Euromarket. We discuss calculations for such CDs later in this chapter.

For reasons grounded in history, the market for Euro CDs has always been and remains basically a market in dollar-denominated paper.

[6] U.S. banks also issue *retail* CDs. However, the face amount of such paper is usually small; also, there's no secondary market for it. Thus, such paper is *not* a money market instrument.

[7] For the appropriate yield conversion, see Chapter 8.

Naturally, as interest rates change over time, this will affect the yield at which an outstanding CD trades. A *rise* in interest rates would, for example, decrease the attractiveness of an outstanding, low-coupon CD, thereby causing a *decrease* in its value, which would be reflected in a rise in the yield at which that CD trades. A *fall* in rates would do the reverse.

Yield Given Price

Almost all CDs issued in the U.S. and Euro markets have a maturity at issue of less than one year and pay simple interest on an ACT/360 basis. The rate of interest paid is the coupon rate, and interest is paid at maturity.

To begin our discussion of CD calculations, we will derive formulas for determining yield given price and price given yield. In deriving formulas for CDs, we will adopt two *important conventions:*

Convention I. *We will always take price, dirty or clean (B or P), to be price per \$1 of face value.* The alternative and widely used convention of expressing price per \$100 of face value (presumably because notes and bonds are priced this way) unnecessarily complicates the price and yield equations for CDs by forcing one to include in them the factor, 100, again and again.

The virtue of working with price or value at maturity per \$1 of face value can be seen in the simple expression we obtain for the value at maturity of a CD carrying a coupon, c. Let

$$T_{im} = \text{days from issue to maturity}$$
$$c = \text{coupon rate}$$

Then,

$$\begin{pmatrix} \text{Value at maturity} \\ \text{per \$1 of face value} \end{pmatrix} = 1 + c\frac{T_{im}}{360}$$

Using that expression, we can easily determine the value at maturity of a CD having a face value, F. Consider, for example, a CD with the following parameters:

$$c = 0.10$$
$$T_{im} = 90$$
$$F = \$1\text{MM}$$

For this CD,

$$\begin{pmatrix}\text{Value at maturity per}\\ \text{\$1 of face value}\end{pmatrix} = 1 + 0.10\left(\frac{90}{360}\right)$$
$$= 1.025$$

and

$$\begin{pmatrix}\text{Value at maturity per}\\ \text{\$1MM of face value}\end{pmatrix} = 1.025(\$1\text{MM})$$
$$= \$1{,}025{,}000$$

Our example perhaps belabors the obvious, but we are breaking with tradition as incorporated in the industry bible, *Standard Securities Calculations Methods.* It seems appropriate to show that this iconoclasm combined with our notation permits us to derive expressions that are far shorter, simpler, and easier to manipulate than are those presented in that book.

Convention II. In the case of CDs, we will also adopt a second important convention: Price is always taken to be the *dirty price,* that is, *the price per $1 of face value with accrued interest, if any, included.* Because of the way yields are calculated and quoted on CDs, this convention greatly simplifies CD price and yield formulas. Also, once a dirty price, *B,* is calculated for a CD, dividing that price into principal and accrued interest is trivial.

CDs are always quoted, at issue *and* in the secondary market, in terms of yield on a simple-interest basis. Recalling the formula for simple interest given in Chapter 4, we can write a formula for the yield that a CD offered at a dirty price, *B,* will pay an investor. Let

$$y = \text{yield on a CD}$$
$$T_{sm} = \text{days from settlement to maturity}$$
$$B = \text{dirty price}$$

Then,

$$y = \left(\frac{\left(1 + c\frac{T_{im}}{360}\right) - B}{B} \right) \frac{360}{T_{sm}}$$

$$= \left(\frac{1 + c\frac{T_{im}}{360}}{B} - 1 \right) \frac{360}{T_{sm}}$$

If a CD is bought on its issue date, then

$$P = B = 1$$

and the expression for y reduces to

$$y = \left(\frac{1 + c\frac{T_{im}}{360}}{1} - 1 \right) \frac{360}{T_{im}}$$

$$= c$$

as would be expected.

The fact that CDs pay interest on the basis of a 360-day year should not be forgotten when CD yields are compared with those on other interest-bearing securities, such as Treasury notes and bonds that pay interest on a 365-day basis. The magic number (0.014) for the conversion from a 365-day to a 360-day basis reminds us that, at the 10% level, getting a year's interest over 360 days is worth

$$0.014\,(0.10) = 0.0014$$

that is, an extra 14bp.

Price Given Yield

Using the formula we've obtained for the yield on a CD, we can derive a formula for the price at which a CD will trade in the secondary market if it's offered at a yield, y. To do so, we solve the expression,

$$y = \left(\frac{1 + c\dfrac{T_{im}}{360}}{B} - 1 \right) \frac{360}{T_{sm}}$$

for B to get

$$B = \left(\frac{1 + c\dfrac{T_{im}}{360}}{1 + y\dfrac{T_{sm}}{360}} \right)$$

Example. Suppose that an investor buys, at a yield of 9.50%, a CD that carries a coupon of 10% and has an original maturity of 90 days, a current maturity of 60 days. The dirty price, *B*, that he will pay per $1 of face value is

$$B = \left(\frac{1 + 0.100\dfrac{90}{360}}{1 + 0.095\dfrac{60}{360}} \right) = 1.009024$$

Breaking Out *AI*

Separating the dirty price *B* paid for a CD into principal and interest is easily done. Let

$$AI = \text{accrued interest}$$

$$T_{is} = \text{days from issue to settlement}$$

On a CD, accrued interest is given by the expression,

$$AI = c\frac{T_{is}}{360}$$

and

$$\begin{pmatrix} \text{Clean price per} \\ \text{\$1 of face value} \end{pmatrix} = P = B - c\frac{T_{is}}{360}$$

Applying these formulas to the preceding example, we find that

$$AI = 0.10\frac{30}{360} = 0.008333$$

and

$$\begin{aligned} P &= 1.009024 - 0.008333 \\ &= 1.000691 \end{aligned}$$

Note that the CD in our example is selling at a *premium.* This is to be expected, since it was traded at a yield of 9.50%, *well below* its 10% coupon.

To finish our example, we assume that the face amount of the CD sold is \$1MM. The price for principal will equal \$1,000,691.00 and accrued interest will equal \$8,333.33 for a total dirty price of \$1,009,024.33.

Basic CD Formulas

Let

c = coupon rate

y = yield at which the security is traded

B = the dirty price per \$1 of face value

P = the clean price per \$1 of face value

T_{im} = days from issue to maturity

T_{is} = days from issue to settlement

T_{sm} = days from settlement to maturity

AI = accrued interest

I. Yield given dirty price:

$$y = \left(\frac{1 + c\dfrac{T_{im}}{360}}{B} - 1 \right) \frac{360}{T_{sm}}$$

II. Dirty price given yield:

$$B = \left(\frac{1 + c\dfrac{T_{im}}{360}}{1 + y\dfrac{T_{sm}}{360}} \right)$$

III. To break B into accrued interest and clean price, note

$$AI = c\frac{T_{is}}{360}$$

and

$$P = B - AI$$

Reserve Requirements and FDIC Insurance: U.S. CDs

An investor who places money in a CD issued in the United States should be aware that cost of that money to the issuing bank exceeds the rate the bank pays on the CD.

Two factors may cause this discrepancy; the first is *reserve requirements.* The Fed used to require banks to deposit with it, as *noninterest-bearing reserves,* a small percentage of the money they raised through the sale of CDs. Today, the reserve requirement imposed by the Fed on time deposits is 0%, but the Fed has the power to raise that rate if it so chooses.

It's easy to calculate the all-in cost to a bank of CD money, when the bank is required to hold, in an idle balance at the Fed, some of this money it raises by selling a CD. Let

c = coupon on the CD

c' = all-in cost to the issuing bank

r_F = reserve ratio imposed by the Fed

Then,

$$c' = \frac{c}{1 - r_F}$$

When the reserve requirement on time deposits is reduced to zero, as is presently the case, this expression reduces, as would be expected, to

$$c' = c$$

The second factor that raises the all-in cost to banks of CD money raised within the United States is the *FDIC premium* for deposit insurance. In early 1993, the rate for FDIC insurance varied, depending on the strength of a bank. To adjust a bank's all-in cost for CD money to take into account FDIC insurance, one simply adds the FDIC-premium rate to the coupon rate paid by the bank. Thus, a bank that was paying an FDIC premium of 28bp, but not required to hold reserves against time deposits had an all-in cost for CD money given by the expression

$$c' = c + 28\text{bp}$$

Currently, U.S. banks do not have to pay FDIC insurance on deposits they take outside of the United States, including deposits they take in the Euromarket.[8] This fact is important to investors, because it explains why a U.S. money center bank will typically offer a rate that's higher on a Euro CD than the rate they offer on a domestic CD of the same size and maturity.

VARIABLE-RATE CDs

Variable-rate CDs were designed to appeal not to the ordinary investor but to money market funds. Such a fund will buy a 90-day, variable-rate CD that pays interest monthly at, say, ⅛ above the 30-day rate and get the selling dealer to give it a *put* on coupon dates. The latter technically gives the fund the right to sell the paper back to the dealer at par on the first and second coupon dates. While it's understood that the put will never be exercised, it serves a purpose; namely, it permits the fund to treat what starts out as 90-day paper as 30-day paper for purposes of calculating the average maturity of its security holdings.

Variable-rate CDs are unattractive from the point of view of liquidity, but the extra return they offer because of compounding should not be neglected by the investor who holds such a CD to maturity. If 30-day CDs were offered at 9⅞ and a 3-month, variable-rate CD were offered at an initial rate ⅛ above that, then with compounding, the true offered rate on the variable-rate CD would be

$$\left[\left(1+\frac{0.10}{30/360}\right)^3-1\right]\frac{365}{90}=0.1222 \text{ or } 12.22\%$$

[8] Congress has threatened to impose FDIC insurance premiums on the deposits U.S. banks take in the Euromarket, but so far, U.S. banks have successfully fought this measure. U.S. banks argue that Eurobanking is a *thin-margin* business and that the imposition of FDIC insurance premiums on the Eurodeposits that U.S. banks take would make it impossible for U.S. banks to compete with the many non-U.S. banks that are also active in the Euromarket.

It is this rate of return, which is 35bp above the 30-day rate, that the investor who holds until maturity should compare to the 90-day rate—assuming, of course, that he does not anticipate a fall in interest rates over the next 60 days.

EURO AND INTERMEDIATE-TERM CDs

CDs, domestic and Euro, may have a maturity at issue of *more than 1 year;* such *intermediate-term CDs* pay interest semiannually or, less typically, annually. Like CDs that pay interest at maturity, intermediate-term CDs (AKA *periodic-pay CDs*) are priced in terms of yield.

Calculating Price Given Yield: Periodic-Pay CDs

The dollar price that a seller of a periodic-pay CD receives equals the stream of all future dollar flows that that CD will throw off, *discounted at the sale yield back to the settlement date.* In other words, the dollar price of the CD equals the *present value,* calculated at the sale yield, of all future dollar flows from the CD minus accrued interest on the CD as of settlement. This sounds simple, but on a periodic-pay CD, the calculation is complex because a separate calculation must be made for the current and for each remaining coupon period.

On a periodic-pay CD, the amount of interest that the CD accrues in each coupon period is calculated as follows:

$$AI = c\frac{A_{\text{In}}}{360}$$

where

A_{In} = *actual* number of days in the coupon period

Since 365/2 = 182.5, consecutive coupon periods are, leap years excepted, always unequal in length. The *actual* number of days in each coupon period is, moreover, taken into account not only in the calculation of interest accrued as of each coupon date but also in the factors by which all future sums to be received are discounted back to the settlement date. For this reason, the present value (price) of a periodic-pay CD *cannot* be calculated using *the standard bond equation* for calculating the price of a bond with a current maturity greater than 6 months.[9] Instead, in pricing such a CD, an *iterative procedure* must be used.

Calculating Price Given Yield: An Example

To illustrate the complexity of calculating the correct price at which a periodic-pay CD will trade when it's sold in the secondary market at a given yield, we next work through an example. The steps in this example correctly suggest the iterative procedure one must use in making any such calculation.

Example. Consider a CD with a 7.55% coupon that was issued on 04/15/76, that will mature on 10/15/77, and that was traded for settlement on 04/19/76 at a yield of 7.50%.[10] To calculate the price that an investor must pay for this security at settlement, we first calculate the *actual* number of days in the current *and* in each future coupon period as well as the *actual* number of days from settlement to the first coupon date (see Table 7–2).

TABLE 7–2
Day Counts Needed to Calculate the Price of a CD that Carries a 7.55% Coupon, Pays Interest Semiannually, Was Issued on 10/15/77, and Was Traded at a Yield of 7.50% for Settlement on 04/19/76

Period	*Dates*	*Number of days*
Issue to first coupon	04/15/76 to 10/15/76	183
Settlement to first coupon	04/19/76 to 10/15/76	179
First to second coupon	10/15/76 to 04/15/77	182
Second to third coupon	04/15/77 to 10/15/77	183
Third to fourth coupon and maturity	10/15/77 to 04/14/78	181

---

[9] The standard bond equation is discussed in Chapter 11.

[10] We've used a dated example because few banks today are issuing term CDs. However, that's not to say that banks may not resume doing so in the future. Another reason for examining the pricing of a term CD is that it illustrates one of the many complexities in bond pricing that can be handled by use of the general bond equation.

Next, we discount the maturity value of the security back to its next-to-last coupon date (Step 1, Table 7–3). We then discount this discounted value (1.00024225) *plus* accrued interest on the next-to-last coupon date back to the preceding coupon date (Step 2, Table 7–3). This procedure is continued until the last period over which the security's value is discounted is the days from settlement to the next coupon (Step 4 in Table 7–3). The value obtained in this step is the dirty price the investor must pay per $1 of face value (Steps 5 and 6 in Table 7–3). This amount can then be adjusted to reflect the security's face value (Step 7, Table 7–3).

TABLE 7–3

A General Formula for Calculating Price Given Yield on a Periodic-Pay CD Traded in the Secondary Market

Step 1: Discount value at maturity back to third coupon date:

$$\left(\frac{1+0.0755\dfrac{181}{360}}{1+0.0750\dfrac{181}{360}}\right)=1.00024225$$

Step 2: Discount sum obtained in Step 1 *plus* coupon interest due on their coupon date back to second coupon date:

$$\left(\frac{1.00024225+0.0755\dfrac{183}{360}}{1+0.0750\dfrac{183}{360}}\right)=1.00047819$$

Step 3: Discount sum obtained in Step 2 *plus* coupon interest due on second coupon date back to the first coupon date:

$$\left(\frac{1.00047819+0.0755\dfrac{182}{360}}{1+0.0750\dfrac{182}{360}}\right)=1.00070426$$

Step 4: Discount sum obtained in Step 3 *plus* coupon interest due on first coupon date back to settlement date. This gives the dirty price per $1 of face value on the settlement date:

$$\left(\frac{1.000704+0.0755\dfrac{183}{360}}{1+0.0750\dfrac{179}{360}}\right)=1.00172735$$

TABLE 7–3 (*Concluded*)

Step 5: Calculate accrued interest on the settlement date:

$$AI = 0.0755\frac{4}{360} = 0.00083889$$

Step 6: Subtract value obtained in Step 5 from the value obtained in Step 4 to get the *clean price, P,* paid per $1 of face value.

$$P = 1.00172735 - 0.00083889 = 1.00088846$$

Step 7: Multiply by $1MM to find the clean price, *P,* of a $1MM CD.

$$P = \$1{,}000{,}000(1.00088846) = \$1{,}000{,}888.46$$

MUNICIPAL NOTES

For investors who are in a position to benefit from tax-exempt income, municipal notes—which when issued with a short original maturity typically pay interest at maturity—are an important money market instrument.

Muni notes, unlike other interest-bearing money market instruments that we've discussed, are usually held by investors from purchase to maturity. Also, because of tax considerations, muni notes are never repoed; and, because of the thin secondary markets in which they trade, muni notes are rarely shorted.

In the United States, muni notes pay interest according to the 30/360 PSA interest-payment convention, described in Chapter 5. Thus, $1MM of muni notes, issued on Jan 15 and carrying a 3.60% coupon would, if held from March 1 to March 31 accrue the following amount of interest:

$$AI = 0.036\left(\frac{30}{360}\right)(\$1{,}000{,}000) = \$3{,}000.00$$

INTEREST-BEARING COMMERCIAL PAPER

The rates quoted on commercial paper are discount rates, and most commercial paper is sold in discount form. However, an investor can, and numerous investors do, request that commercial paper sold to them be structured as interest-bearing paper. Normally, issuers are quite willing to sell their paper in interest-bearing form, since doing so requires only that they adjust the simple yield they quote on interest-bearing paper so that the latter is *equivalent* to the discount rate they're quoting on discount paper of the same maturity.

Example. To illustrate, on Friday, Aug 27, 1993, GE Capital (the biggest U.S. direct issuer of commercial paper) was quoting a discount rate of 3.22% for 180-day money. Suppose that Fidelity Management and Research, one of the biggest U.S. managers of mutual funds, had on that day wanted to buy $50MM of 180-day GE Capital paper. Had Fidelity bought this paper in discount form, they would have paid $49,195,000; and 180 days later on Wednesday, Feb 23, 1994, they would have received $50MM in face value.

Alternatively, Fidelity could have asked GE Capital to sell it $50MM of commercial paper in interest-bearing form. In that case, GE Capital would have quoted Fidelity a simple yield (money market basis) for 180-day money of 3.272690%; Fidelity would have paid GE Capital $50MM in principal for the paper it bought; and 180 days later, GE Capital would have paid Fidelity $818,172.58 of interest plus $50MM to redeem the paper held by Fidelity.

In Chapter 4, we gave a formula for converting a discount rate to the equivalent simple yield, 360-day basis. Using it, check that converting a 3.22% discount rate for 180-day money to the equivalent money market yield raises the rate quoted to 3.272690%.

THE NEXT CHAPTER

In the next chapter, we return to discount paper. There, we describe various ways in which imaginative traders and investors can use, *to their profit,* the basic calculations for discount paper that we developed in Chapter 6.

CHAPTER 8

DISCOUNT PAPER: APPLICATIONS

In this chapter, we apply the formulas developed in Chapter 6 to determine the possible outcomes of strategies frequently used by money market people who trade and invest in discount paper.

COMPOUNDING REVISITED: DISCOUNT SECURITIES

Some of the results we'll derive are relevant for an investor choosing between two alternatives. For example, a portfolio manager might say: "In three months, I've got a tax-payment date coming up; and I have money to invest until that date. Should I buy a three-month bill and mature it or should I *roll* a 1-month bill (i.e., buy three *consecutive* 1-month bills)?"

To evaluate these alternatives, we must revisit a key fundamental: the importance of comparing rates on a *directly equivalent* basis—apples to apples. Suppose, to continue our example, that the yield curve at the short end of the market is flat and that 30- and 90-day bills are both offered at a 9.00 rate of discount. Using the formula,

$$y_{365} = \frac{365d}{360 - dT_{sm}}$$

we calculate that on a simple 365-day yield basis, the 30-day bill would offer our investor 9.19, and the 90-day bill 9.34 (see Table 8–1). These numbers correspond to the bond equivalent yields, y_{be}, asked for these bills.

TABLE 8–1
Comparison, on Different Bases, of the Yield on a 30-Day Bill to That on a 90-Day Bill

			y_c, *Effective Yield with Compounding (365-Day Year)*	
	d, Rate of Discount	y_c *Equivalent Bond Yield*	*Investment Period Is 90 Days*	*Investment Period Is 365 Days*
30-day bill	9.00%	9.19%	9.260%	9.588%
90-day bill	9.00%	9.34%	9.340%	9.674%
Difference in yield	0bp	15bp	8.0bp	8.6bp

Converting the 9.00 discount rates asked for the 30- and 90-day bills to their respective bond equivalent yields shows that simple yield on the 90-day bill is 15bp greater than that on the 30-day bill. We'd expect this result because, from the formula for y_{365}, we see that y_{365} will be higher the greater the number of days, T_{sm}, over which a given discount rate, *d,* is earned.

So far so good, but the rates on the 30- and 90-day bills are still *not directly comparable.* The 30-day bill is worth something extra to the investor because, if he buys it, he'll receive his first interest payment, $F - D_p$, in 30 days, and he'll be able to reinvest that interest payment. More accurately, if our investor were able to roll, over 90 days, three consecutive 30-day bills, each offered at a 9.00 discount rate, he'd earn more than a 9.00 discount rate over that period because he'd be able to *reinvest* earnings *twice.* In short, our old friend from Chapter 4, *compounding,* comes into play.

Compounding: Investment Period Is Less Than One Year

In Chapter 4, we derived a formula for calculating *effective return,* y_c, when a *simple yield, y,* is compounded *n* times over an investment period that's *less than a full year.* Let

n = compounding periods *during* 1 *year*

n' = compounding periods *during the investment period*

T = days in the investment period

then, if T is less than 365,

$$y_c = \left[\left(1+\frac{y}{n}\right)^{n'} - 1\right]\frac{365}{T}$$

Substituting into this formula the bond equivalent yield on the 30-day bill, which we calculated to be 9.19, we conclude that rolling a 30-day bill over a 90-day investment period would give the investor a *compound yield* of

$$\begin{aligned} y_c &= \left[\left(1+\frac{0.0919}{365/30}\right)^{3} - 1\right]\frac{365}{90} \\ &= 0.0926 \text{ or } 9.26\% \end{aligned}$$

Comparing properly compounded (and thus directly comparable) yields, we find that rolling the 30-day bill at a 9.00 discount rate over 90 days would yield the investor only 8bp less than buying and maturing the 90-day bill (see Table 8–1).

With this number in hand, our investor might reason as follows: In my view, the Fed's likely to tighten and soon; also, the cost to me, if the Fed doesn't tighten, of staying short [of buying a 30- versus a 90-day bill] will be at most 8bp. So I'll stay short and hope to capture the rate rise I anticipate.

Compounding: Investment Period Is a Full Year

Some money market people, facing a situation similar to the one in our example, might say, "OK, one investment alternative offers an opportunity for compounding, so I'll compound, over *a full year,* the yields on each of my investment alternatives; then I'll compare their compound yields." In Chapter 4, we gave a simple formula for calculating compound yield when the investment period is a full year:

$$y_c = \left(1+\frac{y}{n}\right)^{n} - 1$$

Applying this formula to an investor choosing between 30- and 90-day bills, we find the following. First, if an investor were to roll the *30-day bill* over a *full year* at a 9.00 discount rate, there would be 365/30 compounding periods, and he would earn a compound yield of

$$y_c = \left(1 + \frac{0.0919}{365/30}\right)^{365/30} - 1 = 0.09588 \text{ or } 9.588\%$$

Second, if an investor were to roll the *90-day bill* over a *full year* at a 9.00 discount rate, there would be 365/90 compounding periods, and he would earn a compound yield of

$$y_c = \left(1 + \frac{0.0934}{365/90}\right)^{365/90} - 1 = 0.09674 \text{ or } 9.674\%$$

A person using these calculations, would conclude that, if rates were to remain flat, staying short (i.e., in the 30-day bill) would, when compounding was taken into account, cost the investor in our example 8.6bp (see Table 8–1). However, it's incorrect to apply this result to our example. Our example concerns an investor whose *investment period is 90 days* and who is choosing between rolling a 30-day bill and buying and maturing a 90-day bill. The numbers in the final column of Table 8–1 are correct *only* for an investor whose *investment period is a full year* and who is choosing whether to roll over for that full year a 30- or a 90-day bill.

The Interpretation of y_c

An investor who calculates y_c on an investment that offers opportunities for compounding can never be certain that he'll receive that rate. His estimate of his investment period may prove *incorrect.* More important, the rate at which he's able to *reinvest* may differ from the rate he projects. Thus, if the investor in our example were to choose to invest for 90 days by rolling the 30-day bill, he could be certain of earning a 9.26 effective yield only if he were certain (1) that his investment period would be 90 days and (2) that he could reinvest on roll dates at a 9.00 discount rate. To obtain certainty at least on the latter count, he'd need a crystal ball.

In selecting securities, an investor seeks those that offer him the best *relative value.* In Street jargon, this means that the investor selects the securities that offer him the best—judged in terms of his investment parameters including his investment horizon—available combination of *risk, liquidity,* and *return.*

In situations where one or more securities would give the investor the opportunity to reinvest earnings during his projected investment period, to properly compare the returns offered to him by alternative securities, he should first properly compound these returns based on the *neutral assumption* that *no* change will occur in either the general level of interest rates or the shape of the yield curve. Once he's made that comparison, the investor may then *superimpose on it his own rate forecast.*

Suppose that, in a given situation, a short security offers the investor as much or more compound yield than does a longer security; if the investor believes rates are likely to rise, his choice is easy—stay short; however, if the investor believes rates will fall, his choice is more difficult. In either case, the calculated value of y_c is at best a *benchmark* designed to help an investor gauge a security's relative value.

FORMULAS, DOLLAR FLOWING, AND APPROXIMATIONS

So far, we've concentrated on deriving formulas that permit us to calculate precisely various money market numbers. The ability to develop and manipulate simple formulas is important for any market participant who wants to "know the numbers."

Unfortunately, in deriving formulas, it's easy to make a mistake. Therefore, one should tackle a *new* problem in steps. First, develop a formula for calculating the new number, say, a break-even price or yield on a new trade; second, apply this formula to a particular numerical example of the new trade; third, *dollar flow* the example created in step two—that is, calculate the *total dollars in* and *total dollars out* that would result if that trade were actually carried out. Steps 2 and 3 amount to making a benchmark calculation. The new formula is assumed to be correct if the numbers produced in Steps 2 and 3 are fully in sync; if not, it's back to the drawing board.

Precision is important to money market traders, but so too is response time. In a rapidly changing market, a trader won't succeed if he's slow at making calculations he needs to respond to changes in the market. Recognizing this, traders have developed various *approximations* that permit them to make quick and dirty estimates of *true* numbers. Every such approximation has a built-in *bias* that makes a particular transaction being evaluated look more or less favorable than it is. Thus, a trader using an approximation needs to know (1) the direction of its bias and (2) how sensitive it is to the length of the transaction and to the level of interest rates. He can determine the first by doing an algebraic check, the second by dollar flowing a few examples.

In situations in which the bias in an approximation becomes large or where it works against the trader, the trader may find it useful to develop a *visual aid*—a printout, produced by a computer program into which current market quotes are inputted.

Illustrations of approximations and of useful visual aids are provided in the discussion of applications that follows these next few words on carry.

CARRY

Broker/dealers have sufficient *capital* to support their market making, arbitrage, and positioning activities, but they lack the billions of dollars they require to *fund* their daily positions. Thus, broker/dealers borrow short-term, each day, huge sums; and generally, they find that the least expensive way to do so is in the *repo* market. Likewise, broker/dealers often find that the least expensive way to *cover their shorts* is to borrow securities—either by *reversing in* the securities they require or by doing an *outright borrowing* of such securities. *Fully funded investors,* such as corporate liquidity portfolios, pension funds, and fixed-income mutual funds, frequently invest in repo; they also provide dealers with securities either via reverses or via securities lendings.[1]

For a fixed-income security, *carry is defined as the interest income received on the security financed minus the interest expense incurred in financing that security;* that is,

$$\text{Carry} = \text{Interest income} - \text{Interest expense}$$

This definition of carry holds for both *long* and *short* positions.

Money and bond market people often talk loosely about *the cost of carry*. Actually, carry may be *positive* or *negative; positive carry is a source of profit, negative carry a source of loss.*

---

[1] Recall from Chapter 7 how interest expense is calculated on repos and reverses.

In Chapters 3, 5, and 7, we defined all necessary relationships for calculating carry: day-count conventions and methods for calculating both accrued interest on a security and interest due on a repo or a reverse. Thus, in calculating carry, the only thing we need to worry about is ensuring that the rates we work with are always *directly comparable.*

FIGURING A TAIL

One common calculation made by money market traders is to *figure a tail.* This calculation is sometimes done using a quick and dirty *approximation.* In our discussion of tails, we will first illustrate the approximation with an example, then investigate the inherent bias in the approximation, and finally check our conclusion about the bias by dollar flowing our example. A better approximation plus a method for figuring the true tail are given in Table 8–2 and the section following it. When interest rates are high, the latter approach should be used.

The Approximation Approach

Dealers and investors sometimes finance securities they position with *term* repo; for example, they finance with a 30-day repo a security with 3 months to run. Often, when they do so, they are creating a *future* security and betting that they'll be able to sell that future security at a profit. In judging the attractiveness of this bet, dealers always rely on explicit predictions of where Fed funds will trade and of what yield spreads will prevail when the term repo comes off.

Here's an example. Assume a dealer is operating in an environment in which the 90-day bill is trading at a rate ⅛ below the Fed funds rate. Assume also that Fed funds are trading at 4⅞, the 90-day bill at 4¾, and 30-day term repo at 4½.

If a dealer were, in this environment, to buy a 90-day bill and finance it with 30-day term repo, he would, over his 30-day *holding period* earn *positive carry* equal to approximately (the two rates are not directly comparable):

$$4\tfrac{3}{4} - 4\tfrac{1}{2}$$

or a profit equal to ¼ over 30 days. He would also have created a *future* 60-day bill, namely, the unfinanced *tail* of the 90-day bill he initially purchased.

TABLE 8–2
Figuring the Tail: An Example

Step 1: The dealer buys $1 million of 90-day bills at 4¾ percent rate of discount.

$$\text{Discount at which bills are purchased} = \frac{dt_{sm}}{360}F = \frac{0.0475(90)}{360}\$1{,}000{,}000 = \$11{,}875$$

$$\text{Price at which bills are purchased} = F - D = \$1{,}000{,}000 - \$11{,}875 = \$988{,}125$$

The dealer finances the bills purchased for 30 days at 4½ percent.

$$\text{Financing cost*} = \frac{0.045(30)}{360}\$1{,}000{,}000 = \$3{,}750$$

Step 2: At the end of 30 days the dealer owns the bills at a net cost figure. Determine what yield this cost figure implies on the future 60-day bills created.

$$\text{Net cost of future 60-day bills} = \text{Purchase price} + \text{Financing cost} = \$988{,}125 + \$3{,}750 = \$991{,}875$$

$$\text{Net discount at which future 60-day bills are owned} = F - \text{Net cost} = \$1{,}000{,}000 - \$991{,}875 = \$8{,}125$$

$$\text{Rate at which future 60-day bills are purchased} = \frac{360D}{t_{sm}F} = \frac{360(\$8{,}125)}{60(\$1{,}000{,}000)} = 0.04875 = 4\tfrac{7}{8}\%$$

Step 3: Future 60-day bills created are sold at a 4⅝ percent discount rate. Calculate dollar profit.

$$\text{Discount at which bills are sold} = F\frac{dt_{sm}}{360} = \$1{,}000{,}000\frac{0.04625(60)}{360} = \$7{,}708$$

$$\text{Profit} = \textit{Net}\text{ purchase discount} - \text{Discount at sale} = \$8{,}125 - \$7{,}708 = \$417$$

Step 4: Figure the annualized yield on a discount basis that $417 represents on a 60-day security.

$$d = \frac{360D}{t_{sm}F} = \frac{360(\$417)}{60(\$1{,}000{,}000)} = 0.0025 = \tfrac{1}{4}\%$$

*Actually less than $1 million has to be borrowed, so the dealer's approach to figuring the tail is only an approximation.

If the dealer thought, as dealers often do, of the carry profit over the initial holding period as raising the yield at which he in effect buys the future security, then by purchasing the 90-day bill at 4¾ and repoing it for 30 days at 4½, he would have acquired a future 60-day bill at a yield of 4⅞.[2] The ¼ *positive carry,* which the dealer earns for 30 days, adds only ⅛ to the yield at which the dealer effectively purchases the future security because the latter has a maturity of 60 days, which is twice as long as the period over which the dealer earns positive carry.

Faced with this opportunity, the dealer would ask himself: "How attractive is it to contract to buy a 60-day bill at 4⅞ for delivery 30 days hence?" The dealer figures he would break even, clearing costs ignored, if he were able to sell that future bill at a rate of 4⅞. Thus, contracting to buy the future bill will be attractive to the dealer only if he believes he can sell that bill at a rate below 4⅞.

The dealer's thoughts on this matter might run as follows: Currently, the yield curve is such that 60-day bills are trading ⅛ below the rate on the 90-day bill. Therefore, if the 60-day bill were to trade at 4⅞ one month hence and if yield spreads did not change, that would imply that the 90-day bill was trading at 5 and Fed funds were trading at 5⅛, that is, at a level ¼ above the present rate. I don't believe that the Fed will tighten or that yield spreads will change unfavorably; therefore, I'll do the trade.

If the dealer's predictions were correct—the Fed did not tighten and yield spreads did not change, he would be able to sell 30 days hence the future 60-day bill he had created at 4⅝, which is the rate that would be the prevailing rate at that time on the 60-day bill.[3] In doing so, he would make, according to his calculation, a profit equal to ¼ (the purchase rate 4⅞ minus the sale rate 4⅝) on a 60-day security.

This approximation, sometimes used by traders to figure the tail on a discount security, can be stated as a simple formula:

$$\begin{pmatrix}\text{Effective yield}\\ \text{at which future}\\ \text{security is}\\ \text{purchased}\end{pmatrix} = \begin{pmatrix}\text{Yield at}\\ \text{which cash}\\ \text{security is}\\ \text{purchased}\end{pmatrix} + \left(\frac{\begin{pmatrix}\text{Rate of profit}\\ \text{on carry}\end{pmatrix}\begin{pmatrix}\text{Days}\\ \text{carried}\end{pmatrix}}{\text{Days left to maturity at the end of the carry period}}\right)$$

[2] Note the *higher* the yield at which a discount security is purchased, the *lower* the purchase price. So buying the future security at 4⅞ is, from the dealer's point of view, better than buying it at 4¾.

[3] Recall the 60-day bill was assumed to be trading at a rate ⅛ below the rate on the 90-day bill, at 4¾ − ⅛ = 4⅝.

Applying this formula to our example, we get:

$$4\tfrac{3}{4}+\frac{\tfrac{1}{4}(30)}{60}=4\tfrac{3}{4}+\tfrac{1}{8}=4\tfrac{7}{8}$$

The notation developed in Chapter 3 enables us to restate the above formula more economically. All we require is the introduction of an asterisk and several subscripts.

A Formula for Approximating the *Tail* on a *Discount* Security Financed with Term Repo*

Let

d = rate of discount at purchase (decimal)

d^* = approximate break-even sale rate

r_r = term repo rate

T_{is} = days from issue (or purchase) to settlement, which is taken to be the date the term repo comes off

T_{sm} = days from settlement to maturity

Then,

$$d^* = d + (d - r_t)\frac{T_{is}}{T_{sm}}$$

*For a more accurate approximation, see Table 8–2 and the accompanying footnote.

The Nature of the Approximation

For people accustomed to thinking in terms of dollars rather than yields, the trader's method of approximating the tail is inherently confusing; such people have difficulty seeing how the method works. To minimize such confusion, we present in Table 8–2 the example we've just worked; Table 8–2 works through this example step by step and always in dollars, not in basis points.

The dealer's method of figuring the tail is an approximation because the two rates used in the calculation are not directly comparable. Both are 360-day rates, but the bill rate, which is a discount rate, is understated relative to the term repo rate, which is a simple yield.

To see the error this noncomparability introduces, note that, in Table 8–2 to get the result implied by the dealer's approximation, we had to figure the financing cost as if the bills were repoed for full face value. Had they been repoed at the discount price paid for them, the financing cost,

$$0.045\left(\frac{30}{360}\right)\$988,125 = \$3,705$$

would have been $45 less than the $3,705 figure shows in Table 8–2. The rate on the tail created by the dealer would thus have been slightly more than 4⅞.

The correct dollar figures for our example are summarized in Table 8–3, which *dollar flows* the transaction. Note that all dollar inflows and outflows recorded there are *dated.* The importance of accurate dating to the calculation is obvious.

Bias

Since the dealer's method of approximating a bill tail *underestimates* his *true* break-even sale rate, the approximation will not cause the dealer to view the bet he's making as being more favorable than it is. Thus, the approximation is justified. This observation suggests an important point. In this type of borrow–invest situation, if the approximation understates the investment rate relative to the borrowing rate, the trader who approximates is on safe ground. If, however, the approximation does the

TABLE 8–3
Dollar Flowing the Tail: An Example

Dollars in		*Dollars out*	
Day 1:			
RP bills at 4½ percent	$ 988,125	$ 988,125......	Buy bills at 4¾ percent
Day 30:			
Sell bills at break-even		988,125......	Repay RP loan
rate of 4⅞ percent..........	991,875	3,705......	Pay RP interest
Total dollars in.............	$1,980,000	$1,979,955......	Total dollars out

(Total dollars in) – (Total dollars out) = $45

opposite, the trader must find a more accurate method of calculation or else dollar flow trades before he does them. Traders who forget this may end up locking in a loss when they think they're locking in a profit.

A final important point about our example of figuring the tail is that the bias in the trader's method of approximating the tail is highly *sensitive to the level of interest rates.* Had we, for example, assumed that the 90-day bill was purchased at a discount rate of 10 and repoed at 9.75, the trader's formula would estimate the rate on the tail as being 10.125 when in fact it would be 10.247. The trader's approximation would have underestimated by almost one-half the gain added by the term repo to the effective yield at which the tail is purchased.

Note finally that our example assumes that the 90-day bill can be financed at *positive* carry. This assumption did not hold during much of the 1980s. When carry is negative, a trader can hope to profit on a bill tail only if the slope of the yield curve is *negative* and *sufficiently steep* to create a high probability that he can sell a tail he creates at a rate far enough below his purchase rate to more than compensate him for *negative carry.*

LOSING YOUR TAIL

The importance of comparing money market rates on the same basis is hard to overemphasize. Here are two cases in point, situations in which traders who forget this rule unintentionally lock in losses—or "lose their tails."

A Repo to Maturity

To illustrate the first case, we set the stage as follows: The Treasury has put out a cash management bill that will mature in 40 days. The bill can be bought in the market at a discount of 9.76, and 40-day *term repo* money can be obtained at 9.90. A trader is considering whether to buy the bills and finance them to maturity. At first, the transaction looks unattractive, *but* the trader realizes that the two rates are not directly comparable. So he looks at the equivalent bond yield on the bill, which is 10%. Now, the transaction takes on some allure. It appears that, by buying the bill and putting it out on term repo to maturity, a profit of 10bp can be locked in over the life of the transaction.

A trader who reasons this way has forgotten an elementary point: The repo rate is quoted on a 360-day basis, whereas the equivalent bond yield on a bill is quoted on a 365-day basis. Therefore, to make the two rates comparable, he *must* convert the figure for equivalent bond yield to a 360-day basis as follows:

$$10\%(360/365) = 9.86\%$$

This simple calculation shows immediately that the proposed purchase and repo to maturity would generate not a profit, but a locked-in loss of 4bp a day. On a $10MM transaction, that would cost the trader around $11 a day plus transaction costs. Note that the size of the loss per day is not sensitive to the time for which the transaction is put on, but the longer the trade is outstanding, the greater will be the locked-in loss.

Paying Daily Interest

Some people think that the major advantage of using term repo financing is the reduction in risk that locking up a certain borrowing rate affords the trader, but more is involved. A trader who rolls *overnight* repo is paying not a *simple* interest rate but a *daily compounded* interest rate.[4]

Using our formula for calculating effective return when compounding occurs, we find that daily compounding increases a 9.90 rate over a 40-day period to[5]

$$\left[\left(1+\frac{0.099}{360}\right)^{40}-1\right]\frac{360}{40} = 0.0995 \text{ or } 9.95\%$$

Thus, if our trader had agreed to pay daily interest on his term repo or had happened to finance his bills *day to day* at 9.90, he would have ended up *locking in not 4bp but a 9bp negative carry* on an

---

[4] Variations exist dealer to dealer and trade to trade with respect to how often repo interest is disbursed. Clearly, it is in the interests of the customer to be paid interest each business day, and if the customer's alternative to rolling repo is to roll overnight Euro deposits, he may well ask for daily payment of repo interest due him.

[5] Assuming compounding over *a whole year;* that is, using the formula

$$y_c = \left(1 - \frac{1}{n}\right)^n - 1$$

would yield too high a figure for the financing cost.

apparently profitable transaction. The power of daily compounding is something neither a trader nor an investor can afford to ignore.

Moral: If you receive or pay out interest on a daily basis, *never* compare that rate with other nondaily rates before compounding it.

The increase in the repo rate—from 9.90 to 9.95—that occurred when we compounded it daily over a 40-day period may suggest to certain readers that some mathematical fiction has crept into the argument. Surely, those traders who willingly agree to pay daily interest on term repo will feel that way. They are wrong, as a dollar-and-cents calculation of interest actually paid out in the two situations will show.[6]

THE COST OF CAPITAL

In our example of figuring the tail, to keep things simple we assumed that the amount borrowed precisely equaled the purchase price of the bills financed. A more typical situation would be that the lender would demand some margin, *haircut* in Street jargon, for protection against failure of the *borrower;* that is, he would value the bills serving as *collateral* (a repo is in essence a collateralized loan) at something less than current market value.

In that case, the difference between the value of the bills purchased and the amount of the repo borrowing would have to be financed out of the dealer's capital. Some cost should be assigned to that capital. Otherwise, the trade would appear to be more profitable than it is because if the dealer's capital were not used for that trade, it could be used for another purpose; thus, a dealer who does a trade that uses his capital always incurs an *opportunity cost.*

There's no hard and fast rule as to how a dealer should measure his cost of capital, but a good rule of thumb is that he should assign to it a cost *at least* equal to the prevailing dealer loan rate at his clearing bank. A dealer always finances some proportion of his total securities position at his clearing bank, and a transaction that uses his capital will therefore require him to increase marginally his borrowing from that bank.

A dealer who takes haircuts on securities he repos uses capital. So,

---

[6] The high interest rates that prevailed in the late 1970s and part of the 1980s taught a lot of traders who had ignored the impact of compounding that that's maybe OK to do, but only in a low-rate environment.

too, does a dealer who pays daily interest on a repo that finances a security such as a bill that pays no return until it's sold or matures. Moreover, the latter cost is not fully reflected even when the repo rate is compounded to allow for the daily payment of interest. The reason is that compounding the repo rate reflects the total dollars of interest that are paid out but *not* the fact that paying out dollars daily requires that the firm either use capital or borrow more dollars during the financing period.

Why did traders, at least in the past, so often ignore the effect of compounding when daily interest was paid? The explanation may lie in the way capital is assigned to traders in some dealerships. Not infrequently, a trader in a dealership will be told that he has been assigned $X million of capital and that some percentage rate on that money will be charged against his profit and loss (P&L) account whether he uses that capital or not. This sort of arrangement may achieve some management goal such as holding down the profit earned by and therefore the bonus paid to the trader, but it also creates a perverse situation in which actions by the trader that cost his firm money are not reflected on his own P&L.

For example, if a trader who is not using all the capital assigned to him wants to do a term repo and the lender requests daily payment of repo interest, the trader is likely to agree readily, since the capital eaten up by the payment of daily interest is a *free good* to the trader who's already being charged for that capital. However, to the trader's firm, that capital is not free. In fact, the opportunity cost of using it may be so high that a transaction that improves the trader's P&L may worsen the firm's P&L.

ANOTHER TAIL QUESTION

Earlier we asked: For a given bill that's going to be repoed for a fixed time at a fixed rate, what will the tail be? A second question traders of tails often ask is: If a given bill is repoed at a fixed spread between the bill and the repo rates, for how many days must the resulting positive carry be earned to add 1bp to the tail?

The answer can be dollar flowed, but that's time-consuming. Fortunately, there's a quick method that gives a good approximation. To see why it works, note that 1bp on a 90-day bill is worth 90 1-day basis points. Similarly, 1bp on a year bill is worth 364 1-day basis points.

Now suppose that the year bill can be repoed at a positive spread of 90bp. This means that the repo adds to the yield on the tail approximately (the two rates are not directly comparable) 90 1-day basis points each day that it's on. Thus, one can estimate that it will take 4 days for the repo to add 364 1-day basis points (i.e., 1bp to the tail of the year bill being financed). Obviously, the more quickly the basis points build up on the tail, the more favorable buying and financing the security will appear to a trader.

Method for Calculating Approximately How Fast Positive Carry Will Increase the Tail on Discount Paper Financed with Term Repo*

Let

y = simple yield, 360-day basis, on discount paper being financed

r_t = term repo rate

T_{sm} = days from settlement to maturity

Then,

$$\begin{pmatrix}\text{Number of days required}\\ \text{to add 1bp to tail}\end{pmatrix} = \frac{T_{sm}}{100(y - r_t)}$$

*For a formula to calculate the *true* break-even rate on the sale of a bill tail, see the formula for d^* on page 143.

The calculation we've just outlined is an approximation. To make it as accurate as possible, the discount rate on the bill should be converted to a simple yield on a 360-day basis before it is compared with the repo rate.

The accuracy of this technique is illustrated by the example in Table 8–4. Note that this technique is an improvement over the formula given earlier for figuring the tail on a discount security.

TABLE 8–4
Estimating the Rate of Tail Pickup on a 10% Year Bill that Is Repoed

Data

$$\text{Bill's current maturity} = 364 \text{ days}$$

$$d = 10.00$$

$$\text{Simple yield, 360-day basis, } y = 11.12$$

$$\text{Term repo rate, } r_t = 10.20$$

$$\text{Carry, } 100(y - r_t) = 92\text{bp}$$

I. Approximate days needed to pick up 1bp

$$\text{Days needed to raise tail yield by 1bp} = \frac{364}{92} = 3.96 \text{ days}$$

$$\text{True tail pickup produced by a 4-day repo} = 0.93\text{bp}$$

II. Approximate yield pickup on a 30-day repo

$$\text{Anticipated yield pickup over 30 days} = \frac{30}{3.96} = 7.58\text{bp}$$

$$\text{True yield pickup produced by a 30-day repo} = 7.47\text{bp}$$

Calculating the True Breakeven Rate of Sale

The *true* breakeven rate of sale on the tail is figured as follows. Let

d^* = break-even sale rate on the tail

d_1 = rate at which bill is purchased

T_1 = days to maturity at purchase

T_2 = days to maturity at sale

r_t = term repo rate

$T_1 - T_2$ = financing period

By setting dollars in equal to dollars out, it's easy to show that

$$d^* = \left[1 - \left(1 - \frac{d_1 T_1}{360}\right)\left(1 + r_t \frac{T_1 - T_2}{360}\right)\right]\frac{360}{T_2}$$

Using this formula, one then calculates the *true* yield pickup on a term repo as follows:

$$\text{True yield pickup} = d_1 - d^*$$

A Visual Aid

If the approximation method we've just outlined is applied to a bill with a current maturity of 6 months or less, calculating the bill's yield on a simple interest, 360-day basis is easy. One merely takes its equivalent bond yield and multiplies by 360/365.

If, however, the bill has a life of more than 6 months, the calculation must be made by converting the discount rate directly to the appropriate simple yield. The formula for doing this:

$$\begin{pmatrix}\text{Simple yield, 360-day basis} \\ \text{on a discount security}\end{pmatrix} = \frac{360d}{360 - dT_{sm}}$$

is not difficult, but in a rapidly moving market a trader or investor may not have the time to apply it.[7] The answer to this dilemma is to use a *visual aid.*

Each morning a bill trader should get a sheet that displays the equivalent bond yield and the true simple yield on a 360-day basis that key long bill issues would yield at an array of rates around those at which these bills closed on the preceding day. Another useful visual aid for a trader who is bidding in a bill auction or trading bills is a sheet showing for 91-, 182-, and 364-day bills the following: price, rate of discount, coupon equivalent yield, and true simple yield on a 360-day basis.

The major trick in creating a useful visual aid is not programming the computer to produce correct numbers but in formatting those numbers in such a way that the trader can consult the sheet with one quick glance.

---

[7] To derive this equation, simply take the expression for y on page 96 and multiple it by 360/365. Doing so yields

$$y = \left(\frac{365d}{360 - dT_{sm}}\right)\frac{360}{365} = \frac{360d}{360 - dT_{sm}}$$

SHORTING

A trader who anticipates an *increase* in rates and a consequent *decrease* in bill prices may choose to *sell* bills *short.* If so, then to prevent a *fail to deliver* (a *fail* for short), the trader must obtain the bills he has sold short (i.e., he must *cover* his short sale) either by *borrowing* those bills or by doing a *reverse repo* (i.e., by reversing in those bills).

The normal fee for borrowing securities is 50bp. Unless the period of the borrowing is fixed at the outset, borrowing securities exposes the trader to the danger that just when interest rates are going up and the short is becoming profitable, the lender may decide to call back his securities because he wants to sell or swap them.

To avoid this difficulty and to cut costs, traders often use reverses to cover shorts. When a trader does a *reverse,* he is *borrowing securities and lending money.* The rate he gets on the money he lends depends on prevailing rate relationships and, in particular, on whether the issue he shorts is one that many traders are shorting. Typically, the reverse rate at which a trader lends will be no more than 50bp below the rate on the bill he shorts; however, if a trader shorts a bill that's a popular short, he will be shopping for what the Street calls a *special issue,* and the reverse rate he gets for the money he lends will be *depressed* by the *large demand* from shorters to borrow that particular issue.

Regardless of how a trader covers a bill short, he will typically experience *negative carry*—either a fee of 50bp charged by the borrower or some spread between the bill rate and the lower reverse rate. In such an environment, the trader can make money on his short only if market rates rise (bill prices fall) sufficiently so that the spread between the prices at which he buys and sells exceeds the cost of putting on and maintaining the short.

In effect a trader who shorts bills is creating a *negative* tail; for him to profit, the rate at which he can purchase that tail must increase over the period of the short. Thus, he faces a breakeven problem that is similar to but opposite in direction to that faced by a trader creating a *positive* tail.[8]

---

[8] Note the investor who creates a tail by buying a security and repoing it wants rates to remain stable or to fall over the repo period.

Specifically, the trader who is contemplating a short wants to know in how many days his negative carry on the short will increase by 1bp the rate at which he must repurchase the bill shorted in order for him to break even on his short. That number, as well as the break even rate on a short for a longer period, can easily be estimated for bills by using the formula for d^* on page 143.

A trader who sells short is borrowing securities, and to borrow securities is simply to run a *negative portfolio*. Thus, on reflection it's obvious, rather than surprising, that formulas for calculating breakevens on tails can also be used to calculate breakevens on shorts.

RIDING THE YIELD CURVE

Frequently, an investor who does a break-even analysis will find an opportunity to make a favorable bet, that is, to take a position, on which the odds favor his making a tidy profit. Here's an example: the break-even analysis of a common and often misunderstood investment strategy—*riding the yield curve.*

Assume that an investor has funds to invest for 3 months. The 6-month (180-day) bill is trading at 8.50, and the 3-month (90-day) bill is trading at 8.10 (Figure 8–1). The alternatives the investor is choosing between are (1) to buy the 90-day bill and mature it and (2) to buy the 6-month bill and sell it 3 months hence. To assess the relative merits of these two strategies, the investor does a *break-even analysis.*

On $1MM of bills, a 90-day basis point is worth $25. If the investor bought the 6-month bill, he would earn 40bp more than if he bought the 3-month bill. Thus, the investor could sell out the 6-month bill after 3 months at a rate 40bp above the rate at which he bought it; that is, at 8.90, and still earn as many *dollars on* his investment as he would have if he had bought and matured the 3-month bill (see Table 8–5). Therefore, the rate on the 3-month bill 3 months hence would have to rise above 8.90 before the investor would earn fewer dollars by holding the 6-month bill for 3 months and then selling it than he would by buying the 3-month bill and maturing it.

How likely is it that the rate on the 3-month bill will rise above 8.90? Note that because of the slope of the yield curve (a 40bp drop between the 6- and 3-month bill rates), the rate at which the 3-month bill trades three months hence would be 8.10 if no change occurred in inter-

FIGURE 8–1
Yield Curve in an Example of Riding the Yield Curve

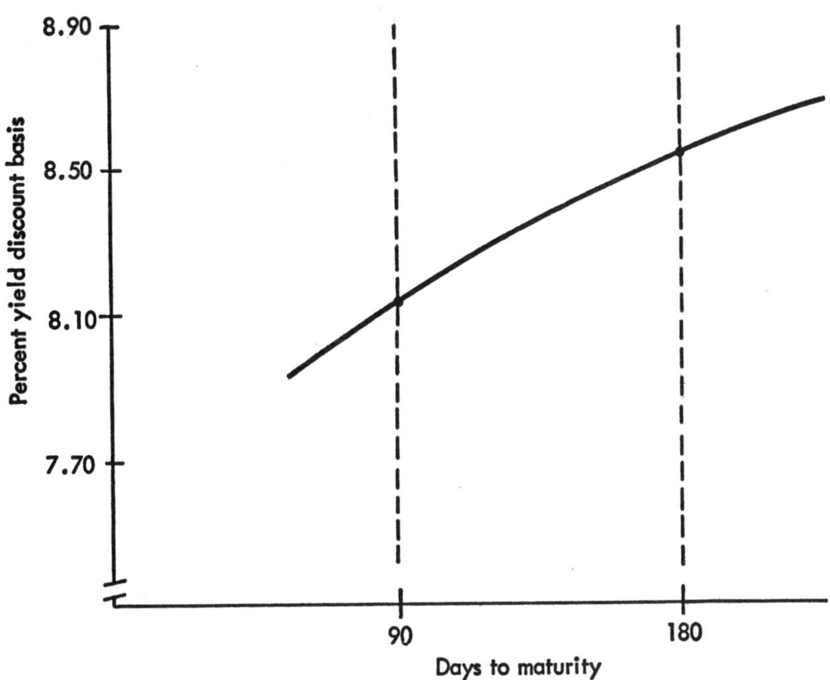

est rates, 80bp below the break-even rate of 8.90. Thus, the investor has 80bp of protection, and the question he must ask in making his choice is: How likely is it that the Fed will tighten in the next 3 months so sharply that the rate on the 3-month bill will rise 80bp? If his answer is that it's unlikely, then he would buy the 6-month bill and ride the yield curve.

HOLDING-PERIOD YIELD ON DISCOUNT PAPER SOLD BEFORE MATURITY

An investor or trader who sells a discount security before maturity will want to know what rate of return his investment has yielded over *his holding period.* The formula for calculating holding-period as a simple yield on a 365-day-year basis is easily derived.

TABLE 8–5
Dollar Calculations of Return in Example of Riding the Yield Curve

I. Buy $1 million of 90-day bills at 8.10 percent and hold to maturity:	
Discount at purchase	$20,250
—Discount at maturity.....	0
Return.................	$20,250
II. Buy $1 million of 180-day bills at 8.50 percent and sell at break-even yield of 8.90 percent:	
Discount at purchase	$42,500
—Discount at maturity.....	22,250
Return.................	$20,250
III. Buy $1 million of 180-day bills at 8.50 percent and sell at 8.10 percent:	
Discount at purchase	$42,500
—Discount at maturity.....	20,250
Return.................	$22,250

To keep our notation simple, we will adopt here a convention that we also use in later chapters:

> When prices and days to maturity on two separate dates before maturity both appear in an equation, we denote the variables referring to the first date with subscript 1, those referring to the second date with subscript 2.

This is preferable to denoting one date as the buy date and the other as the sell date because the equation may be equally useful for calculating the outcome of a reverse-type transaction. For example, the equation we are about to derive for *holding-period yield* on a bill can also be used to calculate the rate of profit or loss on *shorting* a bill.

Let

P_1 = dollar price at the beginning of the transaction

P_2 = dollar price at the end of the transaction

d_1 = rate of discount at the beginning of the transaction

d_2 = rate of discount at the end of the transaction

T_1 = days to maturity at the beginning of the transaction

T_2 = days to maturity at the end of the transaction

y_{hp} = holding-period yield

Then, from the formula for simple interest on page 45, it follows that the holding-period yield earned on a *buy-sell* of a discount security is given by

$$y_{hp} = \left(\frac{P_2 - P_1}{P_1}\right)\frac{365}{T_1 - T_2}$$

which, if we substitute appropriate expressions for P_1 and P_2, reduces to

$$y_{hp} = \left(\frac{1 - \frac{d_2 T_2}{360}}{1 - \frac{d_1 T_1}{360}} - 1\right)\frac{365}{T_1 - T_2}$$

If we want holding-period yield earned on a simple-interest, 360-day basis, we merely multiply this value for y_{hp} by 360/365.

Example. Suppose an investor buys the 90-day bill at a 10.10 rate of discount, that is, at a bond equivalent yield of 10.51. Seven days later, he sells the issue at the same 10.10 rate of discount. Over the 7-day holding period, he will have earned a simple yield, on a *365–day-year basis,* of

$$y_{hp} = \left(\frac{1 - \frac{0.101 \times 83}{360}}{1 - \frac{0.101 \times 90}{360}} - 1\right)\frac{365}{7} = 0.1051 \text{ or } 10.51\%$$

and, on a *360-day-year basis,* of

$$10.52\%\left(\frac{360}{365}\right) = 0.1036 \text{ or } 10.36\%$$

The Repo Pitfall or Opportunity

We've already pointed out one example of how carry that looks *positive* can, in fact, be *negative.* Here's a second and more subtle example—one that illustrates, for an investor who can get away with it, a method to generate a locked-in profit *plus* capital on an arbitrage in bills.

Suppose the 90-day bill is trading at 10, which implies a simple yield on a 360-day basis of 10.26. Suppose also that 7-day repo money can be obtained at 10.10. It would appear that, by purchasing the 90-day bill and repoing it for 7 days, a trader could lock in positive carry of 16 bp.

Whether carry is positive or negative depends, however, on how the repo is done. Every repo is technically a sale and a repurchase, but repos can be and are set up in different ways. Typically, a repo is *priced flat,* which means, on a discount security, that the purchase and sale prices are identical and interest is paid on the amount "borrowed" (i.e., the sale price, at the agreed-upon repo rate). An alternative, however, is for the borrower to sell the security at one rate and later buy it back at another rate with no payment of interest. Some investors prefer the latter approach because it allows them to show the repo on their books as a bona fide purchase and sale as opposed to a camouflaged collateralized loan. Let

$$r_{rp} = \text{repurchase (rp) rate, also known as the repo rate}$$

Anyone who has not massaged the numbers might guess that in our example—$d = 10$, $r_{rp} = 10.10$—it makes no difference which approach is used. The truth, however, is quite different. To understand, recall our discussion in the preceding section concerning how the return earned on a bill sold before maturity is determined. The formula we derived there can be used to calculate the *true* rate paid by a dealer for financing if he does an outright sale and repurchase of a bill as opposed to a flat-priced repo. The example we presented there shows that if our dealer, who is financing 10% 90-day bills for 7 days, agreed to do an outright sell-and-buy-back repo at 10.10, as opposed to a flat-priced repo at 10.10, the true repo rate he would be paying would be 10.36 on a 360-day basis. Thus, the dealer who does the latter type of repo would turn a locked-in positive carry of

$$0.26\% - 10.10\% = 0.16\% \text{ or } 16\,\text{bp}$$

into a locked in negative carry of

$$0.26\% - 10.36\% = -0.10\% \text{ or } -10\text{bp}$$

For an investor who has wide parameters and understands the contrast on a discount security between the true repo rate paid when pricing is flat and that paid when the transaction is a strict sale and repurchase, there is an interesting arbitrage possibility. If in the above situation, the investor (1) reversed in for 7 days at a 10.10 rate 90-day bills on a straight sale–repurchase basis, and (2) offset this transaction by repoing at 10.10 the same securities priced flat at 10.00, he could lock in a positive carry of 26bp *and* generate available funds equal to $250 per $1MM, which is the difference between pricing $1MM of bills at a 10.00 rate of discount and pricing them at a 10.10 rate of discount; that is,

$$\$975{,}000 - \$974{,}750 = \$250$$

Discount Securities Worldwide

As we noted in Chapter 6, the number of days in the year in quoting discount securities varies from country to country. To allow for this, we next restate the formula we derived for holding-period yield on a discount security with the *assumed number of days in the year as a variable.*

Recall the distinction we made at the end of Chapter 6 between T variables and A variables. In this section, we again use A_d as a *variable* that denotes the number of days in the year for quoting a discount security.

The Formula, Worldwide, for Holding-Period Yield on a Discount Security

To calculate holding-period yield on a discount security sold before maturity, we need one additional symbol. Let

A_d = assumed number of days in a year for a discount security

Then,

$$y = \left(\frac{1 - \frac{d_2 T_2}{A_d}}{1 - \frac{d_1 T_1}{A_d}} - 1 \right) \frac{365}{T_1 - T_2}$$

gives holding-period yield earned on a *365-day basis,* while

$$y = \left(\frac{1 - \frac{d_2 T_2}{A_d}}{1 - \frac{d_1 T_1}{A_d}} - 1 \right) \frac{360}{T_1 - T_2}$$

gives holding-period yield earned on a *360-day basis.*

BILL PARITY OR THE IMPLIED FORWARD RATE

The observation is often made that the yield curve in the bill market displays implicitly investors' expectations with respect to future interest rates. To illustrate why, note that to earn a return of 9.90 over 6 months, an investor who buys a 3-month bill at 9.80 must—simple averaging suggests—be able to reinvest 3 months hence in a second 3-month bill at 10.00. Therefore, if a 3-month bill is trading at 9.80 and the 6-month bill at 9.90, intuition suggests that investors must anticipate that the 3-month

FIGURE 8–2
The Bill Parity Problem Visualized

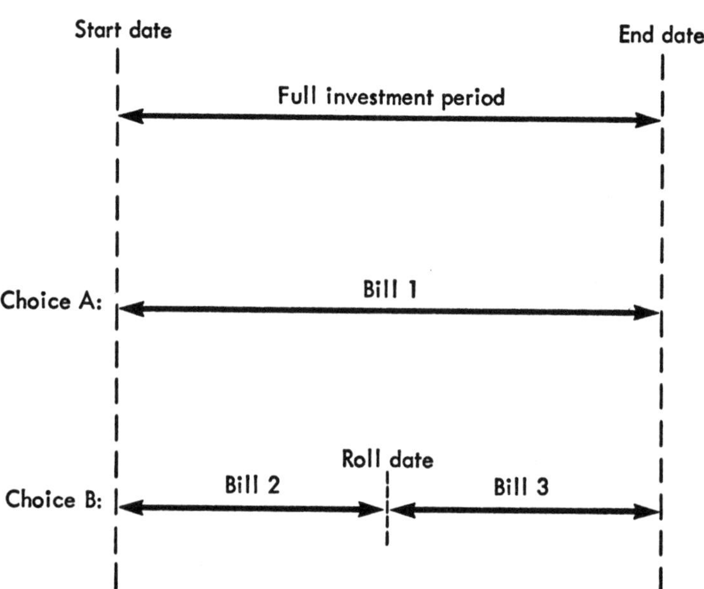

bill 3 months hence will trade at least 10.00 because, if it they didn't think it would, they would buy the 6-month bill in preference to two consecutive 3-month bills.

This observation raises the topic of *bill parity.* Specifically, it leads us to ask: If an investor is choosing between *a long bill* and *two consecutive short bills,* what rate must he get on the second short bill to earn—when reinvestment of earnings on the first short bill is assumed—the same rate on the two short bills that he would earn on the long bill?

To derive a formula for this number, we start by picturing the choice visually in Figure 8–2. The investor is selecting between (1) choice A: an investment in a single long bill, bill 1; and (2) choice B: an investment in two consecutive shorts bills, bills 2 and 3. If we use subscript 1 to denote numbers associated with bill 1, subscript 2 to denote numbers associated with bill 2, and subscript 3 to denote numbers associated with bill 3, we can easily derive a formula for the break-even level for d_3. First, we observe, that if a *principal amount I equal to 1 is invested in both bill 1 and bill 2,* then F_1 and F_2 (which are *unequal*) are derived as follows:

$$\begin{aligned} F_1 &= 1 + D_1 \\ &= 1 + F_1 \frac{T_1 d_1}{360} \end{aligned}$$

which reduces to

$$F_1 = \frac{1}{1 - \dfrac{T_1 d_1}{360}}$$

Similarly,

$$F_2 = \frac{1}{1 - \dfrac{T_2 d_2}{360}}$$

Let

d^* = break-even (bill parity) rate on the second short bill, bill 3

D_{p3} = dollar discount on bill 3

By definition,

$$d_3 = \frac{D_{p3}}{F_3}\left(\frac{360}{T_1 - T_2}\right)$$

If

$$d_3 = -d^*$$

that is, if the investor would earn as much investing $I =$ in choice B as he would investing $I =$ in choice A, then it is necessary that

$$r_{rp} = \text{repurchase (rp) rate, also known as the repo rate}$$

and that

$$F_3 = F_1$$

But if this is so, then from the definition of d_3, it follows that $d_3 = d^*$ implies that

$$d^* = \left(\frac{F_1 - F_2}{F_1}\right)\frac{360}{T_1 - T_2}$$

If we now substitute into this equation for d^* the expressions obtained earlier for F_1 and F_2 and simplify, we get

$$d^* = \left(1 - \frac{1 - \frac{d_1 T_1}{360}}{1 - \frac{d_2 T_2}{360}}\right)\frac{360}{T_1 - T_2}$$

or, alternatively,

$$d^* = \left(1 - \frac{P_1}{P_2}\right)\frac{360}{T_1 - T_2}$$

Example. To illustrate, let's use the numbers in the example with which we began our discussion of bill parity; namely, for bills 1 and 2 respectively:

$$d_1 = 0.099$$
$$T_1 = 180$$
$$d_2 = 0.098$$
$$T_2 = 90$$

Inserting these numbers into our expression for d^*, we get

$$d^* = \left(1 - \frac{1 - \frac{0.099(180)}{360}}{1 - \frac{0.098(90)}{360}}\right)\left(\frac{360}{180 - 90}\right)$$
$$= 0.1025 \text{ or } 10.25\%$$

Calculating d^* shows us that the investor who faces the choice described at the beginning of this section must, when he rolls a short bill, get a higher rate parity between choices A and B—he must buy bill 3 not at a discount of 10.00, but at a discount of 10.25.

The 25bp discrepancy between the break-even rate suggested by mathematical inspection and the rate indicated by more careful reasoning is simply explained. Our calculation of d^* requires that the same yield y be earned on choices A and B. As noted, the difference between a rate of discount d and the equivalent simple yield y is larger the larger T is. In the case at hand, $T_1 = 2T_2$, a factor that outweighs the compounding permitted when choice B is selected.

The number for bill parity, d^*, that we've just calculated is also often referred to, especially by academics, as an *implied forward rate.* This designation suggests the following: (1) Investors are rational, and (2) investors anticipate that a bill covering the time gap between the short and long bills will trade on the date the short bill matures at a rate such that they (the investors) should be indifferent, at the prevailing yield spread, between the short bill and long bill.

CONCLUDING REMARKS ON DISCOUNT PAPER

Throughout our discussion of applications of calculations for discount securities, we've talked about bills. Much of this discussion applies equally well to other discount securities, but there's one exception: *shorting;* because of their *heterogeneity,* commercial paper and BAs cannot be shorted.

THE NEXT CHAPTER

In the next chapter, we return to interest-bearing paper. There, we describe various ways in which imaginative traders and investors can use, *to their profit,* the basic calculations for discount paper that we developed in Chapter 7.

CHAPTER 9

INTEREST-BEARING PAPER: APPLICATIONS

In this chapter, we focus on applications of calculations for money market *interest-bearing* paper. As we do so, we find that we have less to say. Whereas bills are liquid, homogeneous—in sum highly tradable—interest-bearing money market paper tends to be heterogeneous and illiquid; thus, the trading strategies that can be applied to such paper are more limited then they are for discount paper. It's in Part 4, where we turn to notes and bonds, that applications of calculations derived for interest-bearing paper come into their own.

Among interest-bearing, money market instruments, CDs used to be the instrument that was—if any such instrument was—a trading vehicle. Today, however, the U.S. domestic CD market, once grand, glorious, and highly liquid, has come upon bad times. U.S. money center banks, formerly big issuers of domestic CDs, have discovered more attractive alternative sources of funding, and they currently issue few domestic wholesale CDs, although they still issue a fair volume of Euro CDs. As a result, U.S. domestic CDs are no longer a liquid instrument, and traders no longer actively position and trade such paper. Thus, we could severely limit our discussion of applications of CD formulas. However, manipulating such formulas is an instructive exercise for the reader, and who knows when the CD market might again come to life.

HOLDING-PERIOD YIELD ON A CD SOLD BEFORE MATURITY

We begin with a derivation of the formula for holding-period yield on a CD sold before maturity. Intuition, which seems to be invariably wrong in money market calculations, suggests that if an investor bought a CD at

10% and sold it before maturity at the same rate, he would earn 10% over his holding period. In fact, he would earn *less*. The reason is our old friend, compounding. It crops up because interest is not paid by the issuer of the CD until some time after the investor sells it; at sale, however, the CD is priced so that the new buyer will earn the offered yield on an amount equal to the dirty price he pays for the CD, that is, on an amount equal to the principal paid *plus* accrued interest.

A New-Issue CD

Consider first a CD that is bought by an investor at issue and later sold before maturity. The yield that the investor will earn over the *holding period*, y_{hp}, is given by

$$y_{hp} = \left(\frac{\text{Dirty sale price} - \text{Dirty purchase price}}{\text{Dirty purchase price}} \right) \frac{360}{T_{is}}$$

where

y_{hp} = holding-period yield

T_{is} = days from issue to settlement of the sale

On a *new issue*, the purchase price, clean or dirty, is 1, so the formula reduces to:[1]

$$y_h = \left(\frac{1 + c\dfrac{T_{im}}{360}}{1 + y\dfrac{T_{sm}}{360}} - 1 \right) \frac{360}{T_{is}}$$

where y is the rate at which the CD is sold.[2]

---

[1] Recall the convention we introduced in Chapter 7.

[2] This can be proved, as can all other equations in this chapter, by making appropriate substitutions—in this case, for the sale price—and doing a few algebraic manipulations.

Calculating Holding-Period Yield Earned on a CD Sold Before Maturity

Case I. The CD is purchased at issue: Let

c = coupon rate

y = yield at sale

y_{hp} = holding-period yield

T_{im} = days from issue to maturity

T_{is} = days from issue to settlement

T_{sm} = days from settlement to maturity

Then,

$$y_{hp} = \left(\frac{1 + c\dfrac{T_{im}}{360}}{1 + y\dfrac{T_{sm}}{360}} - 1 \right) \frac{360}{T_{is}}$$

Case II. The CD is purchased in the secondary market: Let

y_1 = purchase yield

y_2 = yield at sale

T_1 = days from purchase to maturity

T_2 = days from sale to maturity

Then,

$$y_{hp} = \left(\frac{1 + y_1\dfrac{T_1}{360}}{1 + y_2\dfrac{T_2}{360}} - 1 \right) \frac{360}{T_1 - T_2}$$

Example. An investor buys a 90-day CD carrying a 10% coupon at issue and sells it 30 days later at a 10% yield. The *holding-period yield* he earns is not 10%, but a lower figure, 9.83. The calculation is as follows:

$$y_{hp} = \left(\frac{1 + 0.10 \dfrac{90}{360}}{1 + 0.10 \dfrac{60}{360}} - 1 \right) \frac{360}{30} = 0.0983 \text{ or } 9.83\%$$

A Secondary CD

Holding-period yield on a CD purchased in the secondary market and sold before maturity can be calculated using a similar, but slightly more complex, formula. See Case II in the box on page 159.

Impact of Yield at Sale and of Time Held

The figures in Table 9–1 show what holding-period yield, y_{hp}, an investor would earn if he sold a six-month CD purchased at 9% after various holding periods and at various rates. Look first at the column labeled 9%. It shows that if the investor resells his CD at the purchase yield, the holding-period yield he'll earn will be higher the longer his holding period is (i.e., the closer the sale date is to the date on which the CD matures and accrued interest is paid by the issuer).

If an investor sells a CD at a rate below the rate at which he bought it, he will receive a capital gain; and over his holding period, he will earn a yield higher than the yield at which he bought his CD; also, as shown by the columns labeled *11.00* and *9.00,* this effect will be smaller

TABLE 9–1
The Holding-Period Yield, y_{hp}, Earned by an Investor on a 9%, 6-Month CD when the CD Is Sold at Various Rates after Various Holding Periods

Holding period (Days)	*Yield at Sale (%)*		
	11.00	*9.00*	*7.00*
30	0.96%	8.67%	18.46%
60	4.82	8.74	12.70
90	6.81	8.80	10.81
120	7.86	8.87	9.88
150	8.59	8.93	9.35
179	8.99	9.00	9.01

the longer the investor's holding period. Alternatively, if, the investor sells his CD at a rate *above* the rate at which he bought it, the impact on his holding-period yield will be opposite in direction; and this impact will be smaller, the longer the investor's holding period.

It's easy to explain why the impact of the yield at sale on the investor's holding-period yield diminishes as his holding period increases. The longer the investor's holding period, the shorter is the time during which the investor earns the yield at which he buys the CD; and therefore, the smaller is the impact of that yield on the dirty price he pays for the CD.

Compounding

We've noted that, if an investor sells a CD he's holding before it matures, his doing so will reduce the yield he earns over his holding period. However, if the investor were to *fully* reinvest all proceeds (the full dirty price) realized from the sale of his CD, the impact of his selling his CD before maturity on the effective yield he earns would tend to be offset by the opportunity, created by subsequent reinvestment, for compounding of his interest earnings.

To illustrate, note that an investor who purchased at issue a $1MM, 182-day CD carrying a 9% coupon and sold it 91 days later at rate of 9% would earn a holding-period yield of 8.80 over those 91 days. If, however, the investor were to immediately reinvest the full sale proceeds ($1,022,750) in a new 91-day CD carrying a 9% coupon, his total interest earnings over the 182-day period would equal the interest he would have earned had he held his original 182-day, 9% CD to maturity.

The Repo Scam

A CD is normally repoed *par flat;* that is, the investor lends to the dealer an amount equal to the par value of the CD being financed rather than its market value *plus* accrued interest. Thus, a dealer who repos a secondary CD uses some of his capital, and the older the CD repoed, the more of his capital he uses. As noted, capital has a cost; and whenever a dealer does a trade that uses capital (e.g., whenever he's financing securities or creating a tail) he should take into account his cost of capital. The high cost that a dealer typically assigns to capital is one reason dealers tend to bid low on "stale dated" CDs that carry a significant amount of accrued interest.

Sometimes, traders who are taking new paper into inventory can find lenders who are willing or prefer to do a repo on an outright sale–repurchase basis. The scam in this is that a trader can offer the naive investor what appears to be a high repo rate but actually finance at a cost below the repo rate.

Here's an example. Suppose a trader buys a 90-day CD at a rate of 10%. He could finance the CD with term repo for a week at 9.90. Instead, he proposes to an investor that she sell the CD outright to the investor at 10.05 and buy it back from him a week later at 10.05. To the investor, who hasn't massaged the numbers, the 10.05 apparent yield looks attractive compared with the 9.90 repo rate, but in reality the investor who did this deal would get a simple yield, *y*, of only 9.82. To check this, use the formula we derived for the simple yield earned on a CD sold before maturity.

The kicker in an outright sale–repurchase transaction works in exactly the opposite direction on a CD financing than it does on a bill financing. Doing an outright sale–repurchase, as opposed to a flat-priced repo, makes the borrower's cost of money *higher* than the nominal borrowing rate in the case of a discount security but *lower* than the nominal borrowing rate in the case of a CD.

For the trader who realizes that it makes a difference how CDs are financed, an *arbitrage* opportunity arises. By reversing in CDs flat and repoing them at even a slightly higher nominal rate on an outright sale–repurchase basis, he can lock in a profit margin *and* generate funds at the repo rate.

RIDING THE YIELD CURVE

An investor can ride the yield curve in CDs just as he can in bills. Before doing so, however, he should do a break-even analysis of the sort described for bills.

To illustrate, consider an investor who has 3-month money and is choosing between a 6-month CD yielding 9.00 and a 3-month CD yielding 8.80. The investor wonders: If I were to buy the 6-month CD and sell it 3 months hence, at what rate would I have to sell in order to earn at least the 3-month rate of 8.80?

Intuition suggests that since the investor picks up an extra 20bp over 3 months by buying the 6-month CD, he could sell that CD after 3 months at a yield as high as

$$9.00 + 0.20 = 9.20$$

and still earn at least 8.80 over his 3-month holding period. Intuition, however, grossly overestimates the investor's *true* break-even rate because the sale of a CD before maturity reduces the return earned by the investor for reasons discussed above. To determine his true break-even rate, the investor needs a precise formula. To obtain it, let

y = simple yield offered by the short CD

y^* = investor's break-even yield on the sale of a longer CD

Next, recall our equation for the simple yield earned by an investor when he buys a CD at issue and sells it at yield y before maturity:

$$y = \left(\frac{1 + c\dfrac{T_{im}}{360}}{1 + y\dfrac{T_{sm}}{360}} - 1 \right) \frac{360}{T_{is}}$$

If we interpret y in this equation to be the rate the investor can get on the short CD, then the y value in the equation is y^*, his break-even rate of sale on the long CD. Thus, solving the preceding equation for y (which equals y^*), we get:

$$y^* = \left(\frac{1 + c\dfrac{T_{im}}{360}}{1 + i\dfrac{T_{is}}{360}} - 1 \right) \frac{360}{T_{sm}}$$

If we now insert the numbers in our example into this formula, we obtain

$$y^* = \left(\frac{1 + 0.090\dfrac{180}{360}}{1 + 0.088\dfrac{90}{360}} - 1 \right) \frac{360}{90} = 0.090 \text{ or } 9.00\%$$

This number tells us that, if our investor buys a 6-month CD at 9% and sells it 3 months later, he must sell it at a rate no higher than 9% in order to earn at least 8.80 over his 3-month holding period. Note the 8.80 figure corresponds to the number given in Table 9–1 for the yield earned on a 6-month CD purchased at 9.00 and sold 3 months later at 9%.

CD PARITY

In Chapter 8, we derived a formula for bill parity. A similar formula can be derived for CDs. Suppose 1-month CDs are trading at 9% and 2-month CDs at 10%. An investor anticipates that CD rates will rise and wonders whether he would earn more by buying and maturing a 2-month CD or by buying and maturing two consecutive 1-month CDs. Answering this query requires a break-even calculation. Specifically, the investor needs to know how much he would have to earn on the second 1-month CD in order to earn a return of 10% over the full 2-month period.

Approximation suggests that, with 1-month CDs trading at 9% and 2-month CDs trading at 10%, the investor would have to be able to purchase 1 month hence a 1-month CD yielding 11% in order to break even on the purchase of a current 1-month CD at 9%. Actually, the correct number is slightly lower. Let

c_1 = coupon on the current long CD

c_2 = coupon on the current short CD

c_3 = coupon on the future CD covering the "gap" between the current long and short CDs

c^* = break-even coupon on this future CD

T_1 = days to maturity on the current long CD

T_2 = days to maturity on the current short CD

Assuming that an amount of principal equal to 1 is invested in both the long and the short CDs on day 1, and assuming reinvestment of interest, *the break-even rate of purchase on the future CD, c^*,* is c_3 in the expression:

$$1 + c_1 \frac{T_1}{360} = 1 + c_2 \frac{T_2}{360} + c_3 \left(1 + c_2 \frac{T_2}{360}\right) \frac{T_1 - T_2}{360}$$

Solving this break-even expression for c^* (which equals c_3), we get

$$c^* = \frac{c_1 T_1 - c_2 T_2}{\left(1 + c_2 \frac{T_2}{360}\right)(T_1 - T_2)}$$

If we now plug the numbers in our example into this equation, we find that

$$c^* = \frac{0.10(60) - 0.09(30)}{\left(1 + 0.09\frac{30}{360}\right)30} = 0.1092 \text{ or } 10.92\%$$

The investor's break-even rate on the second CD is not 11.00, but 10.92. The approximation overestimates the break-even rate on the second 1-month CD because it fails to allow for the compounding that can occur if the investor purchases two consecutive 1-month CDs.

THE NEXT CHAPTER

In Part 3, we turn from money market paper to bonds. The topic of bond calculations covers a lot of territory. We begin in Chapter 10 with a discussion of bond basics, including the many concepts of yield commonly applied to bonds.

PART 3

BONDS: THE BASICS

CHAPTER 10

BONDS: MEASURES OF YIELD AND OTHER BASICS

So far we've focused on *money market instruments,* discount and interest-bearing. Now, in Part 3, we turn to *bonds.*

For different purposes, people are interested in different measures of yield on a bond. We begin our discussion of bonds by describing the different and sometimes confusing measures of bond yield that people calculate and by discussing what each such measure means.

BOND PRICE QUOTES

It is market practice to quote the prices of bonds as so and so much per a given amount of principal or face value. For example, in the United States, bond prices are quoted as so and so much per $100 of face value. Also in the United States, bond prices are rounded to the nearest 1⁄32 or fraction thereof—1⁄64 or whatever. The same practice is followed in the United Kingdom. Elsewhere in the world, bond prices are rounded to the nearest 2 (or more) decimal places; practice varies market to market.

The *clean price* of a bond is the price the buyer pays for principal. The prices quoted for bonds are always clean prices. The *dirty price* of a bond, which is the price a buyer actually pays for a bond, is the bond's clean price *plus* any accrued interest on the bond. In our notation,

$$P = \text{clean price of a bond}$$
$$B = \text{dirty price of a bond}$$

MEASURES OF BOND YIELD

For different purposes, people are interested in different measures of yield on a bond. In the first part of this chapter, we describe the different and sometimes confusing measures of bond yield that people calculate, and we discuss what each such measure means.

Current Yield

The simplest measure of yield on a bond is *current yield,* which is defined as the bond's annual coupon in dollars divided by its clean price in dollars. Let

$$y_c = \text{current yield}$$
$$cF = \text{annual coupon in dollars}$$
$$P = \text{clean price of a bond}$$

Then,

$$y_c = \frac{cF}{P}$$

For example, if a bond is selling at par (i.e., at a dollar price of $100) and pays a 10% coupon (i.e., $10 of coupon interest per $100 of face value per year), its current yield is 10%. However, if the same bond were trading at a dollar price of $200, its current yield would be only 5%.

Current yield is a way for an investor to make a quick check of multiple short-dated bonds. Such an investor might reason that he'd rather invest $90 than $103 to get a current yield of say 10%, provided that he doesn't intend to hold the bond he's buying to maturity. If the investor does intend to hold the bond to maturity, he ought to be concerned about whether, over the bond's remaining time to maturity, he'd experience a capital loss or earn a capital gain.

As a bond matures, the price at which it trades (assuming no credit problem attaches to the bond) is inexorably *pulled to par,* (i.e., to the dollar price of 100 at which it will be redeemed). If an investor buys a bond at a *premium* (a price *greater than* 100), *drag to par* will cause the investor to suffer a *capital loss* due to the *amortization* of this premium as the bond approaches maturity. Conversely, if an investor buys a bond at a *discount* (a price *less than* 100), *drag to par* will reward the investor with a *capital gain* due to the *accretion* of this discount as the bond approaches par.

Actually, investors today don't rely much on current yield. A portfolio manager investing, say, pension money, who buys a bond with a long current maturity and who intends to hold that bond for some time now worries about other things; he looks at yield to maturity (Chapter 11) and also duration and convexity, concepts that we cover in Part 4.

In times past, however, when bond investors were less sophisticated, they tended to compare and to buy bonds on the basis of the current yields offered by available bonds. If bond A offered a higher current yield than bond B, they bought bond A.

Redemption Value and Face Value

In discussing money market instruments, we were always dealing with instruments that paid the investor *face value* or par at maturity. There are certain bonds that promise to pay the investor at maturity not face value, but a formula-determined *redemption value.* For this reason, in presenting equations to calculate bond yields, we will, in order to make our equations more general, typically use

$$R = \text{redemption value}$$

in place of

$$F = \text{face value}$$

to denote the amount that the bond pays at maturity. This practice ensures that all of our equations will cover the case where a bond pays at maturity its redemption value as opposed to its face value. However, the reader should bear in mind that, for most bonds, promised redemption value at maturity equals face value.

Simple Yield to Maturity

The concept of simple yield to maturity takes into account the *drag to par* that will inevitably occur if a bond is bought at either a *premium* or at a *discount* and then held to maturity at which time it is redeemed at par. Thus, an investor who looks at *simple yield to maturity* assumes that he's going to hold a bond he buys until it matures. Ignoring any risk of default, he also assumes that, at that time, he will be paid par or 100 for his bond.

It's easy to express simple yield to maturity in symbols. Let

y_s = simple yield to maturity
F = face value
R = redemption value
P = clean price of a bond
cF = annual coupon in dollars
T_{sm} = days from settlement to maturity
(according to the appropriate day-count convention)

Then,

$$y_s = \frac{cF + \dfrac{R-P}{T_{sm}/365}}{P}$$

As one would expect, when an investor buys a bond at *par,* the simple yields he earns reduces to the bond's current yield, which in turn equals the bond's coupon rate. If an investor buys a bond at a *premium, drag to par* will cause the investor to suffer a *capital loss* due to the *amortization* of this premium as the bond approaches maturity; consequently, the simple yield to maturity earned by the investor on his premium bond will be less than the coupon on that bond. Conversely, if an investor buys a bond at a *discount, drag to par* will reward the investor with a *capital gain* due to the *accretion* of this discount as the bond approaches par; and the simple yield to maturity earned by the investor on his discount bond will exceed the coupon on that bond.

The concept of simple yield to maturity takes into account, albeit without great precision, two questions that are important to a buyer of bonds. First, for how long is a given bond going to pay its promised coupon to the investor (i.e., what is the bond's remaining term to maturity)? Second, is the investor buying the bond at a premium that he will eventually lose as his bond trades down to par, or is he buying the bond at a discount that he will eventually earn as his bond trades up to par?

Simple yield certainly has one thing going for it. It is *simple* to calculate. Also, it's the method by which bond yields are currently calculated and quoted in Japanese markets.

Yield to Maturity

When an investor plans to or might hold a bond to maturity, the measure of yield in which he's most interested is *yield to maturity,* a concept we first mentioned in Chapter 4. A bond or note held over any period will throw off a number of cash payments: (1) during its life, periodic coupon payments and, (2) at maturity, a payment of principal (i.e., par) plus a final coupon payment. A note or bond also offers the investor the opportunity to earn additional interest during the life of the security by *reinvesting coupon interest.* The key characteristic of yield to maturity is that it *explicitly* recognizes the importance of points in time at which different cash payments from a bond are to be received and at which these cash payments may, before the bond matures, be reinvested.

Whereas we could write a *closed-form* formula for simple yield to maturity, we cannot do so for yield to maturity. In Chapter 11, we derive *the bond equation* for calculating yield to maturity; here, we simply note that a bond's yield to maturity is the value of the discount rate in the bond equation that equates the present value of all future cash payments thrown off by the bond to the current market price of that security.

Implicit in this definition of yield to maturity is the assumption that the investor will be able to reinvest all coupon payments dropped by his bond prior to its maturity at a rate equal to the yield to maturity at which he bought his bond. Since the reinvestment rates that will prevail in future periods are unknown, an investor cannot calculate with certainty *ex ante* what yield to maturity he will in fact earn over the life of a bond.

For example, an investor who bought, in November 1981 *at par,* a U.S. Treasury *long* (30-year) *bond* carrying a 14% coupon may have thought that with semiannual compounding he was locking in, over 30 years, a yield to maturity that exceeded 14%.[1] After all, he'd bought the long bond, at issue, at a 14% yield to maturity. However, due to falling reinvestment rates, it appears today that such an investor is highly unlikely to hit his bogy. Reflecting the secular decline in interest rates that occurred after 1981, the 14s of 11 were trading on January 6, 1994, at a

[1] When we discussed, in Chapter 6, bond equivalent yield on a long T bill, we noted that the yield-to-maturity calculation on a semiannual-pay bond does not take into account the impact on the yield that the bond holder might earn if he were to reinvest coupon interest and thus take advantage of the opportunity for semiannual compounding.

huge premium; specifically, they were priced in the market at 160-09, and available reinvestment rates in the Treasury market were all single digit.

Holding-Period Yield

An investor who calculates *holding-period yield,* either does not intend to hold the bond he's buying to maturity, or alternatively, even if he thinks he might hold it until maturity, he wants to know whether, over a particular period, he'd be better off buying bond A or bond B. It turns out that the calculation of holding-period yield will furnish a certain and exact result only if it's done *ex post.*

A investor who wants to calculate what holding-period yield he might earn on a given bond over a given period is making an *ex ante* calculation. Better, he's making an *ex ante* estimate because his calculation must be based on his *best estimate* of where that bond will trade at the end of his intended holding period.

Still, investors face this sort of calculation all the time. Consider an investor who has cash he could invest but who knows that, say six months hence, he'll need some or all of that cash. The yield curve is upward sloping, but the investor's view is that interest rates will stay flat or fall over the next six months. The investor could simply buy 6-month bills and mature them. Alternatively, he could buy, say, a 2-year note with a higher current yield and plan to ride that note down the yield curve and sell it six months later, hopefully at a gain.[2] In one guise or another, investors face choices of this sort all the time. Maybe the investor is running a liquidity portfolio and anticipates having to make a tax payment on a fixed future date or maybe he works for a company that's planning to make an acquisition a half year hence.

The tough part of estimating holding-period yield on a bond is estimating (1) the rate at which any *dropped coupons* (i.e., coupons received during the holding period) can be *reinvested* and (2) the *terminal price* that the bond will command at the end of the holding period. Once those estimates are made, the actual calculation of holding-period yield is trivial.

---

[2] With an upward sloping-yield curve, the 3-year note could be paying a current coupon that's higher than the yield the investor could get on a maturing bond; and the 3-year note, because it carries a current coupon, could still be trading at par.

We can restate succinctly the definition of holding-period yield as follows. Let

$$y_{hp} = \text{holding-period yield}$$

Then,

$$y_{hp} = \frac{\text{Terminal market value} + \text{Income received}}{\text{Beginning market value}}$$

To restate this definition of holding-period yield in symbols, we must define a number of variables. Let

B_1 = dirty price at which bond is bought

B_2 = dirty price of bond on terminal date

K = number of dropped coupons

C_k = kth *periodic* coupon payment in dollars

r_{re} = rate at which *all* coupons are reinvested

T_2 = terminal date

T_k = date on which the kth coupon is paid

$T'_k = T_2 - T_k$ = reinvestment period for the kth coupon

A_y = year base for r_{re}

Note that T'_K is the number of days between the receipt of the kth coupon and the end of the holding period.

Using these symbols, we can write the precise formula for holding-period yield as follows:

$$y_{hp} = \frac{B_2 + \sum_{k=1}^{K} C_k \left[1 + r_{re} \frac{T'_k}{A_y} \right]}{B_1} - 1$$

Yield to Call and Yield to Put

A number of bond issuers add a call feature to their bonds; typically, this feature permits the issuer to call some or all of a bond issue at some future date, usually at par or at a premium.

The U.S. Treasury used to issue notes and bonds that were callable at par on a date five years preceding their maturity. Prior to the early

1990s, the Treasury did not call any eligible issue, partly because it issued most of its bonds when the secular trend in interest rates was upward. Therefore, calling an outstanding long bond would not have given the Treasury the opportunity to replace an outstanding issue with a new issue carrying a lower coupon. However, since the early 1990s, the Treasury has called every eligible issue on its first callable date. These calls reflect the dramatic drop in yields during the bull market of the early 1990s. Corporate and muni borrowers have a history of calling bonds they've issued whenever it's advantageous, for one reason or another, for them to do so.

The right to call a bond is an *implied option* that the issuer of the bond sells to the bond buyer; this option is packaged by the issuer with the bond in its indenture. A bond buyer should charge a price for granting a call option to the issuer of a bond he buys; thus, in a rational world, a bond issuer should have to put a higher coupon on a callable issue than he would have to put on a noncallable, but otherwise identical, issue.

Since a call feature on a bond is really an option exercisable by the issuer of the bond, the proper place for us to discuss callable bonds is in another book. Here, we merely note that, if it looks as if a bond may well be called, the investor should be interested not in a bond's yield to maturity, but in its *yield to call.* The technique used for calculating yield to call is the same as that used in Chapter 11 to calculate yield to maturity. The only difference is that, in calculating a bond's yield to call, the bond's call date is substituted for its maturity date, and its call price is substituted for its redemption value at maturity. Naturally, the calculation of yield to call assumes that, once a bond is called, no further coupon payments will be made on that bond.

Sometimes, bonds are issued with a put feature. No national government debt is puttable, but the debt of some Canadian provinces is puttable. Puttable debt is debt that incorporates an implied *put option* that may be exercised by the holder of the debt. An investor holding puttable debt may be interested in yield to put, as opposed to yield to maturity. To calculate *yield to put,* one simply modifies appropriately, for the security in question, the formula for calculating yield to maturity.

Yield to Average Life

In fixed-income land, the term, *yield to average life,* is used in differing contexts. First, it is applied to mortgage-backed securities in which the assets collateralizing the securities issued are a pool of mortgages on which each of the mortgagors has the right to prepay his mortgage. Estimating the average life of mortgage-backed securities is risky because interest rates and living patterns change over time.

The term, *average yield to life,* is also used in a second, quite different context. The indentures of some bond issues provide for *scheduled redemptions.* In the simplest case, an issuer of 20-year bonds might state in his bond's indenture that he will redeem, by lottery, ¼ of the issue at the end of the 10th year. In that case, an investor buying, say, 100 of these bonds might take the view that, in effect, he's most likely buying 25 10-year bonds and 75 20-year bonds. In that case, the investor could calculate a weighted yield to average life based on the yield to maturity formula given in Chapter 11.

Actually, of course, the investor in such an issue might have all or none of his bonds called. To refine his calculation of yield to average life, the investor might want to use a probabilistic approach—to use sampling with replacement if he has many bonds, sampling without replacement if he has only a few bonds.

THE NEXT CHAPTER

In the next chapter, we'll derive the bond equation, obtain a closed-form expression for the price of a bond as a function of its yield, and also consider several special cases, including price-yield calculations for zero-coupon bonds.

CHAPTER 11

THE BOND EQUATION

In this chapter, our focus is the standard bond equation: First, we derive it. Next, we restate this equation in annuity form. Then, we consider various special cases such as zero-coupon bonds and bonds in their last coupon period.

The only place in this chapter where the math may appear—but really isn't—formidable is the section where we restate the bond equation in its annuity form. This section is crucial reading only for someone who wants to program the bond equation. Other readers should, however, try to follow though this section as the approach we use there will prove useful in Chapters 12 and 13 where we discuss and derive expressions for duration and convexity.

BONDS AND THE BOND EQUATION

Whenever a coupon-bearing security (e.g., a note, a bond, or a CD) is sold, the price it will command in a competitive market equals the sum of the present values of all future cash payments discounted back to the valuation date (e.g., to the date on which the trade settles).

We've already encountered a coupon-bearing, periodic-pay security in Chapter 7, namely *term CDs*. In calculating the price of a term CD, one must know precisely how many days (182, 183 or whatever) there are in the current and in *each* remaining coupon period; this is what makes the step-by-step calculation of the price of a term CD so arduous. The procedure used in making price calculations for term CDs is referred to as *the true yield version of the bond equation.*

Before the advent of computers, it was impractical to calculate yield to maturity for a long bond (1) taking into account the exact number of days in each coupon period, and (2) making allowance for coupon dates or a maturity date that would fall on a nonbusiness day. Consequently, in bondland, a simplified version of this equation—*one based on remaining coupon periods*—became *the standard bond equation* that everyone knows and with which everyone works. Actually, people just call this equation *the bond equation.*

In quoting bond prices and yields all dealers rely on *the* bond equation, but they realize that the yields they calculate using this equation may be slightly off, especially when they are calculating yields to maturity on notes or bonds that mature on or that have coupon dates on one or more nonbusiness days. Recognizing this, some dealers put an asterisk or some other sign on their quote sheets next to such bonds. Nonetheless, dealers and others still quote note and bond yields on the basis of *the bond equation.* That's *market practice*—the *market standard* for quoting yield to maturity on notes and bonds.

DERIVING THE BOND EQUATION

In deriving the bond equation, we begin by solving for price given yield. Then, we do the flip calculation: solve for yield given price.

Price Given Yield

The initial question we seek to answer is as follows: How can we determine the price that a bond of a given current maturity—2 years, 20 years, whatever—will command if we know the yield to maturity at which that bond is trading? First, note that the buyer of a bond that is more than 6 months from maturity will receive *a stream of future payments* from that bond. For example, an investor who buys at issue a 30-year Treasury bond, will, if he holds that bond to maturity, receive 60 successive payments of coupon interest and a redemption payment at maturity.

In Chapter 10, we pointed out that the Street prices a bond that pays periodic interest at the present value of the stream of dollar flows—coupon interest plus redemption value at maturity—that the bond offers an investor. We also noted that the rate of discount used in this calculation is the yield to maturity at which the bond trades in the market.

Our task here is to develop a general formula that will permit us to calculate the price at which *any bond* more than one coupon payment from maturity would sell if it were traded at a specific yield for settlement on a specific date. We begin our discussion of the bond equation with an example based on a Treasury note.

Example. On Thursday, March 14, 1996, the T note,

N $7\frac{1}{4}$ 11/30/96

was being offered for settlement on March 15, 1996, at a yield to maturity of 5.432%. Using this information, we want to derive the corresponding dollar price at which this security must be offered.

To do so, we first look at the time framework in which the dollar flows associated with an investment in this note would occur. Part A of Figure 11–1 pictures this. Specifically, it shows that the settlement date is slightly more than halfway through the note's next-to-last coupon period. Figure 11–1 also correctly indicates that, to calculate the present value of the dollar flows generated by this note, we must discount both the approaching coupon payment and the maturity value of the issue *back to the settlement date.* To do this requires that precise numbers be put on the time periods involved; this is done in Part B of Figure 11–1.

March 15, 1996, the settlement date, is 77 days before the next coupon date, and the number of days in the coupon period is 183. Thus,

FIGURE 11-1
Calculating Price Given Yield on a Bond in Its Next-to-Last Coupon Period: An Example

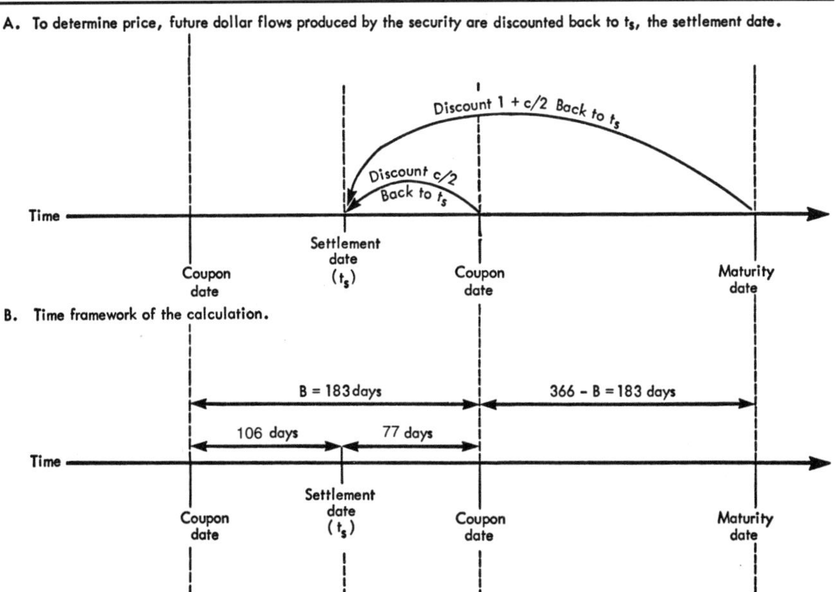

to receive the approaching coupon payment, the investor must wait a fraction, 77/183, of a coupon period. Given that yield to maturity at the offered price is 5.432%, the factor by which the next-to-last coupon must be discounted is

$$\left(1+\frac{0.05432}{2}\right)^{77/183}$$

To obtain the maturity value of the security, the investor must wait the full final coupon period plus a fraction, 77/183, of the next-to-last coupon period (i.e., 1+77/183 coupon periods). Thus, the factor by which the security's maturity value must be discounted is

$$\left(1+\frac{0.05432}{2}\right)^{1+77/183}$$

Since the investor pays a dollar price, *P,* plus accrued interest for the note, and since this amount equals the present value of the coupon payments that the note will drop plus the note's value at maturity, the offered price per $100 of face value must be *P* in the following expression:[1]

$$P+AI=\left[\frac{\frac{0.07250}{2}}{\left(1+\frac{0.05432}{2}\right)^{77/183}}\right]+\left[\frac{1+\frac{0.07250}{2}}{\left(1+\frac{0.05432}{2}\right)^{1+77/183}}\right]$$

which reduces to

$$P=1.0333817675-AI$$

Next, we note that the settlement date is 106 days after the last coupon date (Figure 11–1, Part B). Therefore, at settlement,

$$AI=\frac{0.07250}{2}\left(\frac{106}{183}\right)=0.0209972678$$

and

$$\begin{aligned}P&=1.0333817675-0.0209972678\\&=1.0123844997\end{aligned}$$

[1] In decimal form, the coupon rate is

$$7.250 \text{ percent} = 0.07250$$

This P value is the price per \$1 of face value. Multiplying P by 100 and rounding to the nearest $\frac{1}{32}$, we get a dollar price of 101-075. We have thus concluded that, since the note is offered at a 5.432% yield, the dollar price asked for it must be 101-075. This was in fact the price at which the issue was offered on March 14, 1996 for next-day settlement.

Price Given Yield in the Next-to-Last Coupon Period

The example we have just worked is a specific case of a general problem—calculating the price of a note or bond in its next-to-last coupon period when yield to maturity is known. Generalizing from this example, we can easily write a formula for solving this problem. Let

$$
\begin{aligned}
P &= \text{price of the note} \\
T_{sn} &= \text{days from settlement to next coupon} \\
A_{ln} &= \text{days in the current coupon period} \\
t_{sn} &= T_{sn} / A_{ln} \\
y_{w} &= \text{periodic yield to maturity} \\
R &= \text{redemption value, typically 100} \\
C &= \text{a coupon payment} \\
AI &= \text{accrued interest}
\end{aligned}
$$

Then,

$$P = \left[\frac{C}{(1+y_w)^{t_{sn}}} \right] + \left[\frac{R+C}{(1+y_w)^{1+t_{sn}}} \right] - AI$$

The Summation Sign, Σ

The procedure we used to calculate price given yield on a note or bond in its next-to-last coupon period can easily be extended to cover the calculation of price given yield on issues any number of coupon periods from maturity. The only problem is that each time current maturity is extended by one coupon period, a new term is added to the expression for P; thus, on a bond with a long current maturity, the expression for P becomes unwieldy. Fortunately, it need not because a shorthand device can be used to represent the discounted value of *all* future coupon payments as a single term. This device is the mathematical operator, Σ, which we introduced in Chapter 3.

Let us now apply Σ to the problem at hand. First, we restate the equation derived above for price given yield on a note in its next-to-last coupon period so that the present value of each coupon payment is a separate term. Doing so gives us

$$P=\left[\frac{C}{\left(1+y_w\right)^{t_{sn}}}\right]+\left[\frac{C}{\left(1+y_w\right)^{1+t_{sn}}}\right]+\left[\frac{R}{\left(1+y_w\right)^{1+t_{sn}}}\right]-AI$$

Once the bond equation is written in this form, it's obvious that a pattern exists in the power to which $[1+y_w]$ is raised in the discounting of coupon periods. This pattern permits us to rewrite the equation using Σ as follows:

$$P=\sum_{n=1}^{2}\frac{C}{\left(1+y_w\right)^{n-1+t_{sn}}}+\frac{R}{\left(1+y_w\right)^{1+t_{sn}}}-AI$$

The Standard Bond Equation for Price Given Yield to Maturity

The manipulations we have just gone through may seem pointless, since the expression for P that we've derived looks neither shorter nor simpler than the one we started with, and in fact, it is not. The payoff from introducing Σ lies elsewhere. Specifically, using Σ permits us to write, using three terms only, the bond equation for the price, given yield, of any note or bond that is one or more coupons from maturity. Let

N = number of remaining coupon payments

Generalizing from our formula for P when $N = 2$, that is, when the security being priced is in its next-to-last coupon period, we note that, on a security with a longer current maturity, the maturity value will be discounted by a factor of

$$\left(1+y_w\right)^{N-1+t_{sn}}$$

We also note that each future coupon payment will be discounted by a factor of $(1 + y_w)^n$.

Once the equation is written in this form, it's obvious that a pattern exists in the power to which $(1 + y_w)$ is raised in the discounting of coupon periods. This pattern permits us to rewrite the equation using Σ as follows:

$$P=\sum_{n=1}^{2}\frac{C}{\left(1+y_w\right)^{n-1+t_{sn}}}+\frac{R}{\left(1+y_w\right)^{1+t_{sn}}}-AI$$

If we generalize the above result for a bond which has N remaining coupon payments, then

$$P = \left[\sum_{n=1}^{N} \frac{C}{\left(1+y_w\right)^{n-1+t_{sn}}} + \frac{R}{\left(1+y_w\right)^{N-1+t_{sn}}} \right] - AI$$

To account for the possibility of an odd-first-coupon period and its irregular coupon payment, C_n, then we have

$$P = \left[\sum_{n=1}^{N-1} \frac{C}{\left(1+y_w\right)^{n+t_{sn}}} + \frac{R}{\left(1+y_w\right)^{N-1+t_{sn}}} + \frac{C_n}{\left(1+y_w\right)^{t_{sn}}} \right] - AI$$

RESTATING THE CALCULATION OF *P* GIVEN *y* USING AN ANNUITY EQUATION

It's possible to derive a *closed-form* solution for the price of a bond given its yield to maturity. This closed-form solution employs a particular result for sums that is referred to as an annuity equation. To simplify the exposition in this section, we have numbered the equations that represent key steps in our derivation.

Consider the value of X_N, where

$$X_N = \sum_{n=1}^{N} v^n \tag{1}$$

and

$$v = \frac{1}{1+y_w} \tag{2}$$

We will show that

$$X_N = \frac{1-v^N}{y_w} \tag{3}$$

Let X_n be the nth partial sum of X_N. Then,

$$X_n = v + v^2 + \cdots + v^n \tag{4}$$

and

$$X_{n+1} = v + v^2 + \cdots + v^n + v^{n+1} \tag{5}$$

Hence,

$$X_{n+1} = X_n + V^{n+1} \tag{6}$$

If we now multiply (4) by v, we obtain the expression,

$$vX_n = v^2 + v^3 + \cdots + v^{n+1}$$

which, substituting from (5), we can rewrite as follows:

$$vX_n = X_{n+1} - v$$

or

$$X_{n+1} = vX_n + v \tag{7}$$

We can now solve for X_n by equating (6) and (7)

$$X_n + v^{n+1} = vX_n + v \tag{8}$$

Rearranging terms, we have

$$X_n = \frac{v(v^n - 1)}{v - 1}$$

or

$$\begin{aligned}\sum_{n=1}^{N} v^n &= \frac{v(v^N - 1)}{v - 1} \\ &= \frac{1 - v^N}{y_w}\end{aligned} \tag{9}$$

Finally, by using equation (9), we can restate the expression derived from the bond equation for P given y as follows:

$$P = v^{t_{sn}}\left[C\frac{v(v^{N-1} - 1)}{v - 1} + Rv^{N-1} + C_n\right] - AI$$

or, alternatively

$$P = v^{t_{sn}}\left[C\frac{(1 - v^{N-1})}{y_w} + Rv^{N-1} + C_n\right] - AI$$

Example. Consider the 6¼% of 8/31/00, a 5-year T-note issued on 8/31/95. For settlement on 9/25/95, the *closing ask yield* was 6.0409%

and the *asked price* was 100-28.[2] The next coupon payment date for this note is 2/29/96. Hence t_{sn} equals,

$$\begin{aligned} t_{sn} &= \frac{T_{sn}}{A_{ln}} \\ &= \frac{2/29/96 - 9/25/95}{2/29/96 - 8/31/95} \\ &= \frac{157}{182} \\ &= 0.86263736 \end{aligned}$$

and the accrued interest for the 25-day period from 8/31/95 to 9/25/95, given a *face value* of 100 and *coupon frequency* of 2 is

$$\begin{aligned} AI &= \frac{cFT_{ls}}{wA_{ln}} \\ &= \frac{.0625 \times 100 \times 25}{2 \times 182} \\ &= 0.42925824 \end{aligned}$$

Given and the yield to maturity equals 6.0409% we have

$$\begin{aligned} v &= \frac{1}{(1+y_w)} \\ &= \frac{1}{(1+006049/2)} \\ &= 0.97068106 \end{aligned}$$

Therefore,

$$\begin{aligned} v^{t_{sn}} &= (0.970681064)^{0.86263736} \\ &= 0.97465688 \end{aligned}$$

and, given the number of remaining coupon payments is 10, we have

$$\begin{aligned} v^{N-1} &= (0.970681064)^{9} \\ &= 0.76504856 \end{aligned}$$

[2] As reported in the September 25, 1995 issue of *Barron's*.

Finally, given a *redemption value* of 100, we have the result

$$P = v^{t_{sn}}\left[C\frac{\left(1-v^{N-1}\right)}{y_w} + Rv^{N-1} + C_n\right] - AI$$

$$= 0.97465688 \times$$

$$\left[3.125\frac{(1-0.76504856)}{.060409/2} + 100 \times 0.76504856 + 3.125\right.$$

$$- 0.42925824$$

$$= 100.874884$$

The *quoted* price in *Barron's* was 100-28 or 100.87500 in decimal terms. The slight difference in the computed result is due to the rounding of the intermediate results and the yield to maturity.

NEWTON-RAPHSON ALGORITHM FOR CALCULATING *y* GIVEN *P*

The bond equation, particularly in its annuity form, is convenient and easy to use when one wants to determine the price of a bond given its yield to maturity. However, this equation, as stated above, cannot be inverted into a closed-form solution for yield to maturity given price. To determine the yield to maturity of a bond, an iterative algorithm must be used. The Newton-Raphson method is a standard, efficient algorithm for finding the roots of a non-linear equation. Given the prevalent use of this algorithm in fixed-income calculations, the analyst should have some familiarity with the underlying methodology.

The Newton-Raphson Method

The Newton-Raphson method is used to solve an equation $f(x) = 0$. Starting with a given initial approximation for the root, x_o, a sequence x_1, x_2, . . . is computed, where the $n + 1$th element of the sequence, x_{n+1} is determined in the following manner. The function, $f(x)$, is approximated by its tangent at the point $(x_n, f(x_n))$; and x_{n+1} is taken as the abscissa of the point of intersection of the tangent with the x-axis. Thus x_{n+1} is determined by the following equation:

$$f(x_n) + (x_{n+1} - x_n)f'(x_n) = 0$$

where $f'(x_n)$ is the first derivative of the function $f(x)$ evaluated at the point.

The Newton-Raphson method is then defined by the following iteration:

$$x_{n+1} = x_n - \frac{f'(x_n)}{f(x_n)}$$

This iteration is continued until the difference between x_n and x_{n+1} is less than the maximum error the analyst is willing to accept.

The Newton-Raphson Algorithm for Determining Yield to Maturity Given Price

To determine the yield to maturity of a bond given its price, the Newton-Raphson algorithm must be applied to the bond equation. In this case, we will use the annuity form of the bond equation, which means that we will solve for the value of the annuity variable v. The yield to maturity will then be given by the expression:

$$y_{tm} = w\left(\frac{1}{v} - 1\right)$$

The equation whose root we seek, $f(v)$, its derivative, and $f'(v)$ the relationship between the annuity variable, v, and yield to maturity are to maturity are as follows:

$$f(v) = v^{t_{sn}}\left[C\frac{v(v^{N-1}-1)}{v-1} + Rv^{N-1} + C_n\right] - AI - P$$

$$f'(v) = v^{t_{sn}-1}\left[C\left(t_{sn} + \frac{1}{1-v}\right)\frac{v(v^{N-1}-1)}{v-1} + C_n t_{sn}\right.$$
$$\left. - v^{N-1}\left\{\frac{Cv(N-1)}{(1-v)} - R(N + t_{sn} - 1)\right\}\right]$$

$$v = \frac{1}{1+y_w}$$

$$y_w = \left(\frac{1}{v} - 1\right)$$

$$y_{tm} = w\left(\frac{1}{v} - 1\right)$$

Next, we define the steps of the iterative algorithm as follows.

Step 1: We define the initial value for v_0 as a function of the bond's coupon rate divided by its coupon frequency.

$$v_0 = \frac{1}{(1 + c/w)}$$

This initial value provides excellent convergence characteristics.

Step 2: We calculate the next value for v using the Newton-Raphson formula as follows:

$$v_{n+1} = v_n - \frac{f'(v_n)}{f(v_n)}$$

Step 3: If the difference in value between iterations is less than the error tolerance, here assumed to be 0.00000005, exit the iteration and go to **Step 4,** otherwise repeat **Step 2.** Given the possibility that Newton-Raphson's method may not converge, a constraint should be placed on the maximum number of iterations. **Step 3** is given as follows:

IF $\left[(x_{n+1} - x_n) < \text{max allowable error}\right]$ go to Step 4
IF $\left[n + 2 < \text{max iterations allowed}\right]$ go to Step 2
otherwise STOP
as algorithm failed to converge within allowable iterations

Step 4: The algorithm converged and determined a root for the annuity formula. In this case, the value for yield to maturity is given by the equation:

$$y_{tm} = w\left(\frac{1}{v} - 1\right)$$

TRUE YIELD TO MATURITY

The relationship between price and yield-to-maturity, as defined by the standard bond equation, assumes that all coupon periods after the current period are of equal length. Thus, the actual dates of receipt of the bond's coupon and principal payments are ignored. This assumption is incompatible with the concept of present value, which is based on the notion of the time value of money.

While the error introduced by this assumption is typically small for long-dated instruments (e.g., a 10-year note) it can be material for shorter-dated instruments (e.g., notes with less than two years to maturity). Hence, it's common for shorter-dated instruments to trade on a *true yield* basis.

To calculate true yield, we must modify the standard bond equation to account for the *exact* number of days between the settlement date and actual date of the receipt of the coupon or redemption payment. This requires that the analyst not only account for weekends but for market holidays.

The standard bond equation for price given yield is:

$$P = v^{t_{sn}} \left[C \sum_{n=1}^{N-1} v^n + R v^{N-1} + C_n \right] - AI$$

To use the bond equation to calculate true yield, we must replace the index n as the measure of time in the exponent of v with the exact time between the settlement date and the receipt of a given payment.

The equation for price given true-yield-to-maturity is:

$$P = \left[C \sum_{n=1}^{N} v^{t_n} + R v^{t_N} \right] - AI$$

where

T_n = number of days between the settlement date and the receipt of nth payment

$$t_n = \frac{wT_n}{365}$$

The above equation cannot be restated as a closed-form expression using the annuity equations because the exponents of v in the summation do *not* equal the integer index value n.

To determine the *true* yield-to-maturity given the price using the Newton-Raphson algorithm, we must take the first derivative of the above equation with respect to v. As before, we define f(v) as follows:

$$\mathrm{f}(v) = \left[C \sum_{n=1}^{N} v^{t_n} + R v^{t_N} \right] - AI - P$$

therefore,

$$f'(v) = \left[C\sum_{n=1}^{N} t_n v^{t_n - 1} + Rt_N v^{t_N - 1} \right] - P$$

NOTES AND BONDS IN THEIR LAST COUPON PERIOD

Yield-to-maturity is well defined for any instrument in its last coupon period. It is market practice in the United States and some other markets to quote securities on a money market yield basis during their last coupon period.

Money Market Yield Given Price

On U.S. Treasuries in their last coupon period, money market yield is calculated, according to the standard industry formula, as a simple-interest yield. Let

$$\begin{aligned} y_{tm} &= \text{yield to maturity} \\ y_w &= y_{tm}/w \\ T_{sm} &= \text{days from settlement to maturity} \\ P &= \text{clean price} \\ AI &= \text{accrued interest} \end{aligned}$$

Then, the industry's formula for calculating yield, y, when the clean price is given, can be written as follows:

$$y_{tm} = \left(\frac{R + C_n}{P + AI} - 1 \right) \frac{wA_{ln}}{T_{sm}}$$

Example. Consider the $4\frac{1}{4}\%$ of 11/30/95, a 2-year T-note issued on 11/30/93. For settlement on 9/25/95, the *closing ask yield* was 6.24% and the *asked price* was 99-26.[3] The next coupon (and *last*) payment date for this note is the maturity date 11/30/95. There are 66 days between

[3] As reported in the September 25, 1995 issue of *Barron's*.

settlement and maturity and 183 days in the current coupon period 5/31/95 to 11/30/95. The accrued interest for the 117-day period from 5/31/95 to 9/25/95, given a *face value* of 100 and *coupon frequency* of 2 is

$$\begin{aligned} AI &= \frac{cFT_{ls}}{wA_{\ln}} \\ &= \frac{.0425 \times 100 \times 117}{2 \times 183} \\ &= 1.35860656 \end{aligned}$$

Given a *redemption value* of 100 and using a price of 99-25 and $^{15}/_{16}$ of a 32nd, we have the result

$$\begin{aligned} y_{tm} &= \left(\frac{R + C_n}{P + AI} - 1 \right) \frac{wA_{\ln}}{T_{sm}} \\ &= \left(\frac{100 + 2.125}{99.810547 + 1.35860656} - 1 \right) \frac{2 \times 183}{66} \\ &= 0.052393 \end{aligned}$$

The *quoted* yield in *Barron's* was 5.24% using a price of 99-26. We used a price of 99 and $^{15}/_{16}$ of a 32nd. Had we used the published price of 99-26 the yield would be 5.2285% instead of 5.2393%. The relatively *large* difference in yield given a *small* difference in price is a function of the very short tenor of the security.

Price Given Money Market Yield

If, alternatively, we want a formula for the clean price given the money market yield on a short Treasury, we can obtain it simply by solving the preceding formula for *P*. Doing so gives us

$$P = \frac{R + C_n}{1 + y_{tm} \dfrac{T_{sm}}{wA_{ln}}} - AI$$

Example. Using the same security information used in the above example we can compute the price of the note given the yield of

5.2393%. We have the result

$$
\begin{aligned}
P &= \frac{R + C_n}{1 + y_{tm} \dfrac{T_{sm}}{wA_{\ln}}} - AI \\
&= \frac{100 + 2.125}{1 + 0.052393 \dfrac{66}{2 \times 183}} - 1.35860656 \\
&= 99.810555
\end{aligned}
$$

or 99-26 as quoted in *Barron's*. If we used the quoted yield of 5.24% the computed decimal price is 99.8104290. In points and thirty-seconds this decimal price converts to 99.25 and ⅞ of a 32nd, or 99-257.

PRICES AND YIELDS FOR ZERO-COUPON BONDS

Especially with the advent of Treasury STRIPS, there is today a large supply of bonds in the market that bear a zero coupon.[4]

Price Given Yield

For a zero-coupon issue, one can calculate P given y by using the bond equation derived above. To do so, one simply sets $c = 0$, which causes the expression for P given y to reduce to the following simple formula:

$$
P = \frac{R}{\left(1 + y_w\right)^{N-1+t_{sn}}}
$$

Note that the dirty price of a zero-coupon bond is trivially equal to its clean price, since no interest accrues on such a security.

Example. Consider the *principal* of the 8¼% of 5/15/20, a 30-year T-bond issued on 5/15/90.[5] For settlement on 9/25/95, the *closing ask yield* was 6.9601% and the *asked price* was 18-17.[6] The next coupon

---

[4] We talked about STRIPS in Chapter 2.

[5] Typically, the principal or corpus of a stripped bond trades at a different price than a *coupon payment* to be made on the same date.

[6] As reported in the September 25, 1995 issue of *Barron's*.

payment date for the bond from which this principal was stripped is 11/15/95. Hence, t_{sn} equals,

$$\begin{aligned} t_{sn} &= \frac{T_{sn}}{A_{ln}} \\ &= \frac{11/15/95 - 9/25/95}{11/15/95 - 5/15/95} \\ &= \frac{51}{184} \\ &= 0.27717391 \end{aligned}$$

Given that the yield to maturity is 6.9601%, the number of remaining coupon payments is 50, and a redemption value of 100, we have the result

$$\begin{aligned} P &= \frac{R}{\left(1+y_w\right)^{N-1+t_{sn}}} \\ &= \frac{100}{\left(1+\dfrac{0.069601}{2}\right)^{50-1+0.27717391}} \\ &= 18.531359 \end{aligned}$$

The *quoted* price in *Barron's* was 18-17 or 18.531250 in decimal terms. The slight difference in the computed result is due to the rounding of the intermediate results and the yield to maturity.

The Price Equation in Annuity Form

For a zero-coupon security, the price equation in annuity form reduces to the following simple expression:

$$P = Rv^{N-1+t_{sn}}$$

One can observe that the bond equation for coupon-bearing bonds reduces to the above expression when the coupon rate, c, is set equal to zero. Hence, when one programs a computer to do price-yield calculations for bonds, it is not necessary to code a separate routine for zero-coupon bonds.

Yield to Maturity Given Price

For a bond that carries a coupon, there is, as noted above, no closed-form solution for calculating y given P. However, for a zero-coupon security, such a solution does exist.

Specifically, for a zero-coupon security,

$$\frac{R}{(1+y_w)^{N-1+t_{sn}}} = P$$

Rewriting this expression, we get

$$(1+y_w)^{N-1+t_{sn}} = \frac{R}{P}$$

Next, we take the $N - 1 + t_{sn}$ root of both sides of the equation to get

$$1+y_w = \left(\frac{R}{P}\right)^{1/(N-1+t_{sn})}$$

Hence, the solution for the periodic yield to maturity, y_w, of a zero-coupon bond given its price, P, is as follows:

$$y_w = \left(\frac{R}{P}\right)^{1/(N-1+t_{sn})} - 1$$

Example. Using the same security information used in the above example we can compute the periodic yield to maturity of the zero-coupon bond given the asked price of 18-17. We have the result

$$\begin{aligned} y_w &= \left(\frac{R}{P}\right)^{1/(N-1+t_{sn})} - 1 \\ &= \left(\frac{100}{18.531250}\right)^{1/(50-1+0.27717391)} - 1 \\ &= 0.034800623 \end{aligned}$$

and the yield to maturity is

$$\begin{aligned} y_{tm} &= wy_w \\ &= 2 \times 0.034800623 \\ &= 0.069601247 \end{aligned}$$

or, 6.9601%.

The *quoted* yield in *Barron's* was 6.96%. The slight difference in the computed result is due to rounding the result.

APPLICATION TO OTHER U.S. BONDS

The bond equation in this chapter can be applied, not only to U.S. Treasury and agency notes and bonds, but to *straight* corporate and muni bonds as well as to *straight bonds* issued outside the United States. To do the latter, one must simply make an appropriate adjustment for the interest payment convention used.

When we refer to *straight bonds,* we mean bonds that do not incorporate special features such as a call or a put or a variable coupon. Bonds of the latter sort must be priced to reflect any special features incorporated in them.

THE NEXT CHAPTER

In the next chapter, we introduce an important concept, *carry.* For bond traders and investors who either finance fixed-income securities or reverse them in order to cover shorts, the ability to calculate carry on a proposed trade is crucial to determining how profitable that trade is likely to be.

PART 4

BONDS: ADVANCED TOPICS

CHAPTER 12

CARRY CALCULATIONS: LONG AND SHORT POSITIONS

In earlier chapters, we discussed the calculation of carry on a money market instrument when a trader or investor (1) buys the instrument and does a repo to finance it or (2) shorts the instrument and does a reverse to cover his short. In this chapter, we focus on *carry on bonds.*

CARRY CALCULATIONS FOR SECURITY POSITIONS

As we've noted, broker/dealers have sufficient capital to support their activities as market makers and arbitrageurs, but they lack the billions of dollars in cash required to *fund* their daily positions. Thus, every broker/dealer manages a *leveraged* portfolio of securities.

In general, broker/dealers find that the least expensive way to *fund* their *long positions* is to *finance* these positions by borrowing money in the *repo market.* Likewise, broker/dealers find that the least expensive way to *cover* their *short positions* is to *reverse* in the specific securities they need to cover their shorts.[1]

A *fully funded* investor—a pension fund, a mutual fund, a corporate liquidity portfolio, whatever—may view the market-determined repo rate as the *opportunity cost of capital* for funds it invests in securities. To this comment, we should add that it is not only broker/dealers who do repos to borrow money and reverses to borrow securities. One can easily find traders who are not strictly broker/dealers as well as portfolio managers, whose principal job is to invest cash, who do leveraged transactions using repo and who also short securities, for example, when doing arbitrages that require them to go long one issue and short another. We've

[1]As we've noted, one man's repo is always another man's reverse, since a repo and a reverse are flip sides of the same transaction. Generally, people speak of a dealer as doing a *repo* when he is seeking financing, and as doing a *reverse* when he is seeking securities.

defined carry on a securities position as *the securities' interest income minus the interest expense* incurred by the entity holding the securities position; this definition is appropriate for both long and short positions.

Our definition of carry is the standard definition of *profit,* except that it's stated in terms of interest flows instead of all flows of income and of current expenses. As such, the term *cost of carry,* often used on the Street, is a misnomer in that carry on a securities position can be either positive or negative—a property that is usually associated with a profit measure, not a cost measure.

In earlier chapters, we defined all of the necessary relationships for calculating carry: the calculation of accrued interest on a security, the calculation of interest due on a repo or a reverse, and the day-count conventions incorporated is such calculations.

Financing a Long Position in Bonds

The carry derived from financing a long position in a bond is a function of the price at which the bond is purchased, the coupon the bond carries, the interest accrued on the bond at the time of purchase, the repo rate paid on the funds borrowed, and the length of the period over which the bond is held.

We can easily express the definition of carry,

$$\text{carry} = \text{interest income} - \text{interest expense}$$

in symbols as follows. Let

r_{rp} = the repo rate

C = coupon payment: $C = (c/w)F$

P = clean price of a bond

AI = accrued interest on a bond

A_{ln} = number of days from the last coupon date to the next

T_{hp} = number of days in the holding period

Then,

$$\text{interest income} = C\frac{T_{hp}}{A_{ln}}$$

and

$$\text{interest expense} = (P + AI)r_{rp}\frac{T_{hp}}{360}$$

Substituting our expressions for interest income and interest expense into our definition of carry, we get,

$$\text{carry} = C\frac{T_{hp}}{A_{ln}} - (P+AI)r_{rp}\frac{T_{hp}}{360}$$

In the above equation, we assume that the bond being financed *drops no coupons* during the holding period, T_{hp}, and that interest on the repo is calculated on the basis of a 360-day year. We can easily account for dropped coupons; to do so, we would add a term to the interest-income calculation to account for the reinvestment of the coupon payment received at the then prevailing reinvestment rate, r_{re}.

In our equation for carry, we also assume that interest on a repo or a reverse is calculated on the basis of a 360-day year. That's the appropriate assumption in the United States where most money market rates are calculated using the ACT/360 day-count convention. Elsewhere in the world, money market rates are more typically calculated using the ACT/365 day-count convention. To calculate carry, when the repo interest is calculated using the ACT/365 day-count convention, we would simply substitute 365 for 360 in our equation for carry.

In calculating carry, it's standard market practice to ignore any *haircuts* or *margins* taken by the lender of money. However, one can easily take margin into account by replacing the repo rate, r_{rp}, with a *weighted average* of the repo rate and the funding rate for the *capital* used to meet the margin requirement. The weights are, respectively, the percentage of the total funding requirement financed with repo and the percentage of the total funding requirement funded at the funding rate.

Covering a Short Position by Reversing in the Issue Shorted

The carry derived from covering a short position in a bond with a reverse depends on the coupon carried by the bond, the reverse rate for that bond, the days the short position is maintained (which we'll call the holding period), the clean price of the bond, and accrued interest on the bond at the time of purchase. Let

$$r_{rv} = \text{the reverse rate}$$

Then, by substituting the reverse rate, r_{rv}, for the repo rate, r_{rp}, in our equation for carry on a long position in bonds and reversing the signs of the terms on the left,[2] we can derive the following expression for carry on a short position in bonds:

$$\text{carry} = (P + AI)r_{rv}\frac{T_{hp}}{360} - C\frac{T_{hp}}{A_{ln}}$$

In the above equation, we assume that the bond shorted does not *drop a coupon* during the holding period. We also assume that interest on the reverse is calculated on an ACT/360 basis.

To account for a dropped coupon, we'd have to add a term to the interest-expense calculation to account for the funding of the coupon payment at the repo rate, r_{rp}. The assumption that interest on the reverse accrues according to the ACT/360 convention is appropriate for the United States. In other areas of the world where the ACT/365 day-count convention is used, to calculate interest on a reverse, we would simply substitute 365 for 360 in the equation for interest expense.

While it's not standard market practice to do so, one can account for any requested haircut or *margin* by replacing the reverse rate, r_{rv}, with a *weighted average* of the reverse rate and an appropriate investment rate for the excess funds generated by the margin requirement. The weights are, respectively, the percentage of the total funds generated by the short-sale invested in the short-covering reverse repo and the percentage of the total funds generated by the short-sale invested at the investment rate.

USING CARRY TO DETERMINE FORWARD PRICES AND BREAK-EVEN FINANCE RATES

Most bonds sold in the United States and elsewhere are technically sold for forward settlement because the settlement date for a trade normally occurs after the trade date. For example, in the United States, a bond that's sold for *regular settlement* will settle on the business day following the trade date, while a bond sold for *corporate settlement* will settle three business days following the trade date. The number of days required to settle a bond trade varies from country to country and is a fac-

[2] For a short position coupon income is an *expense,* since the short-seller has sold a bond which he does not own and he, not the issuer, is responsible for all interest payments on the bond. Likewise, while repo is a method for funding the purchase of a bond, reverse repo is a method for covering a short position in the bond. To do so the short-seller *invests* in a reverse repo. The collateral for the reverse repo will be the shorted bond.

tor a dealer who trades sovereign bonds issued by different countries must track carefully to avoid inadvertent *fails.*

When money and bond market people speak of the forward price for a bond, they are talking about the price of that bond when the agreed settlement date is some number of days beyond the date that would be the normal settlement day. Here's a simple example of a routine situation in which a forward trade would be done. A U.S. insurance company sells a *guaranteed investment contract* (a *GIC*). The sale of the GIC is consummated today, but the buyer won't pay for the GIC until a date two weeks hence. Meanwhile, by selling a GIC, the insurance company has locked itself into paying, starting two weeks hence, a specified rate of interest on X million dollars for some specified period.

Presumably, the insurance company chooses the rate of interest it will guarantee to pay on the basis of the general level of rates prevailing today in the market. Thus, the forward settlement (by two weeks) of the GIC exposes the insurance company to *interest rate risk,* namely that the general level of interest rates might move unfavorably to it (specifically *down*) during the two weeks it must wait to receive the X million it is to invest. To hedge this risk, a routine trade for an insurance company in this position would be to lock in, on X million, today's general level of interest rates by buying today for settlement two weeks hence (i.e., by buying for *forward settlement*) X million of Treasury notes or bonds of a maturity appropriate given the life of the GIC.

Calculating a Forward Price

The *forward price* of a bond is the *carry-adjusted* price of that bond as of a specified *forward settlement* date. To determine this forward price, which is today's price adjusted for the carry that will be earned or lost over the specified holding period, we must analyze the so-called *cash-and-carry trade;* this trade calls for a dealer (1) to buy the bond today, (2) to finance it with repo over a predetermined holding period, and (3) to sell it *today* for *forward settlement* on the end date of the predetermined holding period, that is, on the agreed upon *forward settlement date.*

The forward price of a bond is a function of the bond's current price, the finance or repo rate for the bond, and the date on which the *forward trade* settles. Let

$$P_{fwd} = \text{the forward price of the security}$$

Then,

$$P_{fwd} = P + \text{carry on a long position}$$

Substituting into this equation, the expression we obtained above for carry gives us:

$$P_{fwd} = P + C\frac{T_{hp}}{A_{ln}} - (P + AI)r_{rp}\frac{T_{hp}}{360}$$

Implied Repo Rates

Often, an investor must match the settlement date of the purchase of securities with the settlement date of a sale of securities or with the date of receipt of investable funds (the insurance company example given above). In this case, the investor can negotiate a forward purchase of the desired security, where the forward settlement date matches the date when the investor will receive funds.

The investor is quoted a forward offer price for the security and must determine if this price is reasonable given the current offer price, that is, the offer price for regular settlement. To determine the reasonableness of the quoted forward price, the investor calculates the repo rate that is *implied* by the difference between the current price and the forward price.

The rate implied by this difference is referred to as the *implied repo rate.* The forward price is considered to be *reasonable* if the implied repo rate equals or is close to the *market* repo rate quoted for financing the security in question over the term in question.

To determine the implied repo rate, we algebraically solve for r_{rp} in the equation for the forward price. The resulting value for the repo rate is referred to as the *break-even implied repo rate.* Let

$$r^*_{rp} = \text{the } \textit{break-even implied repo rate}$$

Then, solving for r^*_{rp}, we get the following expression,

$$r^*_{rp} = \left(P + C\frac{T_h}{A_{ln}} - P_{fwd}\right)\frac{360}{T_h(P + AI)}$$

In the United States, as a matter of practice, an institutional investor wanting to buy, from a national dealer, bonds for forward settlement really has *two options.* He can buy the bonds for regular settlement and then ask the dealer's repo desk to finance his purchase until the date at which he anticipates receiving moneys to fund his purchase. Or he can ask the dealer to do a trade for forward settlement. A large investor dealing with a national dealer will find that, due to interdealer competition, he'll get about the same price whichever way he does the trade. One reason such an investor might choose to do a forward buy over a financed buy is that his investment parameters preclude him from borrowing.

THE NEXT CHAPTER

An investor who buys a bond is subject to *uncertainty* with respect to what the level of interest rates and the shape the yield curve will be in *future* periods. Uncertainly implies *risk* to the investor—risk that he wants to measure and, if possible, to control. Among investors, one popular measure of risk is duration. In the next chapter, we introduce the concept of duration, show how to calculate it, and then discuss its interpretation.

CHAPTER 13

DURATION

According to modern portfolio theory, an investor will assume risk only if he's compensated for doing so. In bondland, risk is attached even to credit-risk-free Treasuries, and that risk varies from issue to issue. Thus, for investors in bonds, a key problem is how to measure the riskiness of a given fixed-income security.

DEFINING RISK

The risk we'll talk about here and in Chapters 13 and 14 is risk that arises because uncertainty prevails with respect to what levels of interest rates and what shapes of the yield curve will prevail in future periods—where the last period of concern may be 30, even 40 years down the pike. On corporate and certain other bonds, credit risk exists and must be analyzed by the investor; however, the analysis of credit risk is a separate discipline from the study of fixed-income calculations; and for that reason, in our discussion of risk, we ignore credit risk.

In Chapter 10, we presented several measures of yield on a bond. Each such measure incorporates its own virtues and its own flaws. For want of a perfect measure of yield, the market, at least in the United States, has adopted yield to maturity, as determined by the bond equation, as the *standard* measure of yield on a bond more than one coupon from maturity.

An investor who focuses on yield to maturity in choosing what bonds to buy creates a portfolio that embodies two sorts of risk. First, there's *reinvestment risk:* the risk that the investor will have to reinvest the future coupon payments he receives at a yield less than the yield to maturity at which he bought his bond. Second, there's the *curve risk,* the risk that the yield curve will change over the investor's holding period.

Curve risk arises when the investor's holding period differs from the bond's remaining term to maturity. Because of both reinvestment and curve risk, the yield to maturity earned by the investor may differ from the yield that he anticipated earning at the time he bought his bond.

To analyze these risks, it's necessary to determine the sensitivity of a bond's price to a *small* change in the yield to maturity at which a bond trades. Two measures are typically used; they are *duration* and *convexity.* In this chapter, we focus on duration.

One common measure of the *price* sensitivity (risk) of a bond to a *small* change in its yield to maturity is *duration.* Over time, the way duration is defined and the way it's interpreted have evolved. In the discussion below, we cover several measures of duration and several interpretations of what these differing measures of duration mean.[1]

Specifically, in this chapter, we will define three common measures of duration and explore the use of each as a measure of the sensitivity of a bond's price to small changes in its yield to maturity. We'll also cover two related sensitivity measures: the *price value of a basis point* (*i.e., the value of an 01*) and the *yield value of 1/32.*

The Bond Equation Revisited

According to the bond equation, the current value of a bond equals the sum of the present values of all future cash flows. The constant yield at which all such cash flows are discounted is to the bond's *assumed* yield to maturity. Thus, an implicit assumption in the bond equation is that the *term structure of interest rates* is *flat.*[2] While this assumption is unrealistic, the degree of the error introduced by this assumption depends on the shape of the yield curve.

From our discussion of present value in Chapter 4, it's clear that the yield used to discount each future cash should equal the zero-coupon yield. This approach to valuing bonds requires the derivation of a term structure of interest rates. As the *true* term structure cannot be observed,

---

[1] The reader to whom duration is a new concept may find it helpful to read Chapter 5 in Stigum's *The Money Market,* Ed III, Dow Jones-Irwin, 1990.

[2] Finance theory makes a distinction between the *yield curve* and the *term structure of discount or zero-coupon yields.* The yield curve is the relationship between yield to maturity and term to maturity for coupon-bearing bonds, whereas the term structure is the relationship between the term yield of zero-coupon bonds and their term to maturity.

we must analytically derive the term structure. In this case, the bond's value will depend on the method's accuracy. Unfortunately, there is no one agreed-upon, best method for deriving the term structure of interest rates. Therefore, most bond-market participants continue to use the standard bond equation to value bonds; and for this reason, it makes sense for us also to use this equation as a basis for our discussion of risk measures for bonds.[3]

MACAULAY DURATION

Duration was originally defined by Macaulay as the *time-weighted average* of the discounted future cash flows. Specifically, Macaulay suggested that duration be calculated as a weighted average of the discounted cash flows where the weight for each cash flow equals the actual time that an investor would have to wait to receive that cash flow.

If we let

$$D_{mac} = \text{Macaulay duration}$$

then, the equation for Macaulay duration is as follows:

$$D_{mac} = \frac{\sum_{n=1}^{N-1} \frac{(n+t_{sn})C}{(1+y_w)^{(n+t_{sn})}} + \frac{(N-1+t_{sn})R}{(1+y_w)^{(N-1+t_{sn})}} + \frac{t_{sn}C_n}{(1+y_w)^{t_{sn}}}}{\sum_{n=1}^{N-1} \frac{C}{(1+y_w)^{(n+t_{sn})}} + \frac{R}{(1+y_w)^{(N-1+t_{sn})}} + \frac{C_n}{(1+y_w)^{t_{sn}}}}$$

Next, we recall that, according to the bond equation, the dirty price of a bond is given by the expression:

$$B = \left[\sum_{n=1}^{N-1} \frac{C}{(1+y_w)^{(n+t_{sn})}} + \frac{R}{(1+y_w)^{(N-1+t_{sn})}} + \frac{C_n}{(1+y_w)^{t_{sn}}} \right]$$

Thus, the divisor in the equation for Macaulay duration is the expression for the *dirty price* of the bond. Hence,

---

[3] Some analysts have extended the definition of duration to measure the sensitivity of a portfolio of bonds to a change in the shape of the yield curve. Such an extension is typically referred to as a *key-rate duration.*

$$D_{mac} = \frac{1}{wB}\left[\sum_{n=1}^{N-1}\frac{(n+t_{sn})C}{(1+y_w)^{(n+t_{sn})}} + \frac{(N-1+t_{sn})R}{(1+y_w)^{(N-1+t_{sn})}} + \frac{t_{sn}C_n}{(1+y_w)^{t_{sn}}}\right]$$

Typically, people divide the right side of the above equation w, the number of coupon payments per year. When this is done, the calculated value for duration is then measured in *units of years* instead of in *units of coupon payment frequency*—typically half-year units.

Later in this chapter, will use the annuity equations to derive a closed-form representation for the above equation for Macaulay duration.

Duration as a Price Elasticity

A standard interpretation of duration is that duration is the *price elasticity* of a bond, where a bond's price elasticity is defined as the ratio of a small *percentage* change in the bond's dirty price divided by a small *percentage* change in the bond's *yield to maturity*. That is,

$$D_{mac} = -\frac{\dfrac{dB}{B}}{\dfrac{dy_{tm}}{1+y_w}}$$

Because of the interpretation of duration as the average time, in years, to receipt by the bondholder of all future cash flows from his bond, duration must be a positive number. Further, since a bond's price is inversely related to its yield to maturity, the derivative in the above equation will always be negative. Hence, we place a negative sign before the derivative to ensure that duration will be a positive number.

Rearranging the terms on the right-hand side of the above equation, we have:

$$D_{mac} = -\frac{(1+y_w)}{B}\frac{dB}{dy_{tm}}$$

Although we will not do so, it can be shown that the two definitions, presented above, of Macaulay duration are equivalent.

When duration is written in the form

$$D_{mac} = -\frac{(1+y_w)}{B}\frac{dB}{dy_{tm}}$$

we can interpret it as a scaled derivative of price with respect to yield to maturity. Hence, duration is a function of the price sensitivity of the bond given a *specific* value for its yield to maturity. In other words, duration is a function of the *slope* of the *tangent* to the bond equation at a specific value of the bond's yield to maturity.[4]

Duration as an Expected Value

Our second equation for Macaulay duration has an interesting *probabilistic* interpretation. To show this, we recall that the *dirty* price of a bond is given by

$$B = \left[\sum_{n=1}^{N-1} \frac{C}{(1+y_w)^{(n+t_{sn})}} + \frac{R}{(1+y_w)^{(N-1+t_{sn})}} + \frac{C_n}{(1+y_w)^{t_{sn}}} \right]$$

Examining the expression, we observe that each term inside the square brackets is the contribution that a given cash flow makes to the total dirty price of the bond. If we divide both sides of the equation for dirty price by *B,* we have

$$1 = \frac{1}{B} \left[\sum_{n=1}^{N-1} \frac{C}{(1+y_w)^{(n+t_{sn})}} + \frac{R}{(1+y_w)^{(N-1+t_{sn})}} + \frac{C_n}{(1+y_w)^{t_{sn}}} \right]$$

In a probabilistic sense, we can interpret the right-hand side of the above equation as a probability density function.[5] Under this interpretation, each discounted cash flow from the bond divided by the bond's dirty price is viewed as a probability.

Taking this probabilistic interpretation of the bond equation, we can interpret Macaulay duration as the *expected value of the time a bond investor must wait to receive all future cash flows.* This interpretation follows from the definition of expected value in probability theory, where

---

[4] In plotting the bond equation, we measure the bond's price along the vertical axis, the bond's yield to maturity along the horizontal axis.

[5] A probability density function gives the probability of occurrence for each possible outcome. Hence, two properties of a density function are the following: (1) the probability of a given outcome must be non-negative and less than or equal to one, (2) the sum of the probabilities for all possible outcomes must equal one.

the random variable in this case is the *time to receipt of each future cash flow.*[6]

Duration as the Term to Maturity of a Zero-Coupon Bond

We can extend our probabilistic interpretation of duration, by noting that the time to receipt of a given cash flow is also the duration of a corresponding zero-coupon bond that matures on the date on which that cash flow occurs. This follows from the fact that there are no intervening cash-flows for a zero-coupon bond. The *expected time to receipt of the single future cash flow* of a zero-coupon bond is the just the bond's term to maturity. That is, in the case of a zero-coupon bond the above equation for duration reduces to the following simple result-the duration of zero-coupon bond equals its remaining term to maturity.

Thus, given that a coupon-bearing bond can be conceived of as a portfolio of zero-coupon bonds whose maturities equal the various dates on which cash flows from the coupon-bearing bond, we can interpret a coupon-bearing bond's duration as the duration of a portfolio of zero-coupon bonds.[7] As we'll show later, this means that one can interpret the *riskiness* of a coupon-bearing bond to be the same as that of a zero-coupon bond having a duration or term to maturity equal to the duration of the coupon-bearing bond.[8]

Deriving a Closed-Form Solution for Macaulay Duration

Analysts typically use the price-elasticity interpretation of Macaulay duration. Analysts prefer the this interpretation because it calls for a calculation that uses derivatives rather than a potentially long calculation that

---

[6] The expected value of a random variable is the sum across all possible outcomes of that variable where each such outcome is weighted by its probability of occurrence.

[7] As we'll show later, duration is *additive,* that is, the duration of a portfolio of bonds equals the weighted sum of the durations of the bonds that comprise the portfolio.

[8] However, we must remember that duration is but one measure of a bond's riskiness. Hence, while the price change of a coupon bond given a *small* change in its yield to maturity is approximately the same as that of a zero-coupon bond with equal duration, the two bonds will nevertheless exhibit different risks for a large change in yield, and for changes in the shape of the yield curve.

uses the summation operator. While taking the derivative of the bond equation is straightforward, implementing this solution on a calculator or personal computer is not.

Fortunately, there's a simple alternative route for calculating duration. Specifically, one can obtain a *closed-form* solution for Macaulay duration by using an annuity equation.

Consider the value of Y_N, where

$$Y_N = \sum_{n=1}^{N} nv^n \tag{1}$$

and

$$v = \frac{1}{1+y_w} \tag{2}$$

We will show that

$$Y_N = \frac{1+y_w}{y_w}\left[\sum_{n=1}^{N} v^n - Nv^{N+1}\right] \tag{3}$$

Let Y_n be the nth partial sum of Y_N. Then,

$$Y_n = v + 2v^2 + \cdots + nv^n \tag{4}$$

Multiplying (4) by v, we get

$$vY_n = v^2 + 2v^3 + \cdots + nv^{n+1} \tag{5}$$

Next, subtracting (5) from (4), we

$$Y_n - vY_n = v + v^2 + \cdots + v^n - nv^{n+1} \tag{6}$$

But the sum of the first n terms on the right hand side of (6) is X_n. So by rearranging terms, we have

$$Y_n = \frac{X_n - nv^{n+1}}{1-v}$$

or

$$Y_N = \frac{1+y_w}{y_w}\left[\sum_{n=1}^{N} v^n - Nv^{N+1}\right] \tag{7}$$

Hence,

$$\sum_{n=1}^{N} nv^n = \frac{1+y_w}{y_w}\left[\sum_{n=1}^{N} v^n - Nv^{N+1}\right]$$

A Closed-Form Equation for Macaulay Duration

The first step in writing a closed-form solution for duration is to substitute the variable v into the equation for duration. Doing so gives us:

$$D_{mac} = \frac{v^{t_{sn}}}{wB}\left[C\sum_{n=1}^{N-1}(n+t_{sn})v^n + \left(N-1+t_{sn}\right)Rv^{(N-1)} + t_{sn}C_n\right]$$

Expanding the above equation we have

$$D_{mac} = \frac{v^{t_{sn}}}{wB}\left[C\sum_{n=1}^{N-1} nv^n + t_{sn}C\sum_{n=1}^{N-1} v^n + \left(N-1+t_{sn}\right)Rv^{(N-1)} + t_{sn}C_n\right]$$

Next, using the annuity equation we presented in Chapter 11 in addition to the annuity equation we derived in the same chapter for the bond equation, we can write a closed-form solution for duration as follows:

$$D_{mac} = \frac{v^{t_{sn}}}{wB}\left[C\left[\frac{1+y_w}{y_w}\left\{\left(\frac{1-v^{N-1}}{y_w}\right) - (N-1)v^N\right\}\right]\right]$$

$$= + \frac{v^{t_{sn}}}{wB}\left[t_{sn}C\left(\frac{1-v^{N-1}}{y_w}\right) + \left(N-1+t_{sn}\right)Rv^{(N-1)} + t_{sn}C_n\right]$$

Example. We use the same information for the 6¼% of 8/31/00 given in Chapter 11. Given the closing yield of 6.0409% for settlement on 9/25/95 the above equation gives a Macaulay duration of 4.305 years.

MODIFIED DURATION

The overwhelming popularity of duration as a measure of risk derives from its use in estimating the change in a bond's value due to a small change in its yield to maturity.

Given the interpretation of duration as the bond's price elasticity, we have

$$D_{mac} = -\frac{(1+y_w)}{B}\frac{dB}{dy_{tm}}$$

We are not interested in the impact on a bond's price of an *infinitesimal* change in its yield, but rather in a change in its yield of one or more basis points. In this case, we have

$$D_{mac} \approx -\frac{(1+y_w)}{B}\frac{\Delta B}{\Delta y_{tm}}$$

Rearranging terms, we can now obtain an expression for the change in a bond's price given a small change in the bond's yield to maturity.

$$\Delta B \approx -\frac{D_{mac}}{(1+y_w)} B\Delta y_{tm}$$

This result is necessarily an approximation, since the value of duration is correct only for a specific value of yield to maturity. As we'll see in the next chapter, a bond's convexity measures the rate at which a bond's duration changes as its yield to maturity changes. Nevertheless, the above result is a useful approximation, and it's the principal reason why duration is such a widely used statistic.

Modified duration, D_m, is defined as Macaulay duration divided by the term $(1 + y_w)$, that is,

$$D_m = \frac{D_{mac}}{(1+y_w)}$$

$$= -\frac{1}{B}\frac{dB}{dy_{tm}}$$

Example. We use the same information for the given in Chapter 11. Given the closing yield of 6.0409% for settlement on 9/25/95 and using the computed Macaulay duration of 4.305 years, the above equation gives a modified duration of 4.179 years.

Using modified duration, our expression for the *approximate* change in a bond's price given a small change in its yield to maturity becomes

$$\Delta B \approx -D_m B\Delta y_{tm}$$

Example. Given a modified duration of 4.179 years and a dirty price of 101.304143, if the yield increases by one basis point then the price of the $6\frac{1}{4}$% of 8/31/00 would be *expected* to decrease by 0.042335 points or 1.35472 thirty-seconds. In dollar terms the expected decrease is $423.35 per million dollars of par.

A GENERAL DEFINITION OF DURATION

Duration has proven to be a useful measure for comparing the relative price sensitivities of different bonds to small changes in their yields to maturity. However, the above definition of modified duration has limited generality because it's based on a specific bond equation.

Given that the principal use of duration is as a measure of the change in the value (price) of a bond given a small change in its yield, we could consider the above approximation for the change in a bond's price, given a small change in its yield to maturity, to be the definition of duration. If we do so, we can then define duration as the percentage change in price divided by the change in yield to maturity, that is,

$$D = -\frac{\Delta B}{B \Delta y_{tm}}$$

The above definition of duration is now standard.

Example. We use the same information for the given in Chapter 11. Given the closing yield of 6.0409% for settlement on 9/25/95 and using the above equation gives a *general* duration of 4.179 years. We note, that in this measure of duration is identical to modified duration. As discussed below this is general result.

In the previous section, we gave the following expression for the approximate change in a bond's price given a small change in its yield to maturity:

$$\Delta B \approx -D_m B \Delta y_{tm}$$

Rearranging terms, we get

$$D_m \approx -\frac{\Delta B}{B \Delta y_{tm}}$$

or

$$D_m \approx D$$

This expression tells us that modified duration is approximately equal to effective duration. However, since modified duration is a function of Macaulay duration, the above result holds only for non-callable, coupon-bearing bonds.

The definition of duration as the percentage change in price divided by the change in yield is a superior to other definitions, since it is general and can be applied to any financial instrument. Henceforth, when we refer to *duration,* we shall, unless we specify otherwise, mean the above definition rather than Macaulay duration.

DURATION AND THE VALUE OF A BASIS POINT

The concept of the *value of a basis point,* V_{01}, was introduced in Chapter 6. In the case of bonds, the value of a basis point is the simplest and most direct measure of the risk to principal given a small change in a bond's yield to maturity. That is,

$$V_{01} = -\frac{\Delta B}{\Delta y_{tm}}$$

Given the definition of V_{01} it is obvious that duration is simply the value of a basis point divided by price.

Since the relationship between price and yield, as defined in the bond equation, is nonlinear, the change in a bond's price resulting from a 1bp change in its yield will result in different values depending on whether the bond's yield rises or falls. Starting from the bond equation,

$$B = \left[\sum_{n=1}^{N-1} \frac{C}{\left(1+y_w\right)^{(n+t_{sn})}} + \frac{R}{\left(1+y_w\right)^{(N-1+t_{sn})}} + \frac{C_n}{\left(1+y_w\right)^{t_{sn}}} \right]$$

we can write the formulas for the change in a bond's price that would result from a *1bp rise* or *fall* in the bond's yield to maturity. Let

$$B_h = \text{a bond's price if its } y_{tm} \text{ were to fall by 1bp}$$
$$B_l = \text{a bond's price if its } y_{tm} \text{ were to rise by 1bp}$$

Using this notation, we define *two* measures of a bond's change in price, the first for a 1bp fall in yield, the second for a 1bp rise in yield.

$$B_h = \left[\sum_{n=1}^{N-1} \frac{C}{(1+y_w-.0001)^{(n+t_{sn})}} + \frac{R}{(1+y_w-.0001)^{(N-1+t_{sn})}} + \frac{C_n}{(1+y_w-.0001)^{t_{sn}}} \right]$$

and

$$B_l = \left[\sum_{n=1}^{N-1} \frac{C}{(1+y_w+.0001)^{(n+t_{sn})}} + \frac{R}{(1+y_w+.0001)^{(N-1+t_{sn})}} + \frac{C_n}{(1+y_w+.0001)^{t_{sn}}} \right]$$

Let

$$\Delta B_h = B_h - B$$

and

$$\Delta B_l = B_l - B$$

Then, the price value of a 1bp change in yield is defined as

$$V_{01} = \frac{\Delta B_h - \Delta B_l}{2}$$ [9]

or

$$V_{01} = \frac{B_h - B_l}{2}$$

Example. We use the same information for the given in Chapter 11. Given the closing yield of 6.0409% for settlement on 9/25/95 and using the above equation gives a value of a basis point of .042334 points or \$423.34 per million dollars of par.

In countries where bond prices are quoted in 1/32nd of a point, it is common practice to multiply the above result for V_{01} by 32. The result is the *value of a basis point in 32nds.*

In these countries, the *yield value of 32nd* is occasionally used by some analysts instead of $_{01}$. Since the bond equation cannot be inverted, it is not possible to get a closed-form solution for yield to maturity given price. Consequently, one should not calculate the yield value of a 32nd by changing the price of the bond by plus and minus 1/32; instead, one should calculate the yield value of a 32nd by transforming $_{01}$. Let,

---

[9] As ΔB_l, $\leqslant 0$ we take the average of the *difference* rather than the sum of the two price changes.

$$V_{32} = \text{the yield value of a 32nd}$$

We know that

$$V_{01} = \left(\frac{B_h - B_l}{2}\right)$$

Hence,

$$V_{32} = \frac{1}{32 \times V_{01}}$$

THE SENSITIVITY OF DURATION TO CHANGES IN A BOND'S CHARACTERISTICS

The duration of a bond is sensitive to changes in the bond's yield to maturity and to its remaining term to maturity. It is also sensitive to the defining characteristics of a bond—its coupon, maturity and the frequency of its coupon payments. We will comment on each of these sensitivities.

The Influence of Yield on Duration

The influence of a change in the bond's yield on the bond's duration is straightforward A *rise in rates across the yield curve* will diminish distant present values more than it diminishes nearby ones. Thus, if rates across the yield curve rise, the relative contribution to the price of a bond made by nearby payments will increase, while the relative contribution made by distant payments will decrease. Hence, *a bond's* duration decreases as *the yield to maturity at which it trades increases,* that is, a bond's duration is an *inverse* function of its yield to maturity.

The Influence of Coupon and Maturity on Duration

The interpretation of duration as the *expected* or *average* time to receipt by the investor of all promised payments from his bond allows for a straightforward analysis of the effect of both a bond's coupon and its maturity on its duration. If we compare two bonds of equal maturity, the bond with the lower coupon will have the longer duration, since the lower coupon implies that it will take longer for the investor to receive all of the moneys promised him by the bond. This is particularly obvious when one compares a zero-coupon bond with a coupon-bearing bond. The duration of a zero-coupon bond always equals its term to maturity, whereas the duration of a coupon-bearing bond is *always* less than its term to maturity.

When one compares two bonds with equal coupons, the bond with the longer *term to maturity will always have the longer duration.* This is most obvious when one compares the durations of two zero-coupon bonds having different terms to maturity.

The Influence of Coupon-Payment Frequency on Duration

If one compares two bonds of equal coupon and equal term to maturity, the bond that pays coupon interest more frequently will have a shorter duration. This follows from the fact that a greater amount of the promised payments will be received earlier for the bond with the higher frequency of payment.

Consider two bonds, which both have a 10% coupon and a 1-year to maturity. The first bond pays interest monthly while the second bond pays interest annually. In this case, it's clear from what we've said that the first bond must have a shorter duration than does the second.

Duration as a Function of Time

Given the interpretation of duration as the expected time to receipt by an investor of all payments promised by a bond and given the associated view of time as the *random variable,* it's obvious that time will exert an influence on duration. Specifically, a bond's duration is a function of all of the future cash payments it is expected to pay. As time passes and these payments are made, the duration of the bond decreases. Time has two different influences on duration-short run and long run.

In the short run, duration *increases* each time a coupon payment is made. However, in between coupon-payment dates duration *decreases* as we move from one coupon-payment date to the next. Hence, a plot of a bond's duration against term to maturity would reveal a *declining saw-tooth* pattern, with the duration of a bond decreasing from a given coupon date as it approaches its next coupon date. On that next coupon date, however, the bond's duration will increase sharply, although the resultant value will be less than the value of the bond's duration at the prior payment date. Hence, duration is an *inverse* function of *accrued interest.*

We know that, in the *long run,* the duration of a bond must tend towards zero; and that, on the bond's maturity date when its final payments are made, a bond's duration must equal zero. Hence, *a bond's duration is a direct function of its term to maturity.*

With respect to the very long run, we can ask: What is the duration of a *perpetual* bond, that is, of a bond that promises to pay periodic coupons forever and to repay principal only at *infinity?* The duration of a zero-coupon *perpetual* is infinite. In the case of a *coupon-bearing perpetual,* it can be shown that the equation for Macaulay duration simplifies to the following expression:

$$D_{mac} = \frac{1 + y_w}{y_w}$$

From this equation, we make two key observations. First, the duration of a coupon-bearing perpetual is *finite*. Second, the duration of a coupon-bearing perpetual is a function of the yield to maturity at which the bond trades but *not* of the coupon rate it bears.[10]

The above results for perpetual bonds imply that, if we were to examine bonds having an increasingly long term to maturity, we'd find that the duration of a coupon-bearing bond selling at a *discount* would behave differently from that of a bond selling at par or at a premium. In the case of a par or premium bond, the duration would increase *asymptotically from below* to the duration of a coupon-bearing perpetual bond as the bond's term to maturity increases. However, the duration of a discount

---

[10] The equation for the duration of a coupon-bearing perpetual is easily derived if one uses the annuity form of the equations for price and duration and sets $T_{sn} = 0$. Taking the limit of the numerator as N goes to infinity gives the following result for the price of a coupon-bearing perpetual

$$P = \frac{C}{y_w}$$

The limit for the numerator is

$$C\left(\frac{1 + y_w}{y_w^2}\right)$$

Hence, the duration for a coupon-bearing perpetual is

$$D_{mac} = C\left(\frac{1 + y_w}{y_w^2}\right) \bigg/ \left(\frac{C}{y_w}\right) = \frac{1 + y_w}{y_w}$$

bond would first increase like that of a zero-coupon bond and then asymptotically approaches the duration of a perpetual bond *from above* as its term to maturity were increased. Hence, coupon-bearing bonds that sell at a discount can exhibit a *decrease* in their duration as the term to maturity increases.

THE NEXT CHAPTER

In this chapter, we've examined duration, the measure of *risk* that bond investors regard as most important. In the next chapter, we examine another key risk measure, namely a bond's *convexity*.

CHAPTER 14

CONVEXITY

The relationship between a bond's price and its yield to maturity, as specified by the bond equation, is *non-linear*—a curve. In the case of *non-callable* bonds, the shape of a bond's price-yield curve is *convex to the origin* (Figure 14–1). A bond's convexity measures the degree of non-linearity or curvature in the price-yield curve. Specifically, it is a function of the *second* derivative of the bond equation.

The value of the *first* derivative—or equivalently the slope of the tangent—changes as a bond's yield to maturity changes. Since duration is a function of the derivative of the bond equation, the value of duration will depend on the *specific* yield to maturity at which it is evaluated. Hence, convexity measures the sensitivity of a bond's duration to a *small* change in that bond's yield to maturity. Let

$$Cx = \text{the convexity of a bond}$$

Formally, convexity is defined as:

$$Cx = \frac{1}{B}\frac{d^2B}{dy_{tm}^2}$$

DISPERSION

The above definition of convexity is rarely used to calculate convexity. Instead, convexity is typically calculated using another risk measure, a bond's *dispersion.* The dispersion of a bond has several interpretations; these are analogous to those of duration with one exception: the dispersion of a coupon-bearing bond cannot be related to that of a given zero-coupon bond.

Dispersion as the Time-Weighted Average of the Cash Flows

Like duration, dispersion is also a time-weighted average of a bond's discounted cash flows. The weights for dispersion are the *squares* of the actual time that an investor would have to wait to receive specific cash flows. Let

$$M_2 = \text{dispersion of a bond}$$

Then, dispersion is defined as follows:

$$M^2 = \frac{\sum_{n=1}^{N-1} \frac{(n+t_{sn})^2 C}{(1+y_w)^{(n+t_{sn})}} + \frac{(N-1+t_{sn})^2 R}{(1+y_w)^{(N-1+t_{sn})}} + \frac{t_{sn}^2 C_n}{(1+y_w)^{t_{sn}}}}{\sum_{n=1}^{N-1} \frac{C}{(1+y_w)^{(n+t_{sn})}} + \frac{R}{(1+y_w)^{(N-1+t_{sn})}} + \frac{C_n}{(1+y_w)^{t_{sn}}}} - D_{mac}^2$$

In the above equation, the divisor is the expression for a bond's *dirty price.* Hence,

$$M^2 = \frac{1}{wB}\left[\sum_{n=1}^{N-1} \frac{(n+t_{sn})^2 C}{(1+y_w)^{(n+t_{sn})}} + \frac{(N-1+t_{sn})^2 R}{(1+y_w)^{(N-1+t_{sn})}} + \frac{t_{sn}^2 C_n}{(1+y_w)^{t_{sn}}}\right] - D_{mac}^2$$

As in the case of Macaulay duration, people typically divide the right side of the above equation by *w,* the number of coupon payments per year.

If we interpret duration as the average time at which an investor will receive all of the payments promised by a bond, then *dispersion measures the sensitivity of that average time with respect to yield.*

Convexity as a Function of Dispersion

Given the above definition of dispersion, convexity is defined as follows:

$$Cx = \left(\frac{1}{1+y_w}\right)^2 \left(M^2 + D_{mac}^2 + \frac{D_{mac}}{w}\right)$$

It can be shown that the above definition of convexity as a function of dispersion is equivalent to the previous definition, that is,

$$\frac{1}{B}\frac{d^2B}{dy_{tm}^2} = \left(\frac{1}{1+y_w}\right)^2 \left(M^2 + D_{mac}^2 + \frac{D_{mac}}{w}\right)$$

It can also be shown that the second derivative of the bond equation with respect to yield to maturity is a non-negative function. Hence, convexity too must be non-negative.

It's interesting to observe that the dispersion of a zero-coupon bond is zero. Therefore, the convexity of a zero-coupon bond is a function of the square of its duration or its term to maturity. Since the dispersion of a zero-coupon bond is zero, it makes sense that the duration of a zero-coupon bond is a function of its term to maturity, but not of its yield to maturity.

Dispersion as an Expected Value

In a probabilistic sense, a bond's dispersion is the *variance* in the time to receipt of all cash flows from that bond, whereas a bond's duration is the *mean time* to receipt of all cash flows from that bond.

This interpretation of dispersion is perhaps the easiest to comprehend. From probability theory, we know that the variance of a population is a measure the degree by which the values assumed by a random variable differ from that variable's mean or expected value; the higher variance, the more spread out or *disperse* are the values that the variable assumes relative to its mean.

It follows from the interpretation of dispersion as an expected value that the dispersion of a zero-coupon bond must be zero. This makes intuitive sense, since the actual time to receipt of the only payment equals the mean time.

For a coupon-bearing bond, dispersion measures how spread out *in time* the bond's payments are relative to its duration. The more spread out the bond's payments are relative to the mean time to payment, the greater is the bond's dispersion. Since convexity is a positive function of dispersion, convexity increases whenever dispersion increases.

Because duration and dispersion are non-negative functions for standard, non-callable bonds, the convexity of such a bond always exceeds zero. In this sense, non-callable bonds are said to exhibit *positive* convexity.

Deriving Closed-Form Solutions for Dispersion and Convexity

As in the case of a bond's price and its duration, it's possible to derive a *closed-form* solution for a bond's dispersion and hence for its convexity. We will now derive another annuity equation which will allow us to define closed-form solutions for a bond's dispersion and for its convexity.

Consider the value of Z_N, where

$$Z_N = \sum_{n=1}^{N} n^2 v^n \tag{1}$$

and

$$v = \frac{1}{1+y_w} \tag{2}$$

We will show that

$$Z_N = \frac{1+y_w}{y_w}\left\{2\sum_{n=1}^{N} nv^n - \sum_{n=1}^{N} v^n - N^2 v^{N+1}\right\} \tag{3}$$

Let Z_n be the nth partial sum of Z_N. Then,

$$Z_n = v + 4v^2 + 9v^3 + \cdots + n^2 v^n \tag{4}$$

Multiplying (4) by v, we obtain the expression,

$$vZ_n = v^2 + 4v^3 + \cdots + n^2 v^{n+1} \tag{5}$$

Next, subtracting (5) from (4), we have

$$Z_n - vZ_n = v + 3v^2 + \cdots + (2n-1)v^n - n^2 v^{n+1} \tag{6}$$

Rearranging terms in equation (6) and solving for $n = N$, we get the expression,

$$Z_N = \frac{1}{1-v}\left\{\sum_{n=1}^{N} (2n-1)\, v^n - N^2 v^{N+1}\right\}$$

which can be rewritten as follows:

$$Z_N = \frac{1}{1-v}\left\{2\sum_{n=1}^{N} nv^n - \sum_{n=1}^{N} v^n - N^2 v^{N+1}\right\}$$

Using equation (2) to substitute for v in the first term, gives us the expression,

$$Z_N = \frac{1+y_w}{y_w}\left\{2\sum_{n=1}^{N} nv^n - \sum_{n=1}^{N} v^n - N^2 v^{N+1}\right\} \quad (7)$$

Hence,

$$\sum_{n=1}^{N} n^2 v^n = \frac{1+y_w}{y_w}\left\{2\sum_{n=1}^{N} nv^n - \sum_{n=1}^{N} v^n - N^2 v^{N+1}\right\}$$

The first step in writing a closed-form solution for dispersion is to substitute the variable v into the equation for dispersion. Doing so gives us the following expression:

$$M^2 = \frac{v^{t_{sn}}}{wB}\left[\sum_{n=1}^{N-1}(n+t_{sn})^2 Cv^n + \left(N-1+t_{sn}\right)^2 Rv^{(N-1+t_{sn})} + v^{t_{sn}}\right] - D_{mac}^2$$

Expanding the above equation we have

$$M^2 = \frac{v^{t_{sn}}}{wB}\left[C\sum_{n=1}^{N-1} n^2 v^n + 2t_{sn}C\sum_{n=1}^{N-1} nv^n + t_{sn}^2 C\sum_{n=1}^{N-1} v^n + \left(N-1+t_{sn}\right)^2 Rv^{(N-1)} + t_{sn}^2 C_n\right] - D_{mac}^2$$

Next, by substituting the three annuity results,

$$\sum_{n=1}^{N-1} v^n = \frac{1-v^{N-1}}{y_w}$$

$$\sum_{n=1}^{N-1} nv^n = \frac{1+y_w}{y_w}\left\{\sum_{n=1}^{N-1} v^n - (N-1)v^N\right\}$$

$$\sum_{n=1}^{N-1} n^2 v^n = \frac{1+y_w}{y_w}\left\{2\sum_{n=1}^{N-1} nv^n - \sum_{n=1}^{N-1} v^n - (N-1)^2 v^N\right\}$$

into the above equation for dispersion, we can obtain a closed-form solution. We will not, however, perform this substitution because the resulting equation is unwieldy and difficult to manipulate. Instead, we recommend that an analyst, who wants to calculate duration, dispersion, and convexity, first calculate the results for the three annuity equations and then substitute the resulting values into the annuity form of the equation for dispersion.

Example. We use the same information for the 6¼% of 8/31/00 given in Chapter 11. Given the closing yield of 6.0409% for settlement on 9/25/95 the above equation gives a dispersion of 21.806. Substituting this value for dispersion and the Macaulay duration of 4.305 into the equation for convexity we find that the convexity of this note equals 20.018.

To aid the analyst, we present all relevant equations in Table 14–1 at the end of this chapter.

THE INFLUENCE OF YIELD ON CONVEXITY

An argument, analogous to that made for the relationship between a bond's yield to maturity and its duration, can be made for the relationship between a bond's convexity and its yield to maturity. An increase in a bond's yield to maturity will have a greater effect on distant present values than on nearby ones. Hence, a bond's convexity will decrease as its yield to maturity increases, that is, a bond's convexity is an *inverse* function of its yield to maturity.

THE INFLUENCE OF COUPON AND MATURITY ON CONVEXITY

When one compares two bonds with *equal terms to maturity,* the bond with the lower coupon will always display greater convexity. While a bond's convexity is an *inverse* function of its coupon, the influence of a bond's coupon on its *dispersion* depends on a bond's coupon and its term to maturity. As noted, a zero-coupon bond has a dispersion of zero. Since a bond's dispersion is non-negative, dispersion will first increase (from zero) as a bond's coupon increases; at some point, however, depending on a bond's term to maturity, its dispersion may decline as its coupon increases.

When one compares two bonds with *equal coupons,* the bond with the longer term to maturity will have the greater convexity. This is particularly obvious when one compares two zero-coupon bonds, since the convexity of a zero-coupon bond is a function of the square of the bond's duration.

CONVEXITY AS A FUNCTION OF TIME

Previously, we observed that a bond's duration goes to zero as its term to maturity goes to zero. Similarly, a bond's dispersion and, hence, its convexity goes to zero as the bond's term to maturity goes to zero. We also observed that the dispersion of a zero-coupon bond is zero. Given this fact, the convexity of a zero-coupon bond is given by the expression,

$$Cx = \left[\frac{1}{1+y_w}\right]^2 \left[(N-1+t_{sn})^2 + \frac{(N-1+t_{sn})}{w}\right]$$

It's clear from the above equation that the convexity of a zero-coupon bond increases quadratically as its term to maturity increases.

We can ask, as we did for duration: What is the convexity of a *coupon-bearing perpetual bond?* By taking the limit of the equation for convexity as N goes to infinity, we obtain the following equation for the convexity of a coupon-bearing perpetual bond:

$$Cx = \frac{1}{y_w^2(1+y_w)}\left[y_w\left(1+\frac{1}{w}\right)+2\right]$$

From this equation, we see that as the current maturity of a coupon-bearing bond increases, its convexity will asymptotically approach the above limit.

A SUMMARY OF THE BEHAVIOR OF A BOND'S DURATION, ITS DISPERSION, AND ITS CONVEXITY

In a box, we summarize the behavior of a bond's duration, dispersion, and convexity with respect to changes in its coupon, term to maturity, yield to maturity, and coupon frequency.

Behavior of Duration, Dispersion and Convexity

	Duration	*Dispersion*	*Convexity*
Increasing coupon maturity fixed	Decreases	Depends on term to maturity	Decreases
Increasing maturity coupon fixed	Increases	Increases	Increases
Increasing yield	Decreases	Decreases	Decreases
Increasing coupon frequency	Decreases	Decreases	Increases

SUMMARY OF THE EQUATIONS FOR PRICE, DURATION, DISPERSION AND CONVEXITY

In Chapters 11, 13, and 14, we have derived a number of important equations. As an aid to the reader, we summarize in Table 14–1 the major equations for the price, duration, dispersion, and convexity of a bond. These results are presented in a form that allows for the direct application of the three annuity results derived in these chapters.

THE NEXT CHAPTER

In the next chapter, we give examples of how duration and convexity can, in particular circumstances, serve as useful measures of *risk* to an investor in or trader of bonds.

TABLE 14-1
Closed-Form Expressions for a Bond's Price, Duration, Dispersion, and Convexity

$$\sum_{n=1}^{N-1} v^n = \frac{1 - v^{N-1}}{y_w}$$

$$\sum_{n=1}^{N-1} nv^n = \frac{1 + y_w}{y_w}\left\{\sum_{n=1}^{N-1} v^n - (N-1)v^N\right\}$$

$$\sum_{n=1}^{N-1} n^2 v^n = \frac{1 + y_w}{y_w}\left\{2\sum_{n=1}^{N-1} nv^n - \sum_{n=1}^{N-1} v^n - (N-1)^2 v^N\right\}$$

$$P = v^{t_{sn}}\left[C\sum_{n=1}^{N-1} v^n + Rv^{N-1} + C_n\right] - AI$$

$$B = P + AI$$

$$D_{mac} = \frac{v^{t_{sn}}}{wB}\left[C\sum_{n=1}^{N-1} nv^n + t_{sn}C\sum_{n=1}^{N-1} v^n + (N - 1 + t_{sn})Rv^{(N-1)} + t_{sn}C_n\right]$$

$$D_m = \frac{D_{mac}}{(1 + y_w)}$$

$$D = -\frac{\Delta B}{B\Delta y_{tm}}$$

$$M^2 = \frac{v^{t_{sn}}}{wB}\left[C\sum_{n=1}^{N-1} n^2 v^n + 2t_{sn}C\sum_{n=1}^{N-1} nv^n + t_{sn}^2 C\sum_{n=1}^{N-1} v^n + (N - 1 + t_{sn})^2 Rv^{(N-1)} + t_{sn}^2 C_n\right] - D_{mac}^2$$

$$Cx = \left(\frac{1}{1 + y_w}\right)^2 \left(M^2 + D_{mac}^2 + \frac{D_{mac}}{w}\right)$$

CHAPTER 15

USES OF DURATION AND CONVEXITY

In the preceding chapters, we introduced duration and convexity, which are the most commonly used measures of the sensitivity of the value of a bond to a *small* change in interest rates. Consistent with our probabilistic interpretation of duration and convexity, we observe that a fixed-income analyst employs duration and convexity to describe the risk inherent in a bond in much the same manner as a statistician employs mean and variance to summarize the behavior of a distribution function. Specifically, by looking at the duration and convexity of a bond, in addition to its yield to maturity, an analyst can compare the relative merits of alternative bonds.

Further, both duration and convexity possess the property of *additivity,* which means that these concepts can be applied not only to a single bond, but to a *portfolio of bonds.* The duration of a *bond portfolio* equals the weighted sum of the durations of all bonds in the portfolio, where the weight applied to each bond is the *market value* of that bond. A similar result holds for the convexity of a bond portfolio.

The additivity of duration allows a fixed-income analyst to quickly assess the impact of substituting or *swapping* one bond for another in a portfolio of bonds. That is, the analyst can determine the change in the inherent risk of a bond portfolio when one bond is swapped for another.

PORTFOLIO RISK MEASURES

The cash flows from a bond portfolio equal the sum of the cash flows of all bonds that comprise that portfolio. Assume for the moment that the market value of each bond in a portfolio equals *one*. In this case, the duration of the portfolio equals the sum of the durations of each bond in the portfolio divided by the number of bonds in the portfolio, that is, the duration of the portfolio equals the *average* duration of the bonds that comprise it. A similar result holds for the convexity of a portfolio of bonds.

Duration of a Bond Portfolio

In the general case, where the market values of the bonds comprising a portfolio are not all equal to one, the duration of a portfolio comprised of J bonds be expressed as follows. Let

D_{port} = the duration of a portfolio comprised of J bonds

Then

$$D_{port} = \frac{\sum_{j=1}^{J} D_j V_j}{\sum_{j=1}^{J} V_j}$$

The *market value* of the jth bond, V_j, is defined as the product of its dirty price times the par amount of it held in the portfolio divided by 100. In symbols,

$$V_j = \frac{B_j \times \text{nominal par amount of the } j\text{th bond}}{100}$$

Many analysts define the *dollar duration* of a bond held in a portfolio as the bond's duration times its market value, that is,

$$dolD_j = D_j V_j$$

If we define the *total value of the portfolio,* V_{port}, as

$$V_{port} = \sum_{j=1}^{J} V_j$$

When this practice is followed, the *duration of a portfolio* can be written as follows

$$D_{port} = \frac{\sum_{j=1}^{J} dolD_j}{V_{port}}$$

Convexity of a Bond Portfolio

Similarly, an expression for the convexity of a bond portfolio, can easily be written. Let

Cx_{port} = convexity of a portfolio comprised of J bonds

Then

$$Cx_{port} = \frac{\sum_{j=1}^{J} Cx_j V_j}{V_{port}}$$

The examples in this chapter make use of the security information presented in Table 15–1.

Using the information in Table 15–1, Table 15–2 presents an example of portfolio duration and convexity.

TABLE 15–1
SECURITY INFORMATION

Maturity Date	*Coupon*	*Dated Date*	*First Coupon Date*	*Force Last Day of Month*	*Clean Price*
6/30/97	5.625%	Fri 06/30/95	12/31/95	Yes	99.23
7/31/97	5.875%	Mon 07/31/95	1/31/96	Yes	100.03
8/31/97	6.000%	Thu 08/31/95	2/29/96	Yes	100.11
2/15/98	7.250%	Wed 02/15/95	8/15/95		102.31
5/15/98	6.125%	Mon 05/15/95	11/15/95		100.18
8/15/98	5.875%	Tue 08/15/95	2/15/96		99.30
6/30/00	5.875%	Fri 06/30/95	12/31/95	Yes	99.11
7/31/00	6.125%	Mon 07/31/95	1/31/96	Yes	100.09
8/31/00	6.250%	Thu 08/31/95	2/29/96	Yes	100.28
8/15/05	6.500%	Tue 08/15/95	2/15/96		101.30
8/15/25	6.875%	Tue 08/15/95	2/15/96		103.24

TABLE 15–2
PORTFOLIO DURATION AND CONVEXITY

Settlement Date: 09/25/95

Security		*Par*	*Price*	*Duration*	*Convexity*	*Market Value*	*Dollar Duration*	*Dollar Convexity*	*Dirty Price*
5.625%	06/30/97	$10,000,000	99.23	1.636	3.156	$10,104,857	$16,531,547	$ 31,890,930	101.0486
5.875%	07/31/97		100.03	1.714	3.441				100.9878
6.000%	08/31/97	1,000,000	100.11	1.794	3.741	1,007,558	1,807,560	3,769,276	100.7558
7.250%	02/15/98		102.31	2.159	5.397				103.7765
6.125%	05/15/98		100.18	2.356	6.453				102.7762
5.875%	08/15/98	1,000,000	99.30	2.606	7.743	1,005,921	2,621,429	7,788,843	100.5921
5.875%	06/30/00		99.11	4.044	18.820				100.7327
6.125%	07/31/00		100.09	4.106	19.383				101.2133
6.250%	08/31/00	1,000,000	100.28	4.179	20.018	1,013,043	4,233,505	20,279,086	101.3043
6.500%	08/15/05	1,000,000	101.30	7.198	63.628	1,026,617	7,389,588	65,321,577	102.6617
6.875%	08/15/25	1,000,000	103.24	12.806	259.370	1,045,160	13,384,314	271,083,058	104.5160
Cash									100.0000
					Portfolio Sums	**$15,203,155**	**3.024**	**26.319**	

BOND SWAPS

Whenever one or more bonds are sold in order to purchase one or more bonds, the transaction is referred to as a *bond swap*. Although the purposes and types of bond swaps are numerous, several swaps are sufficiently common such that they are referred to by name.

Two-bond swaps are the most common class of swaps and are executed for a variety of purposes. Some of the purposes are summarized in Tables 15–3 and 15–4.

Duration-Neutral Swaps

Typically, when two bonds are swapped, the interest rate risk of the portfolio changes. To keep interest rate risk constant, the investor typically imposes a *duration neutrality constraint*. That is, the investor, in pursuit

TABLE 15–3
Common Bond Swaps

Name	*Purpose of the Swap*
Yield pickup or yield enhancement swap	To increase yield by selling a lower yielding bond and buying a higher yielding bond
Liquidity enhancement swap	To increase liquidity by selling a bond with lower liquidity and buying a bond with higher liquidity
Quality enhancement swap	To increase quality by selling a bond with lower quality and buying a bond with higher quality
Capital appreciation swap	To increase return by selling a bond when it is relatively *rich* and buying a bond when it is relatively *cheap*, with the expectation that the cheap bond will out perform the rich bond during the holding period
Sector swap	To switch from rich sector or issuer class to a *cheaper* sector or issuer class (*e.g.*, selling a *government* bond issued by the U.S. Treasury to buy a *corporate* bond issued by IBM)

TABLE 15–4
Common Duration-Constrained Bond Swaps

Name	*Purpose of the Swap*
Duration-constrained extension swap	To increase duration by selling a bond with shorter duration and buying a bond with longer duration
Duration-constrained contraction swap	To decrease duration by selling a bond with longer duration and buying a bond with shorter duration
Bullet-barbell convexity enhancement swap	To increase convexity by selling *one* bond (*the bullet*) with a medium duration and buying *two* bonds (*the barbell*), one with a shorter duration than the bullet and one with longer duration than the bullet
Barbell-bullet convexity reduction swap	To decrease convexity by selling *two* bonds (*the barbell*), one with a shorter duration than the bullet and one with longer duration than the bullet, and buying *one* bond (*the bullet*) with a medium duration

of one of the purposes listed in Table 15–1, sells bond 1 and buys bond 2 while holding portfolio duration constant.[1]

If an investor holding a portfolio of bonds does a duration-neutral swap, he will typically require that the *dollar durations* of the two bonds be approximately equal. This constraint allows the investor to determine how much of bond 2 he should buy, given the amount of bond 1 he's selling, so as to maintain the portfolio's current duration.

Let

$$D_j = \text{the duration of bond } j$$
$$V_j = \text{the market value of bond } j \text{ held}$$
$$dolD_j = \text{the dollar duration of bond } j$$

Given the constraint that the dollar durations of the two bonds be approximately equal, we have

---

[1] Often, it's not possible to hold duration constant. In this case, the investor will typically require that the duration of bond 2 equal approximately that of bond 1, for example, that the difference in the durations of the two bonds swapped not exceed some small fraction of a year, typically 0.1 or 0.25 years.

$$dolD_1 = dolD_2$$

Given that

$$dolD_j = D_j V_j$$

we can determine the market value of bond 2, V_2, that the investor must buy when he sells V_1 of bond V as follows:

$$V_2 = \frac{D_1 V_1}{D_2}$$

The par amount of bond 2 is determined as follows:

$$\text{par amount of bond } 2 = \frac{100 V_2}{B_2}$$

Using the information in Table 15–1, Table 15–5 presents an example of portfolio duration and convexity.

Duration-Constrained Extension Swaps

If an investor swaps into a bond having a duration that exceeds the duration of the bond he's selling under the constraint that the swap not increase the duration of his portfolio, the swap is referred to as a *duration-constrained extension swap.*[2]

Under the duration neutrality constraint, it will be impossible for the investor to fully reinvest the proceeds he receives from the sale of the shorter-duration bond into a purchase of the longer-duration bond. Instead; he will have to hold some portion of his sale proceeds as *cash,* that is, in an instrument with a duration of *zero.*[3]

The proportion, x, of the proceeds that the investor realizes from the sale of a shorter-duration bond to be invested in the longer-duration bond and the proportion $(1 - x)$ that must be held as cash can be calculated as follows. Let

---

[2] In discussing duration-constrained bond swaps, it's helpful to introduce specific classes of bonds as well as notation to denote them. We will define three types of bonds, those having respectively a short, an intermediate, and a long duration; to distinguish among these three types of bonds, we will use respectively the subscripts *sd, id,* and *ld.*

[3] By *cash* we mean any investment whose principal is constant.

TABLE 15–5
DURATION-CONSTRAINED EXTENSION SWAP

Settlement Date: 09/25/95

Action	*Security Description*	*Par*	*Clean Price*	*Duration*	*Convexity*	*Duration Weights*	*Market Value (proceeds)*	*Dollar Duration*	*Dollar Convexity*	*Dirty Price*
Sell	5.625% 06/30/97	($10,000,000)	99.23	1.636	3.156		$10,104,857	($16,531,547)	($31,890,930)	101.0486
Buy	6.250% 08/31/00	$3,904,931	100.28	4.179	20.018	0.391	($3,955,862)	$16,531,547	$79,188,442	101.3043
	Cash					0.609	($6,148,996)	$0	$0	100.0000
					Sum of Duration Weights	**1.000**				
					Portfolio Sums Before Swap		**$10,104,857**	**1.636**	**3.156**	
					Portfolio Sums After Swap		**$10,104,857**	**1.636**	**7.837**	
					Change in Portfolio Measures		**$0**	**0.000**	**4.681**	

D_{sd} = duration of the short-duration bond

D_{ld} = duration of the long-duration bond

D_{cash} = duration of cash

x = proportion of sale proceeds to be invested in the long-duration bond

Imposing the duration-neutrality constraint, we have

$$D_{sd} = xD_{ld} + (1 - x)D_{cash}$$

Given that the duration of cash, D_{cash}, is zero by definition, it follows that the proportion of the sale proceeds to be invested in the longer-duration bond is

$$x = \frac{D_{sd}}{D_{ld}}$$

The remaining proportion, $1-x$, must be held in cash.

Using market values, and letting

V_{sd} = the market value of the short-duration bond

V_{ld} = the market value of the long- duration bond

we have

$$\begin{aligned} V_{ld} &= xV_{sd} \\ &= \frac{D_{sd}V_{sd}}{D_{ld}} \end{aligned}$$

and,

$$\begin{aligned} \text{cash} &= (1 - x)V_{sd} \\ &= V_{sd} - V_{ld} \end{aligned}$$

Using the information in Table 15–1, Table 15–5 presents an example of a duration-constrained extension swap.

Duration-Constrained Contraction Swaps

If an investor swaps into a bond having a duration that's shorter than the duration of the bond he's selling under the constraint that the swap not decrease the duration of his portfolio, the swap is referred to as a *duration-constrained contraction swap*.

Since a duration-contraction swap is the mirror image of a duration-extension swap, it's obvious that the proceeds that the investor realizes from the sale of the longer-duration bond will be insufficient for him to buy the exact amount of the shorter-duration bond that keeps the duration of the bond portfolio constant. This follows from the fact that the proportion, *x,* of the proceeds that the investor realizes from the sale of the longer-duration bond to be invested in the shorter-duration bond is greater than 1. That is, in a duration-constrained contraction swap,

$$x = \frac{D_{ld}}{D_{sd}} > 1$$

since

$$D_{ld} > D_{sd}$$

Hence the amount, measured in market value, of the shorter-duration bond that the investor must buy is given by the expression,

$$V_{sd} = xV_{ld}$$

$$= \frac{D_{ld}V_{ld}}{D_{sd}}$$

The amount of cash that the investor must add to his sale proceeds is:

$$\text{cash} = V_{sd} - V_{ld}$$

Duration-Constrained Bullet-Barbell Convexity Swaps

In *bullet-barbell* (or *dumbbell*) *swaps,* the duration of the *bullet* bond must be greater than the duration of the shorter-duration bond and less than that of the longer-duration bond. We will denote the bullet bond by the subscript *id.* Typically, the purpose of a bullet-barbell swap is to change the *convexity* of the portfolio while holding its duration constant.

The two barbell securities are a *synthetic* substitute for the bullet security. For example, an investor might replace a 5-year Treasury note with a combination of 2- and 10-year Treasury notes. If the 5-year bullet is sold and, on a duration-weighted basis, the 2- and 10-year barbell is bought, then the convexity of the portfolio will be *increased.* This swap is referred to as a *bullet-barbell convexity enhancement swap.* Conversely, if the 2- and 10-year barbell is sold and, on a duration-weighted

TABLE 15–6
DURATION-CONSTRAINED CONVEXITY SWAP

Settlement Date: 09/25/95

Action	*Security Description*	*Par*	*Clean Price*	*Duration*	*Convexity*	*Duration Weights*	*Market Value (proceeds)*	*Dollar Duration*	*Dollar Convexity*	*Dirty Price*
Buy	6.000% 08/31/97	$7,936,344	100.11	1.794	3.741	0.790	($7,996,330)	$14,345,416	$29,914,270	100.7558
Sell	6.125% 07/31/00	($10,000,000)	100.09	4.106	19.383		$10,121,332	($41,558,187)	($196,181,769)	101.2133
Buy	6.875% 08/15/25	$2,033,184	103.24	12.806	259.37	0.210	($2,125,002)	$27,212,771	$551,161,685	104.5160
					Sum of Duration Weights	**1.000**				
					Portfolio Sums Before Swap		**$10,121,332**	**4.106**	**19.383**	
					Portfolio Sums After Swap		**$10,121,332**	**4.106**	**57.411**	
					Change in Portfolio Measures		**$0**	**0.000**	**38.028**	

basis, the 5-year bullet is bought, then the convexity of the portfolio will be decreased. This swap is referred to as a *bullet-barbell convexity reduction swap.*

If an investor, who wants to hold the duration of his portfolio constant, *sells a bullet bond and buys a barbell,* he must allocate his sale proceeds in fixed proportions between the longer- and the shorter-duration bonds that he buys. Let x be the proportion of his sale proceeds that the investor must invest in the shorter-duration bond and $1-x$ be the proportion he must invest in the longer-duration bond. We can solve for the proportion, x, as follows:

$$D_{id} = xD_{sd} + (1-x)D_{ld}$$

$$x = \frac{D_{id} - D_{ld}}{D_{sd} - D_{ld}}$$

The amounts, measured in market value, of the barbell bonds that the investor must buy are:

$$V_{sd} = xV_{id}$$

$$V_{ld} = (1-x)V_{id}$$

Alternatively, the bullet bond may be *bought.* If so, than to hold the duration of the portfolio constant, the investor must sell the shorter-duration and the longer-duration bonds in the proportions, x and $1-x$, respectively.

Using the information in Table 15–1, Table 15–6 presents an example of a duration-constrained convexity swap.

THE NEXT CHAPTER

So far we've focused principally on U.S. securities. In Part 5, we examine strategies for cross-border investing and calculations for bonds worldwide.

PART 5

FIXED-INCOME SECURITIES WORLDWIDE

CHAPTER 16

COVERED INTEREST ARBITRAGE

As any investor in international markets will quickly observe, significant differences exist among the short-term rates offered by similar instruments denominated in different currencies. For example, differences exist between the rates quoted on a Euro time deposit denominated in dollars and one denominated in deutsche marks (DM), between U.S. and U.K. Treasury bills, and between top-rated U.S. and Canadian commercial paper.

If an investor holding dollars sought only to obtain the highest short-term interest rates available, he would rarely invest in dollar-denominated paper. By buying paper denominated in a foreign currency, however, he would incur a considerable *foreign exchange risk;* that is, a risk that the exchange value of the currency in which he had invested might fall relative to the dollar. Most investors are unwilling to incur a foreign exchange risk in investing short-term money. Thus, a portfolio manager who invests dollar balances in an instrument denominated in a foreign currency will typically *hedge* his resulting *long* position in that currency by doing a *swap;* that is, at the time he buys foreign currency in the *spot* market (foreign exchange market for cash delivery) to purchase an instrument denominated in a foreign currency, he will simultaneously sell that foreign currency *forward,* thereby eliminating his long position in foreign exchange and with it his exposure to a foreign exchange risk. By doing a swap, the investor locks in a fixed rate of return on his investment.

ESTIMATING THE SWAP COST

When a portfolio manager invests dollars in an instrument denominated in a foreign currency on a hedged basis, he is engaging in what is called *covered interest arbitrage.* The return he earns on this arbitrage will equal a *net* rate—the yield on the instrument minus (plus) a second rate, the cost of (yield on) the swap. Thus, to determine whether a domestic instrument or a similar foreign instrument purchased on a hedged basis would yield more, he must calculate this second rate.

An investor who swaps dollars into a foreign currency is in effect buying the foreign currency and then selling it. This suggests that the rate of return on the swap should be calculated as follows:

$$\begin{pmatrix}\text{Rate of return on}\\ \text{swap as a decimal}\end{pmatrix} = \left(\frac{\text{Selling rate} - \text{Buying rate}}{\text{Buying rate}}\right)\frac{360}{T}$$

where

$$T = \text{days transaction is outstanding}$$

We can restate this succinctly in symbols. In this chapter only, let

S = spot rate quoted on U.S. *direct terms;* that is, *dollars per unit of foreign currency*

F = *outright* forward rate in U.S. terms

Then, on a swap out of dollars into a foreign currency:

$$\text{Rate of return on swap} = \left(\frac{F-S}{S}\right)\frac{360}{T}$$

$$= \left(\frac{F}{S} - 1\right)\frac{360}{T}$$

Using this formula for the return on the swap, the investor holding *dollars* can determine what rate he would earn by investing, on a hedged basis, in an instrument *denominated in a foreign currency.* Let

r_{fx} = rate offered by an instrument denominated in a foreign currency

r'_{fx} = net rate offered by this instrument; that is, r_{fx} plus the rate of return on the swap

Then,

$$r'_{fx} = r_{fx}\left(\frac{F}{S} - 1\right)\frac{360}{T}$$

COVERED INTEREST ARBITRAGE

Let

$r_{\$}$ = rate of return on a dollar-denominated instrument similar to a foreign instrument paying r_{fx}

Whenever r'_{fx} exceeds $r'_{\$}$ that is, whenever a foreign instrument offers a greater return on a hedged basis than an instrument of the same maturity and quality (i.e., credit risk) in the domestic market, investors who hold dollars have an incentive to invest those dollars abroad in the foreign instrument. Such *arbitrage* will in turn tend to reduce the profitability of the transaction by raising the spot rate on the foreign currency and depressing the forward rate.

Thus, in markets where arbitrage is active because it is not prevented by exchange controls or other factors, one would expect the net return offered on a hedged basis by an instrument denominated in a foreign currency to equal the rate offered by a similar instrument denominated in dollars. In symbols, this can be stated more succinctly as follows: Where arbitrage is active, it should be that

$$r_{\$} = r'_{fx}$$

$$= r_{fx} + \left(\frac{F}{S} - 1\right)\frac{360}{T}$$

This in turn implies that the difference between the foreign and domestic rates, which we call *the rate differential, should equal minus the rate of return on the swap; that is,*

$$r_{fx} - r_{\$} = \left(1 - \frac{F}{S}\right)\frac{360}{T}$$

In markets, such as that for Eurocurrency time deposits that are heavily arbitraged, the above relationship does in fact often prevail. Consequently, an investor will find that on a net basis the rate he can earn by investing dollars in a time deposit will be the same whether he invests his dollars in a deposit denominated in dollars or, on a hedged basis, in a deposit denominated in a foreign currency.

In markets that are less heavily arbitraged, investing in a foreign instrument on a hedged basis may offer an investor holding dollars a greater return than that offered by a similar dollar-denominated instrument. Thus, an investor whose horizon extends beyond the domestic market will need a new type of break-even number, namely, the rate differential, $r_{fx} - r_{\$}$, that must prevail between a given pair of markets in order that a hedged foreign instrument yield the same rate as does a similar domestic instrument.

As noted, such break-even rate differentials are usually calculated as follows:

$$\left(1-\frac{F}{S}\right)\frac{360}{T}$$

which equals

$$\left(\frac{S-F}{S}\right)\frac{360}{T}$$

The Street, however, does not usually phrase the calculation this way. The reason is that, in the foreign exchange market, forward rates are not quoted on an *outright* basis, but rather as the difference between the spot and forward rates. This difference, $S - F$, is known as the *swap rate;* and in Street descriptions of hedging foreign investments, the formula for calculating the break-even rate differential is written as follows:

$$\left(\frac{\text{Swap rate}}{\text{Spot rate}}\right)\frac{360}{T}$$

CALCULATING THE TRUE BREAK-EVEN RATE DIFFERENTIAL

The preceding formula for calculating the break-even rate differential on a hedged foreign investment is, like many Street calculations, an approximation. In particular, it fails to take into account hedging of the foreign exchange earned in the form of interest on the foreign instrument. When interest rates are low, the discrepancy between the approximate return on a swap and the true rate is small, but when rates are high, it can rise to 50bp or more on a long transaction. The precise formula for calculating the true break-even rate differential is not appreciably more difficult than the one given above, and it is therefore the one that should be used.

To derive this precise formula for the break-even rate differential on a hedged foreign investment, consider an investor who has $1 to invest.

If he invests this \$1 for T days in a domestic instrument yielding $r_\$$ he will have at maturity a sum of dollars equal to

$$1+r_\$\frac{T}{360}$$

If, alternatively, he invests his \$1 in an instrument that is denominated in a foreign currency and that yields r_{fx}, the units of foreign currency he invests will be $1/S$, and the units of foreign currency he will hold T days hence will be

$$\frac{1}{S}\left(1+r_{fx}\frac{T}{360}\right)$$

If he sells this sum of foreign currency forward, the amount of *dollars* he will have at the end of his investment period will be

$$\frac{F}{S}\left(1+r_{fx}\frac{T}{360}\right)$$

Assume that investing in the dollar-denominated instrument and investing in the foreign instrument on a hedged basis both yield the portfolio manager the *same* sum of dollars, that is,

$$1+r_\$\frac{T}{360}=\frac{F}{S}\left(1-r_{fx}\frac{T}{360}\right)$$

By manipulating this equation, it is easy to show that

$$\left(r_{fx}-r_\$\right)^*=\textit{true}\text{ break-even rate differential}$$

is given by the following expression:

$$\left(r_{fx}-r_\$\right)^*=\left(\frac{S}{F}-1\right)\left(\frac{360}{T}+r_\$\right)$$

WEAK AND STRONG CURRENCIES

If a foreign currency is strong (i.e., is expected to *appreciate* in value relative to the dollar) then the forward rate will exceed the spot rate, and the left side of the preceding equation will be negative. This tells us that the investor who swaps dollars into a strong currency will *gain* on the swap and that, in order that a hedged investment in an instrument denominated in that currency will yield him the same rate as a similar dollar-denominated instrument, r_{fx} must be less than $r_{\$}$.

If, alternatively, the foreign currency is *weak* (i.e., is expected to *depreciate* in value relative to the dollar) the spot rate will exceed the forward rate, and the left side of the equation will be positive. For a hedged investment in an instrument denominated in such a currency to yield more on a *net* basis than $r_{\$}$, r_{fx} must exceed $r_{\$}$ by more than the percentage loss on the swap.

The General Rule

Bearing the above in mind, we can state the following general rule:

> The hedged foreign instrument is preferable to the domestic instrument whenever the interest rate differential existing in the market exceeds the true break-even rate differential, that is, whenever
>
> $$r_{fx} - r_{\$} > \left(\frac{S}{F} - 1\right)\left(\frac{360}{T} + r_{\$}\right)$$

The only confusing thing about this rate is that $r_{fx} - r_{\$}$ may, as noted, be positive or negative. If it is negative (for example, $r_{fx} - r_{\$} = -3\%$), then the foreign instrument will be preferable if the amount

$$\left(\frac{S}{F} - 1\right)\left(\frac{360}{T} + r_{\$}\right)$$

is either a smaller negative number (e.g., -2.5%) or any positive number. If, alternatively, $r_{fx} - r_{\$}$ is positive, the interpretation of *greater than* is clear; it means any larger positive number. To illustrate, we give the following two examples.

Calculating the Break-Even Rate Differential on a Hedged Investment in an Instrument Denominated in a Foreign Currency

Let

r_{fx} = rate on a 360-day-year basis offered by an instrument denominated in a foreign currency

$r_\$$ = rate on a 360-day-year basis offered on a dollar-denominated instrument similar to the foreign instrument paying r_{fx}

T = days the transaction is outstanding

$(r_{fx} - r_\$)^*$ = *true* break-even rate differential between an investment in the dollar-denominated instrument and a hedged investment in the foreign instrument

Case I: The foreign exchange quotes are in *U.S. direct terms,* that is

S = spot rate quoted as dollars per unit of foreign exchange
F = *outright* forward rate quoted as dollars per unit of foreign exchange

Then

$$(r_{fx} - r_\$)^* = \left(\frac{S}{F} - 1\right)\left(\frac{360}{T} + r_\$\right)$$

Case II: The foreign exchange quotes are in *European* terms, that is:

S' = spot rate quoted as units of foreign exchange per dollar
F' = *outright* forward rate quoted as units of foreign exchange per dollar

Then

$$(r_{fx} - r_\$)^* = \left(\frac{F'}{S'} - 1\right)\left(\frac{360}{T} + r_\$\right)$$

Case III: If $i_\$$ and i_{fx} are quoted on a 365-day-year basis, change 360 in the above equations to 365.

The Break-Even Formula When Quotes Are in European Terms

So far in our discussion, we have assumed that exchange rates are quoted in U.S. direct terms. If exchange rates are quoted in *European terms* (i.e., as units of foreign exchange per dollar), the formula for the true break-even rate differential must be adjusted accordingly. Let

S' = spot rate quoted in *European terms* (i.e., in units of foreign exchange per dollar)

F' = *outright* forward rate in European terms

Obviously,

$$S = \frac{1}{S'}$$

$$F = \frac{1}{F'}$$

From this, it follows that

$$\left(r_{fx} - r_{\$}\right)^{*} = \left(\frac{F'}{S'} - 1\right)\left(\frac{360}{T} + r_{\$}\right)$$

Example I: The Foreign Currency Is Strong. Consider an investor who held, on a day in early 1980, dollars that he wanted to invest for 3 months.[1] He could have invested in a straight Eurodollar time deposit or he could have invested on a hedged basis in a 3-month Euro DM deposit. On the date in question, rates were as follows:

$$S' = 1.732000 \text{ DM per dollar}$$

$$F' = 1.707473 \text{ DM per dollar}$$

$$r_{\$} = 14\tfrac{7}{8}\%$$

$$r_{DM} = 9\%$$

Plugging the first three of these numbers into our break-even equation, we find that

$$\left(r_{DM} - r_{\$}\right)^{*} = \left(\frac{1.707473}{1.732000} - 1\right)\left(\frac{360}{90} + 0.14875\right)$$

$$= 5\tfrac{7}{8}\%$$

that is, a hedged investment in a Euro DM deposit would have yielded the same return as a straight Eurodollar time deposit if the rate on the Euro DM deposit had been $5\tfrac{7}{8}$ percentage points less than $r_{\$}$. This was

[1]These examples give accurate illustrations of the arbitrage we're describing. Foreign exchange rates as well as the weaknesses and strengths of individual currencies do change over time, but the equations for covered interest arbitrage do not change.

so, due to arbitrage; and consequently, a hedged Euro DM time deposit offered our investor of dollars no advantage over a Eurodollar deposit.

Example II: The Foreign Currency Is Weak. Consider now a portfolio manager who, in the same time period used in Example I, had to choose between a 3-month Eurodollar time deposit and a hedged 3-month investment in Eurosterling (£). On that date, rates were

$$S = \$2.2000 \text{ per } £$$
$$F = \$2.1895 \text{ per } £$$
$$r_\$ = 14\tfrac{7}{8}\%$$
$$r_£ = 16\tfrac{7}{8}\%$$

Inserting the first three of these numbers into our equation, we find that[2]

$$\begin{aligned}(r_£ - r_\$)^* &= \left(\frac{2.2000}{2.1895} - 1\right)\left(\frac{365}{90} + 0.14875\right)\\ &= 2\%\end{aligned}$$

Because sterling (£) was a weak currency, our investor would have had to earn 2 percentage points more on a Eurosterling deposit than on an Eurodollar deposit in order to break even on a hedged investment in a Eurosterling deposit. On the date in question, rates were such that this investment offered no advantage over a straight Eurodollar deposit. Again, arbitrage was at work.

Shopping

We've suggested that, in markets where arbitrage is not prevented by exchange control or other government regulations, it will tend to equalize the return offered by hedged investments in similar instruments. Our Eurocurrency deposit examples, which were constructed from a bank quote board, support this contention.

These examples should not, however, be taken to imply that it isn't worthwhile for a corporate account that wants to invest in size to shop

---

[2] Sterling deposit rates, unlike other Eurodeposit rates, are quoted on a 365-day basis. An accurate estimate of the break-even rate differential, $(r_£ - r_\$)^*$, can be obtained by substituting 365 for 360 in the break-even calculation, as we did.

around to determine whether a hedged investment would be more profitable than a straight dollar-denominated investment. Major banks that deal in foreign exchange tend to view large corporate accounts as holders of *cold* money (as opposed to *warm* money, which is loyal to one or more banks); and for that reason, they give such accounts quotes based on what fits their own dealing positions at the moment. A large corporate account may, therefore, especially in active markets, get quite different quotes from different banks; moreover, it may be able to put together a hedged investment in an instrument denominated in a foreign currency that pays more than a similar dollar-denominated instrument. In such a situation, a corporation is likely to find itself doing different legs of the arbitrage with different banks.

THE NEXT CHAPTER

In the next chapter, we delve into calculations for *floating-rate notes, FRNs* for short.

CHAPTER 17

FLOATING-RATE INSTRUMENTS

Over the last twenty years, interest rates have exhibited a high degree of volatility. One response to this high level of volatility is the widespread acceptance of debt instruments whose coupons change as interest rates change. Floating-rate instruments have many different names; often they carry a proprietary name given to them by the financial institution that first issued the product. Some people have attempted to classify floating-rate paper; unfortunately, such classifications are hard to apply in practice and therefore add little, if anything, to a discussion of floating-rate paper.

All floating-rate instruments share one important characteristic—the future coupon rates to be paid by the floating-rate paper depend on future interest rates, the values of which are unknown, or at least uncertain. Thus, the future coupon rates that a floating-rate instrument will pay are unknown at the time of its issuance. This uncertainty in the value of the coupon rate is the principal difference between floating-rate and fixed-rate instruments. Bonds on which the coupon rate changes in a *predetermined* or *deterministic* manner (e.g., a *stepped-coupon bond*) are not considered floating-rate instruments.

It's market convention to refer generically to floating-rate instruments as *floating-rate notes* (*FRNs* for short). Henceforth we'll adopt this jargon. Borrowers have issued a wide variety of FRNs, but all such notes *share several common parameters.* In the next section, we list and describe these shared parameters. Then, we talk about the different calculations that analysts have developed for valuing FRNs.

FRN CHARACTERISTICS

To identify a particular fixed-coupon issue for the purpose of making price-yield calculations, we need to know the following key parameters:

issue date, maturity date, coupon-payment frequency, coupon rate, and the interest-payment *dates.* To identify a particular FRN for the purpose of making price-yield calculations, we need to know the values of several additional parameters. We list and define these parameters below.

Reference Index

Every FRN has a *reference index* upon which the calculation of each successive new coupon is based. A few examples of the many reference indices in use are 1-month LIBOR (the London Interbank Offered Rate for Eurodollar deposits), the U.S. 3-month T-bill rate, the prime rate, and the 1-week CP (commercial paper) rate.

Quoted Margin to Reference Index

Often, an issuer of an FRN specifies that each new coupon paid by that issue will be set at a *quoted margin* or *spread* to the specified *reference index.* On each reset date, this spread will be added to or subtracted from the reference index to determine the coupon rate the issue will pay over its next coupon period.

Reset Frequency

Among FRNs, the rules for determining the dates upon which a given issue's coupon will be reset vary. Examples of *reset-frequency* rules are the 15th of every month; the last day of March, June, September, and December; and the 30th of June.

Typically, the coupon-payment frequency is the same as the reset frequency. However, on some FRNs the coupon *resets faster than it's paid;* for example, the coupon rate might be reset *monthly,* but coupon interest might be paid only *quarterly.*

The *market standard* for an FRN is that coupon-reset frequency is identical to coupon-payment frequency. Therefore, in discussing calculations for FRNs, we will assume that coupon-reset frequency equals coupon-payment frequency unless we explicitly specify otherwise.

Observation Date

The rules for determining the dates upon which the value of the reference index is observed for the purpose of setting the next coupon vary. The rule for specifying the *observation date* generally includes not only a specific time, but a specific place. For example, the observation date for

3-month LIBOR might be specified as the average offered rate for 3-month Eurodollar deposits at a list of reference banks in London at 12 noon on the second business day preceding the reset date.

FRN NOTATION

In Chapter 3, we discussed the criteria we used in selecting our notation. Also, at the end of that chapter, we listed all of the notation that we'd routinely use in this book (Table 3–1).

FRNs are a special breed of debt securities with which unique parameters and concepts of yield are associated. For this reason, we need to introduce some additional notation to discuss calculations for FRNs. A summary of the notation that we will use in this chapter is presented in Table 17–1; some of this notation is new, some we've been using all along; we repeat definitions of the latter for the reader's convenience. In creating notation specific to FRNs, we have striven to keep our new notation as simple as possible and as consistent as possible with the notation we've used previously. In the case of British index-linked gilts, the required notation is presented with the equations.

FRN MARGIN CALCULATIONS

Because the values of the parameters that specify a given FRN vary widely, it's difficult for an investor to compare directly two different FRNs. For example, how is an investor to compare (1) a 2-year FRN that resets monthly and is spread 10bp over 1-month LIBOR and (2) a 3-year FRN that resets quarterly and is spread 30bp over 3-month LIBOR? The fact that the parameters of FRNs may be and are set over a wide range has precluded the establishment of a standard method for valuing FRNs.

To value an FRN, an investor cannot use the standard present-value calculation he would use to value a fixed-coupon note or bond, unless he's willing to make an *explicit forecast of the future path of interest rates.* Specifically, to apply the bond equation to an FRN, the investor must forecast the value of the reference index on each of the remaining reset dates—and thereby the coupon rate that the FRN will pay in each of its remaining coupon periods.

Analysts and investors use different methods to compare and value

TABLE 17–1
Notation: Conventions Used for FRNs

m_q = quoted margin or spread to the reference index
m_s = simple margin for FRNs
m_{as} = adjusted simple margin for FRNs
m_t = total margin for FRNs
m_{at} = adjusted total margin for FRNs
m_d = discounted margin
F = face value or par
R = redemption value
P = clean price (price excluding accrued interest)
P_a = adjusted price (price adjusted for one-time carry effect)
AI = accrued interest: last coupon date to settlement date
N = remaining number of coupon payments
T_{sm} = days from settlement to maturity
T_{sn} = days from settlement to next coupon payment
T_n = days from settlement to nth coupon payment
A_y = assumed number of days in a year for interest earned
C = coupon payment
C_n = next coupon payment
w = number of coupon payments per year
r_f = finance rate from settlement to next coupon date
r_i = reference index rate
r_{ic} = reference index rate for the current coupon period
r_{ik} = reference index rate for the kth coupon period
r_{ia} = assumed average index rate over remaining life of an FRN
y_{tm} = yield to maturity
v_d = the discount factor, $v_d = \left[1 + \left(r_{ia} + m_d\right)h\right]^{-1}$
h = approximate length of compounding period, $h = \dfrac{365.25}{A_y w}$

FRNs. No one method is inherently better than another. Thus, the choice an investor makes as to which method he'll use to compare FRNs typically depends on his preferences and on the set of investment vehicles among which he's choosing.

The use of margin calculations to value and compare FRNs originated when banks began to issue FRNs to fund their floating-rate loan portfolios. Naturally, the issuing bank was interested in the *margin* or *spread*[1] between the rate on the asset (floating-rate loan) it was funding and the rate on the liability (FRN) it was incurring when both rates were based on the same reference index.

Below, we present several of the standard margin methods used by analysts and investors to value FRNs. We begin our discussion of margin calculations with the definitions of current yield and rollover yield. Although these yields are *not* margins, they are the basis for the standard margin calculations.

Current Yield

The current yield of an FRN is analogous to that of a fixed-coupon note or bond. Thus, the current yield of an FRN is defined as its *current* coupon rate times its face value divided by its clean price. Let

y_c = current yield

r_{ic} = reference index rate for the current coupon period

m_q = quoted margin or spread to the reference index

F = face value

P = clean price

Then, for an FRN, current yield is calculated as follows:

$$y_c = \frac{(r_{ic} + m_q)F}{P}$$

The calculation of the current yield offered by an FRN has one virtue: it's quick and dirty. However, this calculation ignores, *inter alia,*

[1] In a discussion of FRNs, the use of the two terms, *margin* and *spread,* can be confusing. *Spread* typically refers to the difference between the *reference index* and the *coupon rate.* Various measures of the return of FRNs are defined as *margins.* However, the two terms mean the same thing—a difference between two interest rates—and may be used interchangeably.

any discount or premium at which the FRN is bought; thus, a comparison of FRNs based on their respective current yields is just as problematic as is a comparison of fixed-coupon notes based on their respective current yields.

Holding-Period Yield

An alternative method for valuing FRNs is based on the notion of a horizon rate of return. When we discussed measures of yield for fixed-coupon notes, we derived a formula for holding-period yield, which is a horizon rate of return (Chapter 10).

We can also determine holding-period yield for an FRN. In this case, we must take the holding period to be the time from the valuation date until the FRN's next coupon-payment date. As in the case for bonds, we must *assume* what the price of the FRN will be on the next coupon-reset date.[2] The holding-period yield of an FRN is also referred to as its *money market or rollover yield.*

The formula for calculating money market yield on an FRN is straightforward. Let

y_{hp} = holding-period yield

r_{ic} = reference-index rate for the current coupon period

m_q = quoted margin or spread to the reference index

F = face value

P = clean settlement price

P_n = assumed clean price on next coupon date

AI = accrued interest from last coupon date to settlement date

A_{ln} = number of days from last coupon date to next coupon date

T_{sn} = number of days from settlement date to next coupon date

A_y = assumed number of days in a year for interest earned

[2] It is commonly assumed that the price of an FRN equals par on reset dates. This is a reasonable assumption given that the FRN resets to a *market rate* and the issuer has a satisfactory credit rating. For example, an FRN with a *binding* cap will not, in general, price to par on the reset date. Likewise, if an issuer's credit rating for their *short-term* debt is unsatisfactory, it is likely that their FRNs will not reprice to par on the reset date.

Then, holding-period yield for an FRN is calculated as follows:

$$y_{hp} = \left[\frac{\left(P_n + \left(r_{ic} + m_q\right)F\,A_{ln}/A_y\right) - (P + AI)}{P + AI}\right]\frac{A_y}{T_{sn}}$$

Simple Margin

During a coupon period, FRNs often trade at a discount or a premium to par. If an investor is valuing an FRN that he either intends or might hold to *maturity,* he will, in his valuation of the FRN, want to take into account amortization of a premium or accretion of a discount. The *simple margin* takes into account any amortization of a premium or accretion of a discount over the FRN's remaining term to maturity.

The simple margin of an FRN is obtained by adding (1) the amortization of a premium or the accretion of a discount over the FRN's remaining term to maturity (measured in basis points) to (2) the FRN's spread over the index rate (measured in basis points). Let

m_q = quoted margin or spread to the reference index, in basis points

m_s = simple margin for an FRN, in basis points

R = redemption value of an FRN

P = clean price of an FRN

T_{sm} = days from settlement to maturity

A_y = assumed number of days in a year for interest earned

Then, for an FRN, simple margin is calculated as follows:

$$m_s = \left[\frac{100(R - P)}{\left(T_{sm}/A_y\right)} + m_q\right]\frac{100}{P}$$

Adjusted Price

A trader who intends to *finance* the purchase of an FRN will want to make a *one-time* adjustment to the FRN's price to account for the carry from the valuation date to the *next* reset date. Given the finance rate, r_f, the *carry-adjusted* forward price, as of next reset date, can be determined. If the trader then discounts this carry-adjusted price by the *assumed* average coupon rate, he gets the FRN's discounted forward price; this price is called the FRN's *adjusted price.*

Specifically, an FRN's adjusted clean price is calculated as follows. Let

P_a = adjusted clean price of an FRN
r_{ic} = reference index rate for the current coupon period
m_q = quoted margin or spread to the reference index, in basis points
F = face value
P = clean settlement price
r_{ia} = assumed average index rate over the remaining term of an FRN
AI = accrued interest from last coupon-payment date to settlement date
T_{sn} = number of days from the settlement date to the next coupon-payment date
A_y = assumed number of days in a year for calculating interest earned
r_f = funding rate

Then, the adjusted clean price of the FRN is given by the expression,

$$P_a = P - \frac{\left[\left(r_{ic} + m_q\right)F - (P + AI)r_f\right]\left(T_{sn}/A_y\right)}{\left[1 + \left(T_{sn}/A_y\right)r_{ia}\right]}$$

Adjusted Simple Margin

We can now *adjust* the simple margin for the one-time carry effect by substituting the adjusted price, P_a, for the settlement price, P, in the equation for simple margin. The equation for *adjusted margin* is:

$$m_{as} = \left[\frac{100\left(R - P_a\right)}{\left(T_{sm}/A_y\right)} + m_q\right]\frac{100}{P_a}$$

Total Margin and Adjusted Total Margin

An FRN *pays* interest on its face value, but an investor who buys an FRN *earns* interest based on the price he paid for it. That is, simple and adjusted simple margin ignore the *current yield* effect. The above definitions of simple and adjusted margin can be extended to include this income effect. If we add the current yield effect to simple margin, we obtain the *total margin, m_t*, for an FRN. Specifically, total margin is defined as follows:

$$m_t = \left[\frac{100(R-P)}{\left(T_{sm}/A_y\right)} + m_q + (R-P)r_{ia} \right] \frac{100}{P}$$

As in the case of adjusted simple margin, total adjusted margin, m_{at}, adjusts total margin for the one-time carry effect. The equation for total adjusted margin is:

$$m_{at} = \left[\frac{100(R-P_a)}{\left(T_{sm}/A_y\right)} + m_q + \left(R-P_a\right)r_{ia} \right] \frac{100}{P_a}$$

FRNs: DISCOUNTED VALUE CALCULATIONS

The above definitions of *margin* are useful measures for comparing different FRNs. These margin calculations are similar in their usefulness to the simple yield concept for fixed-coupon notes and bonds. From our discussion of present value, a superior valuation method is to discount the cash flows that an FRN will pay out in the future back to the present. However, to apply the discounted cash flow technique, we must assume values for the reference index on each of the future reset dates.

Before continuing, we note that, while the definition of v that we use in this chapter differs from the one we have used elsewhere in this book, the meaning of v and its use is always the same.

Yield to Maturity

Several definitions of an FRN's yield to maturity can be defined depending on the assumptions and forecasts that the analyst is willing to make. We present below the standard assumptions and resultant equations.

Equal Coupon Rates and Periods

The *bond equation* can be used to determine the present value, or price, of an FRN as the discounted value of its future cash flows. To do so, we must forecast the *average* value of the reference index over all future reset dates and assume that all payments made by the FRN, after the next coupon payment, occur at equal intervals during a 365.25 day year. Let

r_{ic} = reference index rate for the current coupon period

r_{ia} = assumed average reference index rate

m_q = quoted margin or spread to the reference index

$$h = \frac{365.25}{A_y w}$$

$$C = (r_{ia} + m_q)Fh$$

$$C_n = (r_{ic} + m_q)F(T_{sn}/A_y)$$

$$v = (1 + y_{tm}/w)^{-1}$$

$$v_{sn} = [1 + y_{tm}(T_{sn}/A_y)]^{-1}$$

Then, the clean price of an FRN is given by the expression:

$$P = v_{sn}\left[C\sum_{n=1}^{N-1} v^n + Rv^{N-1} + C_n\right] - AI$$

To determine an FRN's yield-to-maturity, y_{tm}, we must use an analytic technique such as Newton-Raphson to solve by iteration for the FRN's yield to maturity given its price.

In Chapter 11, we presented a *closed-form solution* for the *price* of a fixed-coupon note or bond. Similarly, we can simplify the above price-yield equation. Using the annuity formula,

$$\sum_{n=1}^{N} v^n = \frac{v(v^N - 1)}{v - 1}$$

we can rewrite the price-yield equation for an FRN as follows:

$$P = v_{sn}\left[C\frac{v(v^{N-1} - 1)}{v - 1} + Rv^{N-1} + C_n\right] - AI$$

where the variables are defined as above.

Equal Coupon Rates and Exact Coupon Periods

If we are unwilling to assume that all payments made by the FRN occur at equal intervals during a 365-day year, then we can use a modified version of the *true yield* or *exact-date* bond equation to determine the present value, or price, of the FRN. While the assumed coupon rate for each reset is equal, the coupon payments will now depend on the length of the coupon period. Let

$$T_k = \text{days from settlement to } k\text{th coupon payment}$$
$$r_{ic} = \text{reference index rate for the current coupon period}$$
$$r_{ia} = \text{assumed average reference index rate}$$
$$m_q = \text{quoted margin or spread to the reference index}$$
$$t_k = wT_k/A_y$$
$$C_k = \left(r_{ia} + m_q\right)F\left(T_k - T_{k-1}/A_y\right)$$
$$C_n = \left(r_{ic} + m_q\right)F\left(T_{sn}/A_y\right)$$
$$v = \left(1 + y_{tm}/w\right)^{-1}$$

Then, the clean price of an FRN is given by the expression:

$$P = \sum_{k=1}^{N-1} C_k v^{t_k} + Rv^{t_{N-1}} + C_n - AI$$

To determine an FRN's yield-to-maturity, y_{tm}, we must use an analytic technique such as Newton-Raphson to solve by iteration for the FRN's yield to maturity given its price.

Different Coupon Rates and Exact Coupon Periods

The general case requires a specific forecast value for the reference index for each future reset date. The only difference between the general case and the equal-coupon-rates and exact-coupon-periods case is the definition of the coupon payment C_k. The price-yield equation is the same in both cases. Let

$$T_k = \text{days from settlement to } k\text{th coupon payment}$$
$$r_{ic} = \text{reference index rate for the current coupon period}$$
$$r_{ik} = \text{assumed reference index rate for the } k\text{th coupon period}$$
$$m_q = \text{quoted margin or spread to the reference index}$$

$$t_k = wT_k / A_y$$

$$C_k = (r_{ik} + m_q) F (T_k - T_{k-1} / A_y)$$

$$C_n = (r_{ic} + m_q) F (T_{sn} / A_y)$$

$$v = (1 + y_{tm} / w)^{-1}$$

Then, the clean price of an FRN is given by the expression:

$$P = \sum_{k=1}^{N-1} C_k v^{t_k} + R v^{t_{N-1}} + C_n - AI$$

To determine an FRN's yield-to-maturity, y_{tm}, we must use an analytic technique such as Newton-Raphson to solve by iteration for the FRN's yield to maturity given its price.

Discounted Margin

The above equation for an FRN's yield to maturity under the assumption of *equal coupon rates and equal coupon periods* can be interpreted as a *discounted* margin over the reference index. Whereas simple and total margin are similar to current yield, discounted margin is related to yield to maturity, since it is a function of the discount rate used to calculate the present value of the FRN's future cash flows.

Discounted margin is defined as margin over the reference index such that the sum of the reference index value and the discount margin equal the discount rate that equates the present values of the FRN's future cash flows to its current price. For each of the above equations for the yield to maturity of an FRN, we can define a discounted margin as follows:

discounted margin = yield to maturity − reference index value

Using the above definition, we can modify the equation for yield to maturity under the assumption of equal coupon rates and equal coupon periods to solve for discounted margin. Let

m_d = discounted margin

r_{ic} = reference index rate for the current coupon period

r_{ia} = assumed average reference index rate

m_q = quoted margin or spread to the reference index

$$h = \frac{365.25}{A_y w}$$

$$C = (r_{ia} + m_q)Fh$$

$$C_n = (r_{ic} + m_q)F(T_{sn}/A_y)$$

$$v = [1 + (r_{ia} + m_d)]^{-1}$$

$$v_{sn} = [1 + (r_{ic} + m_d)(T_{sn}/A_y)]^{-1}$$

Then, the clean price of an FRN is given by the expression:

$$P = v_{sn}\left[C\sum_{n=1}^{N-1} v^n + Rv^{N-1} + C_n\right] - AI$$

To determine an FRN's discounted margin, m_d, we must use an analytic technique such as Newton-Raphson to solve by iteration for the FRN's discounted margin given its price.

Discounted Margin for Perpetual FRNs

In the late 1980's many European-based banks issued *perpetual* FRNs, that is, FRNs with *no* maturity date. For a perpetual FRN, it can be shown that the summation in the formula for discounted margin is an example of the sum of an infinite geometric series. Hence, the formula for the discounted margin of a perpetual FRN can be written as follows:

$$P = v_{sn}\left[C_n + \frac{(r_{ia} + m_q)F}{(r_{ia} + m_d)}\right] - AI$$

where

$$v_{sn} = [1 + (r_{ia} + m_d)(T_{sn}/A_y)]^{-1}$$

INDEX-LINKED BONDS

A *fixed-coupon,* index-linked bond is a specific type of *floating-rate* instrument. In a strict sense, index-linked bonds are not FRNs because their coupon is fixed. They are however variable-rate instruments, since their coupon payments vary as a function of some specified index. While the coupon rate is fixed, the coupon payments vary as a function of some specified index. Both the redemption value, *R,* and the face value, *F,* are periodically adjusted as the value of the index changes. Since a bond's coupon payment is the product of the bond's coupon rate times its face value, it follows that the coupon payment will increase as the value of the index increases and vice versa.

To adjust for the observed changes in the index since the issuance of the bond, the face and redemption values are adjusted by the ratio of the current index value to the value of the index at the time of issuance. When one calculates changes in the index, it's important to note that *time* is measured between *observation* dates for the index and *not* between reporting or publication dates.

While the amount of the various coupon payments will vary with changes in the value of the index, the coupon-rate for the bond is fixed for the life of the bond. However, as *future* coupon payments can only be determined given an *unpublished* value for the index, the bond's future cash flows can only be valued by assuming future values for the index. Nevertheless, the constant coupon rate allows the analyst to value an index-linked bond using the true-yield version of the bond equation.

Typically, the face and redemption value of index-linked bonds adjust as a function of the consumer price index. In this way the periodic coupon payments adjust upwards and downwards as the inflation increases and decreases. This relationship between the cash flows of the bond and the rate of inflation means that the bond pays a *real* rate of interest. Hence, such index-linked bonds are also referred to as *real-rate* bonds.

Currently, Australia, Canada, Mexico, Sweden and the United Kingdom issue index-linked bonds. The United States Treasury has studied the issuance of index-linked bonds but has not, as yet, issued any. We will now discuss an example of index-linked bonds: British RPI-linked gilts.

United Kingdom RPI-linked Gilts

RPI-linked gilts are index-linked securities issued by the British government. They carry a fixed coupon and have been issued occasionally since March of 1981 with various tenors. Both the face and redemption values adjust for periodic changes in the consumer price index, General Index of Retail Prices (RPI). In the case of index-linked gilts, the current face and redemption values are a function of the value of the RPI *eight months prior* to the most recent coupon date. The use of the RPI value as of eight months prior rather than the most current value is a function of the desire to know the value of the coupon payment well in advance of the payment date and to account for the thirty-seven day ex-dividend period.

First, the face and redemption values are adjusted for changes in the RPI from eight months prior to the date of issuance to the value eight months prior to the most recently known value. This value is then adjusted for the inflation rate implied by the two most recent values for the RPI for the period from the most recently known RPI to the next coupon date. Given the *current* face and redemption values, we can calculate prices and nominal and real rates of return.

Price/Yield Equation

If we assume rates for future monthly inflation, we can determine the price, nominal yield, and yield to maturity of an RPI-linked gilt as follows. Let

RPI_k = RPI value for month k

RPI_c = current value for RPI; most recently published value

RPI_{k-8} = value for RPI eight months prior to the kth month

RPI_b = base value of RPI; value of RPI eight months prior to date of issuance

t_{ck} = time in years, between RPI observation dates in months c and k.

i_{ck} = estimated or assumed rate of inflation between RPI observation dates in months c and k.

C_k = the adjusted kth coupon payment

R_N = the adjusted redemption payment

T_k = number of days between the settlement date and the receipt of kth payment

$$t_k = \frac{wT_k}{365}$$

Given current and past values for the RPI and an inflation-rate forecast i_{ck}, we can forecast the value for the RPI in month k as follows

$$RPI_k = RPI_c\left(1+i_{ck}\right)^{t_{ck}}$$

In this case, the adjusted n^{th} coupon payment is given by

$$C_k = C\frac{RPI_{k-8}}{RPI_b}$$

and the forecast redemption value is given by

$$R_N = R\frac{RPI_{k-8}}{RPI_b}$$

From the above calculations for the adjusted coupon payments and the redemption value, we can calculate the price of an RPI-linked gilt as follows:

$$P=\left[\sum_{k=1}^{N} C_k v^{t_k} + R_N v^{t_N}\right] - AI$$

The above equation cannot be restated as a closed-form expression using the annuity equation because the exponents of v in the summation are *not* equal to the integer-index value k and the coupon payments are a function of k.

To determine the yield-to-maturity given the price using the Newton-Raphson algorithm we must take the first derivative of the above equation with respect to v. As before, we define $f(v)$ as follows:

$$\mathrm{f}(v)=\left[\sum_{k=1}^{N} C_k v^{t_k} + R_N v^{t_N}\right] - AI - P$$

and, therefore,

$$\mathrm{f}'(v)=\left[C\sum_{k=1}^{N} t_k v^{t_k-1} + R_N t_N v^{t_N-1}\right] - P$$

Converting Between the Nominal and Real Rates of Return

Given the nominal rate of return and the periodic inflation rate, one can determine the equivalent real rate of return on any security. Hence, the real rate of return of a RPI-linked gilt is given by the Fisher equation, which relates real and nominal rates.

Let

i_{ann} = annual inflation rate

y_w = (nominal) yield to maturity compounded w times per year

$y_{w,real}$ = real yield to maturity compounded w times per year

then,

$$y_{w,real} = \left(\frac{1+y_w}{1+i_{ann}} - 1 \right)$$

The above equation for the real rate of return, given the nominal rate, can be inverted to solve for the nominal rate given the real rate. That is,

$$y_w = (1+i_{ann})(1+y_{w,real}) - 1$$

THE NEXT CHAPTER

In the next and final chapter, we describe the various sorts of sovereign debt issued by the major countries in whose debt international investors most typically invest. We also present price/yield equations for all of the sovereign debt we describe.

CHAPTER 18

FIXED-INCOME SECURITIES WORLDWIDE: CALCULATIONS

A comprehensive book on the topic of money market paper and bonds worldwide could easily run several thousand pages, and it would need to be updated *at least* every two or three years. Our focus has been and continues to be on *calculations* for money market paper and bonds that pay a fixed or a variable rate and that are neither puttable nor callable, that is, instruments that have *no* imbedded options.

Most investors who venture *cross-border to buy money market paper or bonds* are financial institutions. Also, the instruments they are most likely to buy are commercial paper, CDs, and sovereign debt; and the related trades they are most likely to do are Eurodollar deposits, repo, reverses, and securities lending.

The category, sovereign debt typically comprises bills (discount paper) and fixed-rate notes and bonds of varying maturities; it may also comprise floating-rate notes and index-linked issues. Typically, sovereign debt is denominated in the currency of the issuing country, but there are exceptions; for example, the U.K., France and Italy issue some national debt denominated in ECUs, a unit of account established by the European *Economic Community* (*EC*) countries as a step in their proposed movement to full economic union and to use of a common currency.

In this chapter, we will confine our discussion in two ways. First, we will consider only instruments issued and traded in the domestic markets of the following countries: the United States, the United Kingdom,

France, Germany, Italy, Japan, and Canada.[1] Second, we will give equations for price-yield calculations only for those instruments that require specific formulas as opposed to the general price-yield formulas that we haven't already covered in this book.

Readers who want to research calculations for the many fixed-income instruments traded worldwide that we do not cover in this chapter should consult the following sources or subsequent editions of them:

CSFB Guide to: Yield Calculations in the International Bond and Money Markets, Crédit Suisse First Boston (Irwin Professional Publishing, 1988).

The European Bond Markets: An Overview and Analysis for Money Market Managers and Traders, Stuart McLean, Ed. (Irwin Professional Publishing, 1993).

Formulae for Yield and other Calculations, a publication of ISMA (the International Securities Marketing Association).

The Global Bond Markets, Lederman, Jess and Park, Keith H. (Irwin Professional Publishing, 1991).

Caveat: As a result of the growing internationalization of markets and of the attempts of various groups (e.g., the EC countries) to harmonize financial practices, this is a time at which anything said today about the classes of securities issued in a country or about how trades of these securities are cleared, internally or cross border, may well be dated tomorrow.

One final note: Jargon varies country to country, so we've made our own rules. Specifically, in discussing sovereign debt, we try to refer to *short-term, discount* paper as *bills;* to *medium-term, fixed- or variable-rate* paper as *notes;* to *long-term, fixed- or variable-rate* paper as *bonds;* and to *medium- and longer-term, zero-coupon* paper as *zero-coupon bonds* or just *zeros.*

---

[1] We include U.S. money market paper and Treasury securities in our discussion because a summary of what we've already said about the terms of such instruments takes little space and may facilitate comparisons by the reader. For example, between U.S. and other sovereign debt. Also, it's useful to sketch briefly the process of settlement and clearing for U.S. instruments because that process is a good paradigm to bear in mind when one tries to follow clearing and settlement procedures in other countries. Generally, the clearing of money market paper and government issues is simpler and quicker under U.S. procedures than under procedures prevailing in other countries.

NON-SOVEREIGN MONEY MARKET PAPER WORLDWIDE

The menu of money market instruments routinely found in the national capital markets we're about to discuss includes some *discount* paper (T bills, commercial paper, and bankers' acceptances), and several interest-bearing instruments: repos, reverses, Eurodollar deposits, CDs (domestic and Euro), and municipal notes. Interest on Eurocurrency deposits is everywhere figured on an ACT/360 basis. In most countries, price-yield calculations for other money market securities (or transactions) are also made on an ACT/360 basis; but in the United Kingdom and Canada, price-yield calculations are made on an ACT/365 basis.[2] In either case, we've already said, from the point of view of calculations, all that needs to be said about such paper.

One point worth making, with respect to money market trades, is that when repo is done outside the United States, the trade is typically structured as a *buy back;* that does not alter the interest calculation associated with the trade, but it does restrict the ability of the lender of money to reprice his collateral. We also note that U.K. government debt, gilts, could not be repoed until recently.

NON-SOVEREIGN NOTES AND BONDS WORLDWIDE

In general, within a given country, the price-yield equation (i.e., *the bond equation*) for non-sovereign issues is the same as that for sovereign issues—be it the former fixed-rate, variable-rate, or zero-coupon. However, when one moves from sovereign to non-sovereign debt, two things typically do change. First, the payment convention changes; in Europe and North America, it's typical that government-guaranteed, public (muni), and corporate bonds pay according to some variant of the 30/360 convention. Second, settlement of non-sovereign issues often takes longer than settlement of sovereign issues; and ex-dividend policy may differ between the two classes of securities. One final point: corporates often

---

[2] Recall that, in Chapter 5, we discussed at length ACT/360 and other interest-payment conventions.

issue a wider class of securities than do other borrowers; a corporate issue may have a sinking fund, be self-amortizing, and so on; to make price-yield calculations for a corporate having any of these features, one must *use the general bond equation.*

ISMA CALCULATIONS

The International Securities Marketing Association (ISMA)[3] has defined standard price-yield calculations for most instruments traded in the world's capital markets. In the following six sections, we present the most important ISMA equations. Examples will not be presented as the ISMA equations for money market instruments and coupon-bearing bonds are identical to those presented earlier in this book. Therefore, in discussing the bond market practices with respect to the sovereign debt of different countries, we will refer to these standard equations. In cases where it is market practice not to use an ISMA equation, we will present this equation and an example of how it's used.

The following are the ISMA price-yield formulas. For consistency with our earlier chapters, we have restated these formulas using our notation.

ISMA FORMULAS FOR MONEY MARKET INSTRUMENTS

ISMA employs the standard equations for money market instruments. The definitions of the variables and all of the discount equations can be found in Chapter 6. For convenience, we repeat only two variants of the equations for discount instruments.

$$d = \left(\frac{R-P}{R}\right)\left(\frac{A_y}{T_{sm}}\right)$$

$$y_{365} = \frac{R}{P}d$$

[3] ISMA was formerly known as the Association of International Bond Dealers (AIBD).

and for interest-at-maturity, coupon-bearing instruments the ISMA equations are:

$$y_{365} = \left(\frac{1 + C\dfrac{T_{im}}{A_y}}{B} - 1 \right) \frac{A_y}{T_{sm}}$$

$$B = \left(\frac{1 + C\dfrac{T_{im}}{A_y}}{1 + y_{365}\dfrac{T_{sm}}{A_y}} \right)$$

ISMA NOTES

ISMA recognizes three variants of the price-yield equation—the standard, the Moosmüller, and the Braess-Fangmeyer methods. The standard method is identical to the standard bond equation defined in Chapter 11. Readers familiar with the price-yield equation employed by the U.S. Treasury will recognize that the Moosmüller formula is identical to that equation. The Braess-Fangmeyer method appears to be used only in Europe, particularly by domestic investors in the German capital market.

The Standard Method

ISMA uses the standard price-yield equation for notes and bonds, that is,

$$P = v^{t_{sn}} \left[C \sum_{n=1}^{N-1} v^n + Rv^{N-1} + C_n \right] - AI$$

$$= v^{t_{sn}} \left[C \frac{v\left(v^{N-1} - 1\right)}{v - 1} + Rv^{N-1} + C_n \right] - AI$$

The Moosmüller Method

The Moosmüller method uses money market discounting from the next coupon date back to the settlement date. This is the only difference between the Moosmüller method and the standard method for calculating prices and yields. This difference is seen in the lead factor of the Moosmüller equation for price given yield. This equation is as follows:

$$P = \left(\frac{1}{1 + t_{sn} y_w} \right) \left[C \frac{v\left(v^{N-1} - 1\right)}{v - 1} + Rv^{N-1} + C_n \right] - AI$$

The above equation is the equation used by the U.S. Treasury to determine, in the auctions of U.S. T notes and bonds, the price of the issue auctioned, given the yield established by the auction process.

The Braess-Fangmeyer Method

The Braess-Fangmeyer method computes prices and yields on an *annual basis,* that is, the relevant time interval is taken to be one year. Hence, coupon payments are annual, periodic yields are converted to annual yields before use, and remaining time to maturity is measured in years. This method contrasts to the standard bond equation where all measures are based on a coupon period; that is, coupon payments are per coupon period; yields are compounded at the frequency of payments per year; and time is measured in number of coupon periods remaining.

We must define several new variables before we present the Braess-Fangmeyer equation. Let

t_{sm} = time from settlement to maturity, in years according to relevant day-count convention

$\lambda = \text{int}\left(t_{sm}\right)$

$\phi = t_{sm} - \text{int}\left(t_{sm}\right)$

$\delta = 1/\left(1 + y_a\right)$

$\varphi = \text{int}\left(w\phi\right)$

$y_a = \left(1 + y_w\right)^w - 1$

AI_{BF} = accrued interest, as defined by the Braess-Fangmeyer method

where int(x) is the *integer function* that returns the *largest integer* that is less than or equal to the input variable, x. Given the definitions of the above variables, the Braess-Fangmeyer equation for price given yield is as follows:

$$P=\left(\frac{1}{1+\phi y_a}\right)\left\{\left[cF\left(1+\left(\frac{w-1}{w}\right)\frac{y_a}{2}\right)\left(\frac{1-\delta^{\lambda}}{y_a}\right)+R\delta^{\lambda}\right]\right.$$

$$\left.+C\left[1+\varphi\left(1+\left(\frac{\varphi+1}{w}\right)\frac{y_a}{2}\right)\right]\right\}-AI_{BF}$$

$$AI_{BF}=C\left[1-\left(wt_{sm}-\text{int}\left(wt_{sm}\right)\right)\right]$$

ISMA ZERO-COUPON NOTES

As in the case of coupon-bearing notes, ISMA recognizes three variants of the price-yield equation for zero-coupon notes and bonds: the standard, the Moosmüller, and the Braess-Fangmeyer methods. The standard method is identical to the standard bond equation for zero-coupon notes defined in Chapter 11. Again, the Braess-Fangmeyer method appears to be used only in Europe, particularly by domestic investors in the German capital market.

The Standard Method

ISMA uses the standard price-yield equation for zero-coupon notes that have a remaining time to maturity greater than one *compounding* period.[4] The ISMA equation is as follows:

$$P=Rv^{N-1+t_{sn}}$$

and

$$y_w=\left(\frac{R}{P}\right)^{N-1+t_{sn}}-1$$

[4] To aid the investor in choosing between alternative investments, zero-coupon yields are typically quoted on the same basis as coupon bonds. Hence, if coupon bonds are quoted on a *semi-annual compounded* basis then the *compounding period* for zero-coupon bonds would be six months, as measured by the appropriate day-count convention.

The Moosmüller Method

The Moosmüller method uses money market discounting from the next coupon date back to the settlement date. This difference is enough to prevent one from inverting the price-yield equation for zero-coupon notes and, hence, from obtaining a closed-form solution for yield given price.

The Moosmüller formula for price given yield is as follows:

$$P = \frac{Rv^{N-1}}{\left(1 + t_{sn} y_w\right)}$$

To solve for yield given price, we must apply the Newton-Raphson iteration technique to the above equation.

The Braess-Fangmeyer Method

The Braess-Fangmeyer method computes prices and yields on an *annual basis.* To give this equation for zeros, we set the coupon rate, c, equal to zero. Repeating the notation for the Braess-Fangmeyer method, let

t_{sm} = time from settlement to maturity, in years, according to relevant day-count convention

$$\lambda = \text{int}\left(t_{sm}\right)$$

$$\phi = t_{sm} - \text{int}\left(t_{sm}\right)$$

$$\delta = 1/\left(1 + y_a\right)$$

$$y_a = \left(1 + y_w\right)^w - 1$$

where int(x) is the *integer function* that returns the *largest integer* that is less than or equal to the input variable, x. Given the definitions of the above variables, the Braess-Fangmeyer equation for price given yield is as follows:

$$P = \left(\frac{R\delta^{\lambda}}{1 + \phi y_a}\right)$$

ISMA ODD-LAST-COUPON PERIOD

Occasionally, notes are issued with odd-last-coupon periods. While such notes are rarely issued in the United States, they are issued by various corporate issuers in the Eurobond market. The true-yield bond equation can obviously be used, without modification, to value notes with odd-last coupons. This follows from the fact that the true-yield bond equation discounts each cash flow using the exact time between the settlement date and the receipt date of the cash-flow.

On the other hand, we can extend the standard bond equation to handle notes with odd-last coupons by explicitly accounting for the *last* coupon payment in the same way that we account for the *next* coupon payment following purchase.

In addition to the variables used in the standard bond equation, we define a variable t_{lm} as the fraction of a *full* coupon period represented by the odd-last-coupon period. Let

T_{lm} = number of days from the coupon-payment date immediately preceeding the maturity date to the maturity date, according to the relevant day-count convention

$A_{l,l+1}$ = number of days from the coupon-payment date immediately preceeding the maturity date to the nominal-next-coupon date after the maturity date, according to the relevant day-count convention

$t_{lm} = T_{lm}/A_{l,l+1}$, the fraction of the nominal-last-coupon period from the next-to-last-coupon date to the maturity date, according to the relevant day-count convention

Then the ISMA price-yield equation for notes with an odd-last coupon period is as follows:

$$P = v^{t_{sn}}\left[C\sum_{n=1}^{N-2} v^n + \left(R + t_{lm}C\right)v^{N-2+t_{lm}} + C_n\right] - AI$$

$$= v^{t_{sn}}\left[C\frac{v\left(v^{N-2}-1\right)}{v-1} + \left(R + t_{lm}C\right)v^{N-2+t_{lm}} + C_n\right] - AI$$

ISMA STEPPED-COUPON NOTES

In the previous chapter, we presented the various valuation formulas for floating-rate notes. There is another class of notes whose coupons vary over time. These are referred to as *stepped-coupon* notes. The major difference between floating-rate notes and stepped-coupon notes is that, at issuance, *all* the future values for a stepped-coupon note are known, that is, the coupon rates and dates of the steps are known in advance. Therefore, no uncertainty exists as to the future values of the coupons as exists with floating-rate notes.

Given this known sequence of coupons, we can use the standard bond equation to relate the price and yield of a stepped-coupon note. To do so, we next present the appropriate ISMA formula for a bond that has two steps and is currently in its *first* step.[5] In this case, we need only account for the fact that the coupon payments will differ after the coupon has *stepped* to its new value; all other factors of the bond equation remain unchanged.

$$P = v^{t_{sn}}\left[C_1\sum_{n=1}^{N_1-1} v^n + C_2\sum_{n=N_1}^{N_1+N_2-1} v^n + Rv^{N_1+N_2-1} + C_n\right] - AI$$

$$= v^{t_{sn}}\left[C_1\sum_{n=1}^{N_1-1} v^n + C_2\sum_{n=1}^{N_1+N_2-1} v^n - C_2\sum_{n=1}^{N_1-1} v^n + Rv^{N_1+N_2-1} + C_n\right] - AI$$

Using the annuity equation, we obtain the following result for a two-step note:

$$P = v^{t_{sn}}\left[C_1\frac{v\left(v^{N_1-1}-1\right)}{v-1} + C_2\frac{v^{N_1}\left(v^{N_2}-1\right)}{v-1} + Rv^{N_1+N_2-1} + C_n\right] - AI$$

The analyst can extend the above equation for a note that has more than two steps.

---

[5] Obviously, if a bond is in its *last* step, the standard bond equation can be used without alteration.

ISMA FLOATING-RATE NOTES

The European Federation of Financial Analyst Societies (EFFAS) recommends the use of the discounted approach to the valuation of FRNs. In particular, they recommend the use of the equal-coupon rates and periods version of discounted margin. As the notation for the ISMA floating-rate note equation uses different definitions for the symbols we used in the bond equation, we shall repeat both the equation and the symbol definitions. For FRNs, the recommended equation by ISMA is as follows:

m_d = discounted margin

r_{ic} = reference index rate for the current coupon period

r_{ia} = assumed average reference index rate

m_q = quoted margin or spread to the reference index

$$h = \frac{365.25}{A_y w}$$

$$C = \left(r_{ia} + m_q\right)Fh$$

$$C_n = \left(r_{ic} + m_q\right)F\left(T_{sn}/A_y\right)$$

$$v = \left[1 + \left(r_{ia} + m_d\right)\right]^{-1}$$

$$v_{sn} = \left[1 + \left(r_{ic} + m_d\right)\left(T_{sn}/A_y\right)\right]^{-1}$$

Using this notation, the clean price of an FRN, according to the ISMA calculation is given by the expression:

$$P = v_{sn}\left[C\sum_{n=1}^{N-1} v^n + Rv^{N-1} + C_n\right] - AI$$

U.S. TREASURY ISSUES

In earlier chapters, we often used U.S. Treasury issues as examples. Here, for the convenience of the reader, we present, for U.S. sovereign debt, the same information that we present below for the sovereign debt of other nations.

Issues Routinely Sold

The U.S. Treasury auctions, according to a regular schedule, three types of securities: bills, notes, and bonds.

Treasury Bills

All Treasury bills are *discount* securities. The Treasury auctions 3-month, 6-month, and 1-year bills according to a schedule that ensures that a new 6-month bill is always a *reopening* of an old year bill, and a new 3-month bill is always a *reopening* of an old 6-month bill.

Occasionally, when it requires extra cash, the Treasury will issue a short-term *cash management bill.* The original maturities of such issues rarely exceed several weeks.

Treasury Notes

All Treasury notes pay a *fixed coupon,* are non-callable, and are redeemed at maturity at face value. Currently, the Treasury regularly auctions notes with original maturities of 2, 3, 5 and 10 years.

Treasury Bonds

The Treasury issues a single *fixed-coupon* bond; it is a *bullet bond* that has an original maturity of 30 years and is redeemed at maturity at face value. Treasury bonds used to be callable five years from maturity; but in recent years, the Treasury has issued only *non-callable* bonds in order to facilitate the stripping of its bonds.

Zero-Coupon Bonds

Currently, all new issues of Treasury bonds and of 10-year notes may be *stripped,* that is, divided into pieces—one piece for each coupon payment the issue will drop before maturity and one piece for the payment of corpus due at maturity. Each such separate piece constitutes a particular *zero-coupon* security, and each carries a unique identifying (*CUSIP*) number. Zero-coupon securities created by stripping Treasury notes and bonds are referred to as *STRIPs.* By combining appropriate STRIPs a dealer may *reconstitute* a strippable Treasury issue.

Method of Issuance

All Treasury securities are sold via *auctions* run by the Federal Reserve Bank of New York, an arm of the U.S. central bank.

Treasury Bills

All Treasury bills are issued through auctions in which bidders submit bids for specific face amounts; each bid is stated as a percentage discount rate carried to 2 decimal places. In a bill auction, the lowest bidders, that is, lowest discount rate, are awarded the full amount for which they bid. Bidders bidding what turns out to be the stop-out discount rate, the highest discount rate accepted, may receive only a prorated share of the dollar amount for which they bid.

Treasury Notes and Bonds

In the past, the U.S. Treasury issued all new notes and bonds via yield auctions in which the lowest bid yield up to the stop-out bid are accepted. Today, the Treasury issues two-year and five-year notes via Dutch auctions. In a Dutch auction dealers and investors are awarded their securities based on the *average accepted bid,* rather than at their submitted bid. The three- and ten-year notes, as well as the thirty-year bond continue to be auctioned under the regular auction rules.

Secondary Market Practices

The secondary market for U.S. Treasury securities, which is made by hundreds of dealers, small and large, is highly liquid. Some 30-odd dealers, domestic and non-domestic, have been designated as *primary dealers* by the Federal Reserve. The interdealer (*inside*) markets that primary dealers make in Treasury securities is brokered by four or five competing firms.

Treasury Bills

In the secondary market, a Treasury bill is quoted on the basis of the current *yield,* carried to *three decimal places,* at which it is bid and offered.

Treasury Notes and Bonds

In the secondary market, Treasury notes and bonds are quoted as a *percentage of face value* plus so and so many *32s*. Thus, a U.S. Treasury bond that was offered at 99.25% of face value would be quoted as being offered at 99-08. Often, note and bond traders fine tune their bids and offers to *64s*. If a bond were offered at a price of 99 and 17/64, the extra 1/64 asked for the bond would be indicated by *a + sign,* and the bond would be quoted as being offered at 99-08+.

Applicable Conventions

Key conventions used in the trading of U.S. Treasury securities are as follows:

Quotes

Bills are quoted in terms of yield. Notes, bonds, and STRIPs are quoted as a percentage of face value carried to the nearest 32nd or 64th of one percent.

The prices quoted for these securities in the *inside market* for Treasuries are disseminated by various brokers whose screens dot the desks of all traders of Treasuries at primary dealers. These price quotes, at which investors are currently dealing, are available to subscribers on various proprietary screens maintained by individual interdealer brokers: the latter include Cantor Fitzgerald, Bloomberg, Telerate, and Reuters.

Settlement and Value Dates

The value date is the settlement date. Trades done for cash settlement settle on the *trade date*. Normal settlement is T+1, where T represents the *trade date*. Corporate settlement is T+3. Other forward settlement dates may be negotiated between the buyer and seller.

Interest-Payment Convention

All Treasury bills are *discount* securities on which the governing day-count convention is *ACT/360*.

All Treasury notes and bonds pay interest *semiannually*. Also, all Treasury notes and bonds accrue interest according to the *ACT/ACT* day-count convention.

All Treasury STRIPs, created by dealers, are *de facto* zero-coupon securities that pay at maturity the face amount purchased. Price-yield calculations for STRIPs are based on the ACT/ACT payment convention.

Coupon-Payment Frequency and Date

Coupon interest is paid semi-annually on notes and bonds. No coupon interest is paid on bills and STRIPs; these discount securities that are redeemed at maturity at par.

Settlement of Trades

Currently, the Treasury issues bills, notes, and bonds only *in book-entry* form. There are *no* physical Treasury securities. Instead, the Federal Reserve tracks, for banks and any *other depository institutions* (*DIs*) that have a book-entry account with it, *the interests* that each such DI has in every Treasury issue. DIs in turn track for what internal and for what customer (including dealer and trust) accounts they are holding Treasury securities.

The Treasury effects payments of coupon interest and redemption of principal for its outstanding issues via the Federal Reserve. The latter credits, over the Fed wire, payments of interest and principal due to the reserve accounts that DIs maintain with it.

All trades of Treasury issues are *settled payment versus delivery*. Payment is made over the Federal Reserve *wire* and results in a corresponding change in the Fed's book-entry records.

Treasury Bills

Early in the day, T bills may be traded for *cash* (*same-day*) settlement. Later in the day, bills can only be traded for *regular settlement,* that is, for settlement on *the next business day* or on any forward date to which the buyer and seller may agree.

Treasury Notes, Bonds, and STRIPs

Treasury notes, bonds, and STRIPs are normally traded for *regular settlement,* that is, the *value date* is T+1. Corporate settlement (T+3) and other forward settlement dates can always be negotiated between buyers and sellers of governments.

Price-Yield Calculations

Price and yield calculations for U.S. Treasury notes and bonds are done according to the standard ISMA equations.

U.K. SOVEREIGN DEBT

In the United Kingdom, *bonds are referred to as stocks;* thus, bonds issued and guaranteed by the U.K. government are known as *gilts* (for *gilt-edged stocks*). Unlike the U.S. Treasury, the U.K. Exchequer has, over time, issued a large, untidy mix of issues; consequently, despite the fact that, for the three fiscal years starting in 1988–1989, the United Kingdom ran a budget surplus and retired debt, there are 100-odd gilt issues outstanding.

Outstanding gilts come in *four* types and carry *nine* names. The four types are: (1) *straight bonds* (most are bullets, but some are callable), (2) *convertibles,* (3) *indexed-linked bonds,* and (4) *irredeemable* (a.k.a. *perpetuals* or *undateds*). The nine names are Exchequer, Treasury, Funding, Redemption, Transport, Gas, Conversion, Consols, and War Loan. Since bonds carrying the above names are all backed by the same U.K. government guarantee, the names have *no* practical significance. In recent years, the U.K. government has issued only Treasuries and Exchequers.

Issues Routinely Sold

As noted, the U.K. issues bills and a wide range of notes and bonds. To distinguish among U.K. notes and bonds, traders and investors, in referring to a gilt issue, always specify the name; the coupon; the maturity date, if any (perpetuals have no maturity date); and the call date, if any (callable gilts are also known as *double-dated* bonds).

It is common for gilts to be issued in *partly-paid* form. On such issues, the investor buys a bond by making a part payment and commits to make, in the future, up to three further part payments or calls.

Most gilts are held in registered form but some issues may be held in bearer form. The registrar for gilts is the Bank of England.

Bills

U.K. Treasury bills are issued by the government in anticipation of future revenues. Some U.K. T bills are issued with an original maturity out to one year, but most such bills are issued with an original maturity of 91 days.

Bullet Bonds

The vast majority of outstanding gilts are fixed-rate bullet bonds with a single, fixed maturity date.

Callable Bonds

Over 10% of U.K. gilts comprise callable bonds that are redeemable at a date prior to maturity on 3-months notice by the U.K. government.

Currently, most outstanding callable issues have call dates between 1998 and 2004. These bonds were issued at a time when interest rates were high; consequently, the market expects these bonds to be called.

Index-Linked Bonds

In the United Kingdom, as elsewhere, high inflation rates caused investors to be concerned about the *real rate of return* they could earn by investing in governments. In response to this concern, the U.K. Treasury began to issue bonds, the coupon payments and final redemption value of which were linked to *the Retail Price Index* (*RPI*). These issues initially offered a real return of just over 2.5%, but that rate is now higher. Indexed gilts were designed for and initially offered only to U.K. pension funds, but the restriction on who could buy them was later lifted.

Perpetual Bonds

The United Kingdom has a small amount of *irredeemable* bonds outstanding. These bonds carry no maturity, but they may be redeemed after a certain date on three months' notice. In all cases, the earliest such date has passed. The United Kingdom issued most of its *perpetuals* in the low-interest-rate environment following WW II; consequently, these securities trade at a discount, and it's unlikely that any of them will be redeemed any time soon.

Convertibles (Bonds)

The amount of *convertible gilts* outstanding is small, and all such bonds have in fact been converted to *bullet* bonds. Two such issues were the only gilts to have *sinking funds*.

Method of Issuance

All U.K. government securities are issued via auction by the Bank of England.

Bills

A new issue of U.K. T bills is auctioned weekly. Historically, the amount of new bills issued each week has been small.

Notes and Bonds

In 1979, the United Kingdom began offering fixed-size, new issues (stocks) through price auctions in which it sets a minimum tender price. If a stock is under subscribed (i.e., bids at or above the *minimum* tender price for the stock are for an amount less than the size fixed for the issue), the Bank of England may issue the balance of the stock via *taps* (reopenings). The Bank of England may also offer *taplets* or *tranchettes* of issues that were previously fully subscribed.

The Bank of England may also do a *new* tender or auction of a fully subscribed, outstanding stock; this new tender is handled like the auction of a new issue; typically, it creates a new issue with a *short* first coupon; once that first coupon is paid, the new issue trades fungible with the outstanding issue that's been reopened. Lastly, the Bank of England has done straight auctions of several new issues. It has also used *reverse auctions* to retire debt.

Secondary-Market Practices

On October 27, 1986, The U.K. had *Big Bang* day—not to recreate the universe, but rather to reform the gilt market. After Big Bang, market-making dealers were permitted to trade both with other market-making dealers and with customers, that is, to trade on *a dual capacity* basis, acting both as *principal* and as *agent*. Post Big Bang, the secondary market for gilts moved off the floor of the London Stock Exchange to an upstairs, dealer-made OTC market. This market is brokered by three inter-dealer brokers.

An investor who buys gilts from a market-making (*primary*) dealer is charged *no* commission. However, an investor who buys gilts from an *agent* is charged a commission, which he would be well advised to negotiate before he buys.

Investors *may not* short gilts, but dealers *may* do so. Dealers are permitted to cover their shorts in one way only—by borrowing gilts (against cash or equivalent collateral) from one of the ten Stock Exchange Money Brokers (SEMBs).

U.K. regulations used to *preclude the repoing of gilts,* but dealers in London have for some time actively engaged in repos and reverses that involve the sovereign debt of other countries and an assortment of currencies. Also, the Bank of England had announced, as of spring 1995, that it intended to create a repo market in gilts.

The secondary market in U.K. bills is thin for two reasons. Issuance is, as noted, small. Also, the British clearing banks must hold such bills as reserves. Therefore, the market in U.K. bills is *thin,* and reflecting this, the bid-offer spread in this market is around 5bp. Normally, U.K. bills trade at a *premium* to the market so they are unattractive to investors, other than banks required to hold them.

Applicable Conventions

Key conventions used in the trading of U.K. gilts are as follows:

Quotes

U.K. bills are quoted on a yield basis.

All gilts are quoted and traded on the basis of *clean* prices; buyers of course pay the full dirty price. Interest-bearing gilts, like U.S. Treasury notes and bonds, are quoted as a percentage of face plus so and so many 32s. Most gilts are quoted with a bid/offer spread between 2/32s and 4/32s. In the gilt market, a quote is good for £5MM.

On domestic trades of gilts, the *settlement date* and the *value date* are the same; and both occur one business day after the trade date, that is, on T+1. However, gilts can trade for *cash* (same day) settlement if the trade is effected before 11 A.M. GMT.

At the time a trade is done, a forward settlement date can also be negotiated. However, the forward settlement date may be no later than 14 days after the trade date. On forward trades, the clean price charged is the market price on the trade date appropriately adjusted for carry.

Interest-Payment Convention

The discount on U.K. bills is calculated on the basis of a 365-day year.

On gilts, the calculation of accrued interest is based on ACT/365. In other words, accrued interest is calculated, assuming a 365-day year, on the basis of the actual number of days between the preceding dividend date and the settlement date.

Coupon-Payment Frequency and Date

Gilts pay coupon interest *semi-annually,* except for 2% *Consols* (perpetuals), which pay coupon interest *quarterly*. Coupon-payment dates vary from stock to stock.

Short First Coupons

As noted, because the U.K. Treasury often chooses to auction a new amount of an outstanding issue, it's common for a *newly* issued gilt to have a *short first coupon*. If so, the new issue will trade fungible with the outstanding issue only after payment of the short first coupon. If the issue is only partly paid, the coupon payment will be further adjusted to reflect that.

Ex-Dividend Policy

Generally, a U.K. gilt goes *ex-dividend* 37 days before its next coupon date; however, due to weekends and bank holidays, the ex-dividend period can range from 32 to 40 days. After its ex-dividend date, a gilt trades with *negative* accrued interest until its next coupon date.

An investor who buys a gilt between its ex-dividend date and its coupon date does *not* receive the next coupon payment; instead that coupon payment goes to the previous owner of the issue. It is for this reason that a gilt trades between its ex-date and its next coupon date with *negative* accrued interest.

However, for gilts that pay coupons on the 5th, 6th, 7th or 8th of January, April, July, and October, the ex-dividend date is the first business day of the preceding month. Also, for gilts with more than five years to maturity, there is a 21-business-day period before the normal ex-dividend date during which a gilt is typically traded *cum dividend* but can also be traded *ex-dividend* (the latter practice is called *special ex-dividend*). During the special ex-dividend period, price may be quoted either way, but *the normal quote is cum dividend.* This practice does not apply to the War Loan 3.50% bonds sold in 1952 and later.

No coupon is paid on a partly-paid gilt. Also, the first coupon paid on such a gilt, after it's fully paid, is normally less than a full coupon.

The messy business of ex-dividend trading in gilts occurs because the ownership of most gilts is still *registered* with the Bank of England. In the United States for example, there is no need for Treasuries to trade ex-dividend because of the U.S. *book-entry system.*

Settlement of Trades

All gilts are available in *registered* form, the registrar being the Bank of England. Certain gilts, including the 3.50% War Loan, may be converted to bearer form.

There is a *limited book-entry system* for gilts. Specifically, the Bank of England maintains a *Central Gilt Office* (*CGT*), via which market makers, the interdealer broker, money brokers, and settlement banks who are members of CGT can settle gilts for their own account on a book-entry basis.

In recent years, the CGT system has been extended to broker/dealers and to investors whose clearing agents are members of CGT. If an investor's clearing agent is not a member of CGT, his trade must be settled via physical delivery. Institutional trades are increasingly cleared via CGT, but small trades are cleared via physical delivery.

Currently, gilts may not be held in either the Euroclear or the CEDEL depositories.

Taxation

Coupons on gilts are paid after deduction of a 25% basic tax rate. Due to double taxation agreements, certain investors, including U.S. investors, may apply for a full rebate of the 25% withholding tax applied.

Foreign investors may also escape British taxation of coupon interest by buying *FOTRA* (*free of tax to residents abroad*) bonds. To receive *gross* interest on such bonds, a non-resident investor must apply to the U.K. Inspector of Foreign Dividends or make an E arrangement with the Board of the Inland Revenue.

Price-Yield Calculations

Price-yield calculations for gilts are done according to the standard ISMA equations, with the exception that the definition of the fraction of a coupon period from settlement to the next coupon payment date differs as noted below.

British Redemption Yield (Yield to Maturity)

The price-yield equation for British gilts differs slightly from the standard bond equation. The day-count convention for U.K. gilts is ACT/365. Whereas most sovereign issuers who employ the ACT/365 day-count also pay interest annually, U.K. gilts pay interest semi-annually.

In calculating accrued interest on an ACT/365 basis, we always use the annual coupon and a year-base of 365. However, in calculating the fraction of a coupon period from the settlement date to the next coupon date, t_{sn}, which is typically defined as $t_{sn} = T_{sn}/A_{ln}$, the question arises as to what value we should assign to A_{ln} when the note or bond pays on a semiannual basis.

In the United Kingdom, the most common approach is to define A_{ln} to be 365 divided by the coupon frequency. Given that U.K. gilts pay interest semi-annually using the ACT/365 day-count convention, the fraction of a coupon period from the settlement date to the next coupon date is $T_{sn}/182.5$. Likewise, the compounding factor for discounting the redemption value is defined as the remaining term to maturity divided by 182.5, that is, $T_{sn}/182.5$, rather than as the number of remaining coupon payments minus one. Finally, the price-yield equation is adjusted depending on whether the gilt is trading ex-dividend.

The Bank of England defines the *Redemption Yield* of a coupon-bearing bond trading *cum-dividend* as follows.

$$P = v^{(T_{sn}/182.5)}\left[C\frac{\left(1-v^{N-1}\right)}{y_w}+C_n\right]+Rv^{(T_{sm}/182.5)}-AI$$

When the bond is trading *ex-dividend,* the next coupon payment, C_n, equals zero and the accrued interest term, *AI,* is replaced by the rebate accrued interest, *RAI.* Let the rebate accrued interest be defined as:

$$RAI = cF\frac{T_{sn}}{365}$$

then the redemption yield of a coupon-bearing trading *ex-dividend* is given by:

$$P = v^{(T_{sn}/182.5)}\left[C\frac{\left(1-v^{N-1}\right)}{y_w}\right]+Rv^{(T_{sm}/182.5)}+RAI$$

Note that the rebated accrued interest *increases* the price whereas accrued interest *reduces* the price paid by the buyer. That is, the buyer receives the rebate accrued interest, as they will not receive the next coupon, but pays the normal accrued interest.

Example. Consider the $8^1/_2$% of 12/07/05, a gilt issued on 9/29/94. Assuming a *redemption yield* of 7.9566% and settlement on 9/25/95, the settlement price was 103-22. The next coupon payment date for this note is 12/07/95. Hence t_{sn} equals

$$\begin{aligned} t_{sn} &= \frac{T_{sn}}{A_{ln}} \\ &= \frac{12/07/95 - 9/25/95}{182.5} \\ &= \frac{157}{182.5} \\ &= 0.4 \end{aligned}$$

and the accrued interest for the 110-day period from 6/07/95 to 9/25/95, given a *face value* of 100, is

$$\begin{aligned} AI &= \frac{cFT_{ls}}{365} \\ &= \frac{.08500 \times 100 \times 110}{365} \\ &= 2.56164384 \end{aligned}$$

Given and the yield to maturity equals 7.9566% and a *coupon frequency* of 2 we have

$$\begin{aligned} v &= \frac{1}{(1 + y_w)} \\ &= \frac{1}{(1 + 0.079566/2)} \\ &= 0.96173913 \end{aligned}$$

Therefore,

$$\begin{aligned} v^{t_{sn}} &= (0.96173913)^{0.4} \\ &= 0.98451631 \end{aligned}$$

and, given the number of remaining coupon payments is 21, we have

$$\begin{aligned} v^{N-1} &= (0.96173913)^{20} \\ &= 0.45829564 \end{aligned}$$

There are 3726 days between the settlement date, 9/25/95, and the maturity date, 12/07/05, hence

$$v^{(T_{sm}/182.5)} = (0.96173913)^{(3726/182.5)}$$
$$= 0.45091028$$

Finally, given a *redemption value* of 100, we have the result

$$P = v^{(T_{sn}/182.5)}\left[C\frac{\left(1-v^{N-1}\right)}{y_w} + C_n\right] + Rv^{(T_{sm}/182.5)} - AI$$

$$= 0.98451631 \times$$

$$\left[4.250\frac{(1-0.45829564)}{0.079566/2} + 4.250\right] + 100 \times 0.45091028$$

$$-\ 2.56164384$$

$$= 103.687570$$

or 103-22.

FRENCH SOVEREIGN DEBT

The French government issues a wide variety of bills, notes, and bonds, all of which are actively traded. France also has a futures market based on such securities.

Issues Routinely Sold

Currently, the French government issues various types of *bills, notes,* and *bonds*. Also, French dealers may *strip* certain government bonds to create *zero-coupon* securities.

Bills

The French government meets some of its funding needs by issuing regularly, through the French Treasury *short-term, discount* bills called *BTFs* (*Bons à Taux Fixe*). These bills are normally issued with maturities of *13, 26, and 52 weeks.*

Occasionally, BTFs *having a 4- to 7-week maturity* are issued by the French Treasury. Such issues are the equivalent of U.S. Treasury cash-management bills.

Notes and Bonds

Currently, the French Treasury issues several types of notes and bonds: fixed-rate, short-term notes and both fixed-rate and floating-rate longer-term bonds.

The French Treasury regularly issues *interest-bearing, fixed-rate* notes, called *BTANs* (*Bons du Trésor à Taux Annuel Normalisé*); these notes have maturities at issue of either 2 or 5 years. Auctions of 2-year BTANs are held in February, May, August, and November, whereas auctions of 5-year BTANs are held in January, April, July, and October. Both 2- and 5-year BTANs mature on the 12th of the month. BTANs are referred to by the French as *medium-term bills,* because, like bills, they are quoted on a *yield basis* (calculated on the basis of either a *365- or a 366-day year*).

Currently, the French Treasury meets the bulk of its long-term funding needs by issuing a new fixed-rate security introduced in 1985, namely *OATs* (*Obligations Assimilables du Trésor*).[6] Each issue of OATs is fungible; it may have an original maturity from 7 to 30 years; and it is typically reopened within a year of its issue date. All OATs are *bullet* issues. Most *fixed-rate* OATs are denominated in *FFr;* however, France was the first EC country to denominate some of its bonds (OATs) in *ECUs,* and it plans to continue doing so. In the secondary market, the most actively traded OATs are the 7- and 10-year issues.

Zeros

The French government was the first EC country to approve the stripping of its bonds. As a result, France now has a market for *stripped OATs* (i.e., *zero-coupon bonds*) that resembles the U.S. market for STRIPs.

Floating-Rate Bonds

The French Treasury issues not only fixed-rate but *floating-rate OATs.* The latter come in four flavors. Two are pegged to short-term indices, two to longer-term indices.

---

[6] Prior to introducing OATs, the French Treasury issued a mix of securities which included exchangeable bonds, bonds with exchange warrants, extendible bonds, indexed bonds, renewable bonds, and one zero-coupon bond.

1. *OAT TMB:* The coupon rate on an OAT TMB is based on the *annual average* of *the average monthly yields* (*bond equivalent yield*) on auctions of *13-week BTFs*. Specifically, the OAT TMB coupon is set equal to the TMB index over the prior 12 months. Coupon interest on OAT TMBs is paid annually. The TMB index is published by the Caisse des Dépôts et Consignations.
2. *OAT TRB:* The TRB index is set each quarter, preceding a coupon payment, to equal the average yield at the eleventh auction of 13-week bills (BTFs). OAT TRBs have short maturities and pay quarterly coupons in arrears.
3. *OAT TME:* The TME index is a monthly average of weekly values of the TME index, which is a weighted average of yields on fixed-rate OATs with maturities of more than 7 years, where the weights are the amounts outstanding of each such issue. The coupon on a TME OAT is set annually to equal the average of the previous year's TMEs. Thus, if the TME index is 5.50 and if yield on the OAT TME is 5.30%, then the OAT TME is quoted at −20bp.

   The French Treasury also issues *TME FRNs,* coupon interest on which is quoted off the TME index and paid *annually.*
4. *OAT TRA:* The TRA index is revised in line with variations in TME. The French Treasury also issues OATs indexed to the TRA index.

Method of Issuance

The French government issues its debt through auctions.

Bills

New issues of BTFs are auctioned according to a quarterly calendar that specifies in advance the maturity of the issues to be sold. Each week, one 13-week BTF is issued; later, this issue is reopened as a half-yearly or yearly BTF. Bids for BTFs are submitted as discount rates figured, on the basis of a *360-day year,* to two decimal places (e.g., the rate bid might be $d = 5.41\%$). BTFs may be traded on a *when issued* (*wi*) basis.

Notes and Bonds

In France, new government notes and bonds are also sold through *price auctions*. Also, in France, as in the United States, *primary dealers* play a significant role both in the distribution of new government issues and in the making of a *secondary market* for outstanding government issues.

French government bonds are listed on the Paris Stock Exchange, but most trading of such issues occurs in a dealer-made, OTC market. To increase efficiency in that market, dealers in French governments have set up *an interdealer broker* who brokers not only buys and sells, but also the lending of government issues.

Secondary Market Practices

Starting in the mid 1980s, the French government instituted a number of financial-market reforms, including the creation of a financial futures market, *MATIF* (*Marché A Terme International de France*), in which French government bonds in the 7- to 10-year sector and short-term bills are deliverable. The introduction of futures trading and other reforms as well have increased the liquidity of French government issues and thereby made these issues more attractive to foreign investors. The French have also developed a reasonably good *repo* market for French government debt.

Applicable Conventions

Discounts on BTANs are calculated on an ACT/360 basis. BTANs and OATs accrue interest according to the ACT/ACT payment convention.

Quotes

BTANs and OATs are quoted as a percentage, to *two decimal points,* of 100 of face; thus, a quoted price might, for example, be 99.73. The price quoted is always a *clean* price.

Settlement and Value Dates

Domestic trades of BTANs and OATs settle two days after the trade date, on T+2. The *value date* is the *settlement date,* so the buyer pays interest accrued as of the settlement date. On both BTANs and OATs, interest accrues according to the ACT/ACT payment convention.

International trades of BTANs and OATs typically settle on T+7, but that number is negotiable. Again, the value date is the settlement date.

Coupon-Payment Convention

BTANs and OATs pay an annual coupon.

Ex-Dividend Policy

OATs and BTANs both trade *cum dividend* until the coupon-payment date. Thus, neither type of issue has an ex-dividend date.

Taxation

France levies a flat 18.1% tax on interest income. However, interest on bonds, BTFs, BTANs, and other short-term instruments held by nonresidents, is exempt from this levy.

Settlement of Trades

Just how trades of French debt are cleared depends on the type of security traded.

Bills and Notes

BTFs and BTANs are cleared *cash versus delivery* through the Saturne system run by the Banque de France. Trades in bills—BTFs and BTANs—can be cleared on the trade date (*spot clearing*). Counterparties using Euroclear or CEDEL must clear through their respective subaccounts with Saturne.

OATs

Like U.S. Treasuries, French OATs are available only in *book-entry* form. A French clearing house and depository, *Société Interprofessionelle pour la Compensation des Valeurs Mobilières* (*SICOVAM*) clears OATs, while the Banque de France settles the cash side. Euroclear and CEDEL are also used to clear trades in OATs, especially if one party or both parties to a trade are nonresidents.

Because there is no delivery versus payment system in SICOVAM, nonresidents typically use Euroclear or CEDEL.

Price-Yield Calculations

Price-yield calculations on OATs are done according to the standard ISMA equations.

GERMAN SOVEREIGN DEBT

In the mid 1980s, a number of steps were taken to liberalize the German capital market, including the market for government bonds. These steps included the admittance of foreign dealers, the creation of a futures/options market, and the elimination of a 25% withholding tax. Today, the Germans also have a fairly active repo market in their debt.

Issues Routinely Sold

The German government issues various discount paper, notes, and bonds to fund its debt.

Unverzinsliche Schatzanweisungen (U-Schatze for Short)

U-Schatzes, which are discount paper, are sold with *maturities up to 2 years.* The Bundesbank sells this *paper* as part of its open market operations; therefore, the liquidity of U-Schatzes is affected by Bundesbank purchases and sales of this paper.

Federal Government Notes Bundeskassenobligationen (Kassen for Short)

Kassen, also called *government notes,* are sold by the German government to satisfy its medium-term financing needs as well as those of its agencies. These issues range in maturity from 2 to 6 years. They are *bullet* issues with no call feature. Generally, Kassen trade at a 30bp spread above Bunds because the latter are more liquid.

Bundesobligationen

Bundesobligationen are *5-year* federal government issues sold in *tap* form. They account for about 20% of the Federal government's outstanding debt.

Bundesobligationen are more attractive to overseas investors than are Kassen. The reasons are several: (1) Bundesobligationen have more than liquidity because the aggregate amount of them outstanding is greater and because typically the size of individual issues is greater. (2) The Bundesbank intervenes to smooth the market for Bundesobligationen, as it does to smooth the market for Bunds. (3) In October 1988, five Bundesobligationen were added to the 18 other government issues, the prices of which are fixed continuously during stock-exchange hours. Also, all future Bundesobligationen over DM 2b will also be traded continuously.

Bunds

Federal government bonds (*Bundesanleihen*) are referred to as *Bunds.* These issues are *bullet* bonds issued with maturities of 6 to 30 years. Currently, a new 10-year Bund is issued each month. The various 10-

year Bunds trade with about the same liquidity, so there's no one benchmark issue. Ten-year Bunds constitute the largest sector of the German government market in terms of both amounts outstanding and amounts traded in the secondary market.

Method of Issuance

The method used to issue German debt varies depending on the type of debt issued.

Treasury Discount Paper: Unverzinsliche Schatzanweisungen

Treasury discount paper (*U-Schatze* for short) is issued by the Bundesbank in connection with its open market operations.

Federal Government Notes: Bundeskassenobligationen

These notes (*Kassen*) are issued irregularly several times a year *by tender*. Specifically, banks make *bids* (*tender offers*) for a new issue; these bids include a fixed coupon, a fixed maturity, and a minimum yield. The size of new Kassen issues varies widely depending on market conditions.

All Kassen are listed on one or more of the German stock exchanges.

Bundesobligationen

These 5-year obligations are issued in *tap* form.

Bunds

Currently, a new 10-year Bund is issued each month, but there's no regular schedule of issuance. Bunds are listed on all eight German stock exchanges.

A fixed syndicate, led by the Bundesbank, underwrites each new issue of Bunds. The selling syndicate includes 70-odd German institutions and 20 foreign banks and broker/dealers. Each new issue to be sold is allocated 80% to German members of the selling syndicate, 20% to foreign members.

Together, the Bundesbank, the government, and the Central Capital Market Committee set the conditions of each new issue. Members of the selling syndicate do not bid competitively for a new issue; instead, each member is allocated a quota that it must take; each syndicate member then reoffers, to the public, the securities allocated to it. The Bundesbank retains 20% of each new issue to use in its open market operations.

Syndicate members are compensated for the *risk* they take in underwriting new issues by being given a *commission* of 1 3/8%, some portion of which they may give up to bank and insurance company buyers as a *reallowance*. For up to a year, the Bundesbank can reclaim this reallowance if it buys, in its open market operations, underwritten bonds at a price less than or equal to their issue price minus the reallowance. The purpose of this scheme is to encourage syndicate members to place Bunds with long-term investors.

To permit implementation of this system, all Bunds have control numbers which allow the Bundesbank to identify a specific bond within a specific issue. Because the Bundesbank cannot reclaim any reallowance on the 20% of a new issue that it takes, Bunds originally in the Bundesbank's intervention tranche may, for up to a year, command a slightly higher price in the secondary market than do Bunds sold by syndicate members.

All Bunds are automatically listed on all German stock exchanges.

Restrictions on Overseas Investors (Kassen and Bunds)

Overseas investors may *not* tender at offer. Also, new issue may not be sold to U.S. investors until it has become *seasoned;* generally that's deemed to be 40 days after issuance.

Non-resident investors may *not* buy *Bundesschatzbriefe* (government savings bonds), *nor* may they buy *Fianzierungsschatz* (small, illiquid Treasury financing notes).

Secondary Market Practices

With respect to German soverign debt, secondary market practices vary depending on the type of security traded.

Kassen

Kassen are listed and traded in the *geregelter Freiverkehr,* which is a regulated, unofficial, *OTC* market. Only notes so listed may be used as collateral for Lombard loans from the Bundesbank.

Bunds

All Bunds are listed on all of the German stock exchanges. However, most trading of such bonds occurs on the Frankfurt Stock Exchange whose regular trading hours are 11:30 A.M. to 5:00 P.M., Frankfurt time. Retail investors may place a buy or sell order on a German stock exchange only through a bank.

Since 1988, the most liquid German Bunds have been traded *continuously* during stock exchange hours. This system, which replaced the previous system of trading Bunds only for the purpose of fixing a price, was made in part to support the opening of a Bund futures contract in Germany.

Short Sales

Because of legal restrictions on the shorting, within Germany, of German sovereign debt, much of the trading in such debt occurs in international marketplaces, particularly in London, which is the largest such marketplace. London derives its importance in the trading of the sovereign debt not only of Germany, but of a number of other countries, because of restrictions and or taxes imposed on the trading of such debt when it's traded in its native (i.e., domestic) market.

Applicable Conventions

Key conventions used in the trading of German sovereign debt are as follows:

Bond Quotes

Prices are quoted as a percentage to two decimal points of 100 or par.

Settlement and Value Dates

In the *domestic market,* for a trade executed on *an exchange,* the *settlement date* is the *second business day* after the trade date, that is, T+2. For an OTC trades, the settlement date is negotiable. In either case, the *value date* is the *same* as the settlement date.

On *international trades,* the settlement date is typically the *fifth business day* after the trade date, that is, T+5; but that's negotiable. The *value date* is the *same* as the settlement date.

Interest-Payment Convention

Interest on German bonds accrues according to the *30E/360* convention.

Coupon-Payment Frequency and Date

Coupons are paid *annually* on either the 1st or the 15th of the month.

Ex-Dividend Policy

The *Kassenverein* (the security clearing association) has set up complex rules for ex-dividend dates and accrued interest:

(1) If the next coupon date falls between the 3rd and the 16th of a month, the ex-dividend date is the first business day after the last day of the previous month.

(2) If the next coupon date lies between the 17th of the current month and the 2nd of the next month, then the ex-dividend date is the first business day after the 15th of the current month. (However, some banks detach the coupons 15 calendar days prior to each coupon date.)

Negative Accrued Interest

If the trade date is the ex-dividend date or later, and if the day before the settlement date is within the current coupon period, the buyer will pay the seller the purchase price *minus* accrued interest from the value date to the next coupon date). Thus, there is *negative accrued interest* (*minuszinsen*), since the seller receives the full coupon on the coupon date. The amount of negative accrued interest is the interest that accrues between the settlement date and the coupon date.

Positive Accrued Interest

On trades *before the ex-dividend date,* the buyer receives accrued interest calculated from the previous coupon date to the value date. If the trade falls *on the ex-dividend date or later and if the day before the settlement day lies in the next coupon period,* then (1) the buyer does not receive the next coupon after the trade date and (2) accrued interest due him is calculated from the next coupon date to the value date.

Settlement of Trades

German bonds are issued in *book-entry* form. Customers and dealers have accounts with clearing banks and the latter have accounts with the *Kassenverein* (*KV*), which are clearing agents of the stock exchanges.

In general, trades in German government securities can be settled either through the Kassenverein or through either Euroclear or CEDEL. However, German counterparties may insist on domestic settlement.

Delivery of most bonds within Germany occurs via book entry in one of two ways:

(1) *Domestic settlement via Kassenverein:* Settlement is cash versus delivery on T+2.

(2) *International settlement via Euroclear or CEDEL:* Settlement and value date are set according to AIBD conventions. Normally,

trades of German bonds outside Germany are settled on T+5, but this is negotiable. Euroclear and CEDEL can also clear trades within the domestic German system on T+2.

German bonds settle on a *price plus accrued interest* basis. Accrued interest is calculated from the most recent coupon date to the value date.

Since the 1970s, the book-entry system administered by the Federal Debt Administration (*Bundesschuldenverwaltung*) has also been used for Kassens. These securities can be cleared either domestically through the Kassenverein or internationally through Euroclear and CEDEL. Because Kassens and Bunds are both available only in book-entry form, physical delivery of recent issues of either security to either domestic or overseas investors is impossible.

Taxation

There is *no* withholding tax imposed on coupon interest received by non-residents holding German government debt.

Price-Yield Calculations

Price-yield calculations are done according to the standard ISMA equations. Domestic investors use the standard, Moosmüller, and Braess-Fangmeyer methods, while international investors tend to use only the standard method bond equation.

ITALIAN SOVEREIGN DEBT

Historically, overseas investors were reluctant to invest in Italian government bonds for various reasons, including lack of liquidity and difficulties associated with clearing such issues. Today, however, due to economic, market, and regulatory reforms carried out by the Italian government, Italian government issues have began to attract more interest from overseas investors.

Issues Routinely Sold

As a result of continuous large federal deficits and consequent large issuance of government securities, Italian government securities today comprise over 80% of the Italian bond market. The market for Italian government securities can be divided into two distinct segments: short-term and medium-term to long-term.

Bills

Italy issues *discount paper* denominated in both *Italian lira* (*Lit*) and ECU.

At the short end of the market, the Italian government issues a lira-denominated T bill or *BOT* (*Buoni Odinari del Tresoro*); these issues have original maturities of 3, 6, and 12 months. Italy also issues *1-year T bill BTE* (*Buoni Ordinari del Tesoro in ECU*) *denominated in ECU.*

Notes and Bonds

The Italian government borrows money by issuing various sorts of notes and bonds. These are described briefly below.

A *CCT* (*Certificati del Credito del Tresoro*) is a floating-rate note. CCTs used to be issued with a 2- to 10-year maturity, but they are now more commonly issued with a 7-year maturity.

A *BTP* (*Buoni del Tresoro Poliennale*) is a fixed-rate bond. BTPS are now issued with 5-, 8-, and 10-year maturities.

A *CTO* (*Certificati del Tresoro con Opzione*) is a fixed-rate bond that carries an option, Generally, CTOs are issued in the 6-year range.

A *BTE* (*Buoni Ordinari del Tesor in ECU*) is a short-term, fixed-rate, ECU-denominated bond.

Method of Issuance

Italian government securities are issued in various ways. *Competitive auctions* are generally used to issue BOTs; in such auctions, bids are accepted from the highest price down; non-competitive bids may also be made, such bids are accepted at the average price accepted plus a small spread.

The Treasury uses *Dutch auctions* to issue BTPs, CCTs, CTOs, CTEs, and BTEs. In such auctions, the Treasury sets a minimum price (maximum rate) below which (above which) bids will not be accepted. Reopenings of a given issue must have the same minimum price because the withholding tax that the investor must pay at maturity is based on the difference between that price and par.

Syndicates are used only for issuing public-sector bonds.

Treasury Bills

Italian Treasury bills (*BOTs*), are issued twice a month. They are subject to a 12.5% withholding tax that is calculated against an amount equal to face value minus issue price. BOTs are the only Italian government issue on which withholding tax must be paid *in advance;* hence, BOTs are quoted on a *net* price basis in the secondary market.

There is no formal *wi* market in BOTs, but some dealers make a *gray* market in to-be-auctioned issues by listing them on their Reuters page prior to their auction date.

BOTs are issued via competitive auctions held by the Bank of Italy at the middle and end of each month. The precise auction schedule is published at the beginning of each year. BOT issues auctioned at the end of the month tend to be for larger face amounts and thus more important than BOT issues auctioned in the middle of the month. The exact amount of BOTs to be auctioned on each auction date is announced several days before the auction and is published on Reuters, page ATIE.

In a BOT auction, each bidder may submit a maximum of five competitive bids. The Bank of Italy fills bids in order of price, until the new issue is fully sold.

Treasury Notes and Bonds

BTEs (*Buoni Ordinari del Tesoro in ECU*) are short-term, ECU-denominated securities. The coupon is paid at maturity. They are issued at par via a Dutch auction. The Bank of Italy determines the amount offered, the maturity, and the maximum coupon accepted.

On auction day, Italian dealers must pay for BTEs in lira at a fixed Lit/ECU exchange rate, which is determined, on the issue date, by the Bank of Italy; nonresidents, however, must pay in ECU. A holder of BTEs must instruct the Bank of Italy, at least one month before maturity, as to whether he wants repayment in lire or in ECU; the Lit/ECU exchange rate applied is the average of the Milan/Rome fixings two business days prior to the maturity date.

CCTs (*Certificati di Credito del Tesoro*) are *floating-rate notes* indexed to BOT yields plus a fixed spread. Generally, CCTs, which are initially offered on the first day of a month, are auctioned in a fixed amount, at a minimum basis price. Withholding taxes are imposed at maturity on the difference between the minimum basis price and par. CCTs may be reopened at any time at their original minimum basis price.

CCTs, which are exempt from withholding tax, are indexed to the net yield on BOTs, while those subject to a 12.5% withholding tax are indexed to the gross yield on BOTs. CCTs. which are subject to a 6.25% withholding tax, are indexed to the gross yield on BOTs adjusted by the factor,

$$(1.1250) \div (1.0625) = 0.933333 \text{ or } 93.333\%$$

This adjustment makes it possible to *compare directly* all net coupons on a given date.

Occasionally, CCTs are quoted before issue (*wi*) in the *gray* market.

The many CCTs outstanding are classified by maturity, by tax rate, by spread, and by annual versus semi-annual coupon.

BTPs (Buoni del tesoro Poliennali) are fixed-rate bullet bonds that pay a *semi-annual coupon* and are issued with maturities of 5 to 10 years. They are issued via Dutch auctions. For each auction, the Bank of Italy defines the coupon, the maturity, the amount issued, and the minimum price. There is only one minimum basis price for BTPs, even if reopened, because like *CCTs* and *CTOs* (which are defined below), taxes are withheld at maturity on the difference between the minimum basis price and par.

CTOs (*Certificati del Tesoro con Opzione*) are fixed-rate, semi-annual-pay bonds that carry a put option. This option gives the investor the right to obtain early redemption at par at end of year three. Most CTOs have maturities in the 6-year range. Normally, the put may be exercised, upon notification to the Bank of Italy, during the 1-month period before the exercise date.

CTEs (*Certificati del Tesoro in ECU*) are ECU-denominated *fixed-rate* bonds that pay an *annual coupon*. They are issued at par, currently in maturities of 5 or 6 years.

Italian underwriters of CTEs must pay for them in lira at a fixed Lit/ECU exchange rate that is determined by the Bank of Italy on the issue date. Coupons and repayments are made in lire at an exchange rate that is the average of the Milan-Rome fixings on the two business days preceding a coupon or maturity date.

Foreign underwriters may pay for CTEs in lira or ECU. If payment is made in ECU, the bonds are placed in a special ECU account at the Bank of Italy; CTEs in this account pay coupons and repay principal in ECU. Nonresidents may pay for CTEs in lira and request that their bonds be put in the special ECU account at the Bank of Italy. This option enables nonresident investors to buy CTEs from Italian dealers and then convert them to the ECU account maintained by the Bank of Italy.

Secondary Market Practices

After issue, Italian bonds may be traded in any one of three markets: the *Milan Stock Exchange,* the *OTC market,* and *the Telematic market.* In practice, stock-exchange trading in Italian government bonds is thin. The OTC market for Italian governments—principally a telephone market with quotes posted on Reuters pages—is also a thin market with bid-offer spreads of 10 to 20bp.

The *Telematic market* was developed to give Italian governments better liquidity; it is a *screen-based* market in which 25 primary dealers post, during working hours on days when the stock exchange is open, prices on more than 75 government issues. In this market, the minimum face amount traded is 5b Lit, and spreads are often as narrow as 1 cent. However, trading in BOTs is concentrated mostly in new issues.

Italian government securities are normally held in book-entry form under a system of accounts operated by the Bank of Italy. An investor wanting physical bonds must specifically request them. All Italian government issues have an ABI identifying number.

Nonresident investors may buy and sell Italian government bonds through an Italian depository (agent) bank that has an account with the Bank of Italy. Such investors may also deal in Italian governments through Euroclear or CEDEL. Nonresident investors holding bonds in the Italian book-entry system may withdraw those bonds for transfer abroad, in which case the bonds are stamped "payable abroad."

Bills

BOTs are not listed on the Milan Stock Exchange, but they are traded in the *Telematic market.* Generally, the liquidity of BOTs falls sharply after they have been outstanding for several weeks.

Notes and Bonds

Secondary-market practices vary depending on the type of note or bond traded. The key differences are as follows:

BTEs are not listed on an exchange. Instead, secondary trades of BTEs are made in an OTC market.

CCTs are listed on the Milan Stock Exchange, but not until they pass their first coupon date. All CCTs are quoted in the Telematic market by primary dealers, with new CCTs being listed a few days after auction. Generally, the bid-offer spread is 1 to 2bp.

BTPs are listed on the stock exchange after they pay their first coupon. Also, the most representative BTPs as well as all new BTPs are listed in the Telematic market in which spreads as narrow as 1 to 3 cents are common.

Some *CTOs* are listed on the Milan Stock Exchange after they pay their first coupon, but most are listed only on the Telematic market. New CTO issues are the most actively traded, with bid-offer spreads ranging from 2 to 10bp. CTOs often trade at yields higher than those at which straight bonds trade; this suggests that the put option incorporated in a CTO is undervalued.

CTEs are listed on the stock exchange; the Telematic screen market quotes only one CTE issue. CTEs placed or transferred abroad are listed on the Luxembourg Stock Exchange.

Applicable Conventions

Key conventions used in the trading of Italian sovereign debt are as follows:

Bond Quotes

Prices are quoted as a percentage to two decimal points of 100 or par.

Coupon-Payment Frequency and Date

Italian government bonds generally pay a *semi-annual coupon*. However, BTEs, CTRs, and CTEs pay an *annual coupon*.

Some CCTs also pay an *annual coupon;* for example, the CCT of 01 May 1997 pays on May 1 of the current year an annual coupon equal to a rate—based on the yields at which 12-month BOTs were issued in February and March of the preceding year—plus a spread of 75bp. Since November 1987, CCTs that pay a *semi-annual coupon* have been indexed to the semi-annual yield equivalent of 12-month BOTs plus a spread of 30 to 50bp.

With respect to other Italian bonds, we note the following: BTPs pay interest semi-annually. With one exception, CTOs have mid-month coupon dates. CTEs pay an annual coupon.

Settlement and Value Dates

Trades in Italian government issues normally settle on T+3 if the trade is settled domestically, but on T+7 if the trade is settled through CEDEL or Euroclear. The value date is the settlement date.

Interest-Payment Convention

Coupon interest on Italian government bonds is calculated on the basis of a 30/360 payment convention. Some Italian bonds have a short first coupon, and the prorated coupon paid on the first coupon date is calculated using the ACT/360 formula.

In contrast to virtually all other capital markets, interest accrues on Italian government debt on both the *first* and the *last* day of the accrual period. In Italy then, accrued interest will typically include one extra day when compared to most other countries.

Interest on money-market instruments is calculated using the ACT/360 formula.

Settlement of Trades

Settlement of trades in Italian governments can be made via the domestic book-entry system or through Euroclear and CEDEL.

Taxation

In the past, Italy has imposed a variety of taxes on income earned on Italian sovereign debt. Currently all bonds issued in Italy are subject to a 12.5% withholding tax. Most Italian government issues are redeemed at maturity *at par,* but *minus the withholding tax* on the difference between the *minimum basis price* and par. The withholding tax is also applied to the coupon interest.

As such, yields in the Italian market are typically quoted on a *gross basis* for investors who are not subject to the withholding tax; and on a *net basis* for those investors subject to the tax. Likewise coupons are quoted on a gross and net basis.

Non-residents may apply to the Italian Ministry of Finance for refunds of withholding tax. Requests for refunds of taxes withheld are currently met within a few months.

Before buying Italian government bonds an investor should check whether his country of residence has a tax treaty with Italy and, if so, what impact that treaty has on the amount and rate of the withholding tax he must pay.

Price-Yield Calculations

Price-yield calculations for Italian government instruments are done according to the standard ISMA equations, with the exception that the definition of an accrual period includes both the first and the last day; and with the exception that the formula must account for withholding taxes.

Italian Tax-Adjusted Yield to Maturity

The price-yield equation for BTPs includes several modifications to the standard bond equation. The incidence of withholding taxes on both coupon interest and the difference between the official issue price and the redemption value must be reflected in the equation. Also, the market practice of accruing interest on both the first and the last day of the accrual period means that accrued interest always reflects one more day than is typical in other countries.

The standard bond equation is

$$P = v^{t_{sn}}\left[C\left(\frac{1-v^{N-1}}{y_w}\right) + Rv^{N-1} + C_n\right] - AI$$

If we let

$$m = \text{withholding tax rate}$$

then, the equation for the price of a BTP given its yield is as follows:

$$P = v^{t_{sn}}\left[(1-m)C\left(\frac{1-v^{N-1}}{y_w}\right) + \left(R - m(R - P_o)\right)v^{N-1} + (1-m)C_n\right] - AI_{net}$$

where accrued interest, net of the withholding tax, is defined as follows.

$$AI_{net} = (1-m)C\frac{(T_{ls}+1)}{360}$$

Note that the above formula follows market convention by adding one extra day to the normal number of days between the last coupon date and the settlement date.

Example: Consider the price of the BTP 12s of 05/01/02 for settlement on March 21, 1994 given a net annual yield of 8.533%. The withholding tax rate is 12.5% and the base price for taxes is 92.70000. Before using the above price-yield equation for BTPs we must convert the market standard quote, which is on an annual basis, to a semi-annual basis. That is, while the BTP is issued with a semi-annual coupon, the market standard is to quote these instruments on a annual basis net of withholding taxes. We can use the following equation to convert from an annual basis to a semi-annual basis. Since we are converting a net yield, the converted yield will also be a net yield. Hence

$$\text{semi-annual yield} = 2\left(\left(1 + \text{annual yield}\right)^{1/2} - 1\right)$$

$$.08358 = 2\left(\left(1 + .08533\right)^{1/2} - 1\right)$$

That is, a net semi-annual yield of 8.358% is equivalent to the quoted net annual yield of 8.533%. We can now apply the price-yield equation for BTPs.

$$P = v^{t_{sn}}\left[(1-m)C\left(\frac{1-v^{N-1}}{y_w}\right) + \left(R - m(R - P_o)\right)v^{N-1} + (1-m)C_n\right]$$

$$-(1-m)C\frac{(T_{ls}+1)}{360}$$

$$= \left(\frac{1}{1+.08358/2}\right)^{\frac{41}{182.5}} \times \left[(1-.125)(6.0)\left(\frac{1-\left(\frac{1}{1+.08358/2}\right)^{16}}{.08358/2}\right)\right.$$

$$\left. + \left(100 - .125(100 - 92.70)\right)\left(\frac{1}{1+.08358/2}\right)^{16} + (1-.125)(6.0)\right]$$

$$-(1-.125)(6.0)\frac{(140+1)}{360}$$

$$= 116.020424 - 4.11250$$

$$= 111.907924$$

JAPANESE SOVEREIGN DEBT

After the U.S. market, the Japanese bond market is the second largest fixed-income market in the world. From the late 1970s on, the Japanese government took a number of steps to liberalize issuance and trading in its markets for fixed-income securities.

Issues Routinely Sold

Japanese government bonds go by the moniker *JGBs*. Actually, the Japanese government issues several types of bonds. In theory, all JGBs are callable at any time, but no JGB has ever been called and the calling of one is viewed as a step that would never be taken. Thus, JGBs may be thought of as being *de facto* bullet bonds.

Japanese Maturity Bonds (Chukoku Bonds)

Chukoku bonds comprise 2-, 3-, and 4-year *fixed-coupon* bonds as well as 5-year discount bonds.

Japanese Long-Term Bonds

Japanese long-term bonds comprise 10-year, *fixed-coupon* bonds and 20-year, *fixed-rate* bonds (*Super Long Bonds*). The latter are currently issued quarterly.

Each of these bonds is numbered serially in order of issuance. For example, bond number 105 is a 5%, 10-year bond maturing on Dec. 22, 1997. In the United States, and most other countries, bonds are referred to by coupon, maturity, and call date (if any). In Japan, a specific bond issue is referred to by the serial number that identifies it by serial order of issuance. Thus, dealers trade Bond 105, Bond 114, and so forth.

Since 1972, the most common maturity in which new JGBs have been issued is 10 years; and since 1975, the Japanese government has issued new 10-year bonds regularly. In late 1986, the Japanese government issued the first of a number of fixed-rate, 20-year bonds. Finally, since 1977, the Japanese government has issued a large number of medium-term bonds.

Method of Issuance

The Japanese government uses two methods to issue its debt.

Issuance by Syndicate

This method is used for discount bonds having original maturities of 5 and 10 years.

The issuance of a new Japanese government issue is authorized by the *Ministry of Finance* (*MOF*) and implemented by the *Bank of Japan* (*BOF*). A *syndicate,* which comprises over 700 Japanese financial institutions as well as some overseas dealers, is responsible for *underwriting* a new issue. Under an annual bond-issuing authority set by the Japanese Diet, the MOF and the BOF set, in consultation with representatives from the underwriting syndicate, the coupon and the size of each new issue. The consultations for the next 10-year issue normally begin during the last week of each month.

Subscriptions for a new issue are allocated among syndicate members via a quota system. A syndicate member must accept and pay for the full amount of a new issue allocated to it even if it's unable to sell in full its allocation.

From month to month, the amount of the new 10-year that's issued varies considerably. Also, month to month, issue sizes vary considerably; and a new issue, once sold, may be *reopened;* on occasion, the same issue will be reopened in several consecutive months. Since the securities sold at each reopening will have *a short first coupon,* these new securities will not trade fungible with the initial issue until the semi-annual coupon date following the reopening or consecutive reopenings has passed.

Issuance by Auction

The Japanese have auctioned, through MOF, 2-, 3-, 4-, and more recently 20-year coupon bonds.

For each issue to be auctioned, MOF announces the maturity date and the coupon. It also decides whether the new issue will be called a deficit-financing bond (*akaji kokusai*) or a construction bond (*kensetsu kokusai*). The one bond may be identical to the other, but because of differences in names, the two types of bonds are not interchangeable.

Securities houses tender secret bids for the issue to the auctioned. Investors may also tender competitive bids for the new issue through securities houses. Bids received are accepted from the highest bid down to a *stop-out bid* (one at which at least 100% of the new issue is sold). The day following the bidding, the MOG publishes a *reserve price,* and all bids at or above the reserve price are met in full at the price bid. In an auction, smaller investors may enter noncompetitive bids.

All members of the selling syndicate may participate in the auction of a Japanese government issue, but as a matter of practice, the bulk of the securities sold is taken down by the Japanese big four: Nomura Securities, Daiwa Securities, Nikko Securities, and Yamaichi Securities.

Hybrid Auctions

In October 1987, 10-year JGBs began to be issued via a *hybrid* auction. What this means is that the selling syndicate is still responsible, under the system described above, for underwriting more than 50% of a new 10-year, but some percentage of the new issue, 40% in 1989, is made available for sale via auction. A would-be bidder in the auction knows the parameters that have been set for the new issue—subscription price, coupon, and size—and his bid is limited to a percentage, 12% in 1989, of the issue to be auctioned.

Issue Cycles

Currently, MOF sells new issues according to regular schedule. A new 10-year bond is issued each month; a new 5-year discount bond and a new 20-year bond are issued quarterly; and new medium-term bonds are usually auctioned during the first or second week of the month.

Secondary Market Practices

There are 100-odd dealers of various ilk that make the domestic OTC market in Japanese government bonds. Inter-dealer trades are brokered by a single broker, the Japan Bond Trading Company; bids and offers as well as trades executed through this broker are posted on the broker's screen and are beamed out to all dealers linked to the system.

All large trades occur in the OTC market, which accounts for 95% of the trading in JGBs. The other 5% occurs on the Tokyo, Nagoya, and Osaka Stock Exchanges on which all JGB issues are listed. There is a requirement that small retail trades be executed on a stock exchange.

The Benchmark Effect

The secondary market for JGBs exhibits *two quirks,* one of which is *the benchmark effect.* Even though a new 10-year JGB is issued every month, over 90% of trading in the market is in a single 10-year issue. Because this issue has lots of liquidity whereas other issues have little liquidity, the benchmark issue typically *trades expensive* to surrounding issues by 30 to 80bp.

Also, unlike in the United States, the Japanese 10-year benchmark bond is not necessarily the most recently auctioned 10-year; it may even be an issue that has been outstanding for a year. Requirements for a bond to be a benchmark bond are as follows: its coupon must be near the prevailing market rate; it must have been widely distributed after issue; and the amount of it outstanding must be large (reopened issues are preferred). The Japanese big four securities houses have a major impact in the choice as to which 10-year issue will be the benchmark 10-year issue.

The Reverse Coupon Effect

The second quirk exhibited by the secondary market for JGBs is *the reverse coupon effect.* Japanese investors—including insurance companies who are allowed to pay dividends out of current income but not out of capital gains—have a strong preference for high current yield. As a result, there is a tendency in Japan for high-coupon bonds (all tax, call and other features taken into account) to trade at lower yields than they would in other countries.

Short Sales

Shorting JGBs is difficult and expensive because of the absence in Japan of a U.S.-style repo market. There is the *Gensaki* market in which dealers can finance their positions for fixed periods from one week out to six months. However, this market is not set up for the reversing in securities to cover shorts. In 1989, MOF tried to introduce in Japan a repo more like the U.S. repo market, but volume is this new market remains modest.

Applicable Conventions

Key conventions used in the trading of Japanese government securities are as follows:

Bond Quotes

JGBs are quoted and traded on a *simple-yield basis* (calculated to 2bp), rather than on a price basis. The calculation of simple yield for a Japanese bond was described in Chapter 10.

For bonds trading at a *premium,* Japanese simple yield is less than yield to maturity. For bonds trading at a *discount,* the reverse is true.

Settlement and Value Dates

For Japanese bonds, settlement occurs on *fixed* days, every fifth business day. The value date and the settlement dates coincide, and they occur 7 to 15 days after the trade date.

Interest-Payment Convention

JGBs accrue interest on an ACT/365 basis. For bonds bought at issue, the interest-accrual period includes both the issue date and the settlement date.

Coupon-Payment Frequency and Date

JGBs pay a semi-annual coupon on the 20th of the appropriate month. If the coupon date is a non-business day, the coupon is paid on the following business day.

Ex-Dividend Policy

JGBs go ex-dividend 14 days before their coupon date. A bond traded during its ex-dividend period is settled on its next coupon date, not on the next settlement date (or on the next business day after its next coupon date if the latter is a non business day).

Settlement of Trades

Trades of JGBs settle on *fixed dates:* the 5th, 10th, 15th, 20th, 25th, and the last day of each month. A trade settles on the first fixed settlement date following the trade date. If this date is not a business day, then the trade settles on the next business day.

Form

JGBs are available in *bearer* form, although Japanese bearer bonds may not be delivered outside Japan. Most JGBs are held in the Japanese version of a *book-entry* system, under which an investor holds, in a custodial account, bonds registered in the name of the custodian. Overseas investors are advised to buy bonds so registered; the time required and the restriction imposed on when a bearer bond may be converted to registered form cause bearer bonds to trade as much as 5bp cheap to registered bonds.

Settlement

JGBs are settled through Japanese clearing banks which have accounts with the Bank of Japan, the ultimate clearing agent. Most bonds are in registered form and are cleared DVP via book-entry.

JGBs may not be settled during the 14 days prior to a coupon date. However, settlement of such bonds may occur on the first business day after the coupon date even if this date isn't a normal settlement date.

Settlement Period

The Japanese have a rather complex arrangement for settling trades with a variable lag between the trade date and the settlement date. They are discussing the benefits of moving to continuous settlement as occurs in the United States and some other countries.

Price-Yield Calculations

Domestic investors use the simple yield equation presented in Chapter 10 to value coupon-bearing notes, while international investors tend to use the standard bond equation presented in Chapter 11. The day-count convention for Japanese simple yield is ACT/365 NL; this means that when one calculates term to maturity one excludes all leap days between the settlement date and the maturity date. For the reader's convenience we repeat the definition of simple yield:

$$y_s = \frac{cF + \dfrac{R-P}{T_{sm}/365}}{P}$$

CANADIAN SOVEREIGN DEBT

The government of Canada meets its domestic funding needs by issuing securities in the C$ bond market. Occasionally, however, the government of Canada also sells offshore bonds denominated in currencies other than the Canadian dollar, the proceeds of which are used to bolster the foreign exchange reserves of the Canadian central bank (the Bank of Canada).

Issues Routinely Sold

The Canadian government issues discount paper (bills), fixed-rate notes, and fixed-rate bonds.

Bills

The Canadian government routinely issues bills, which are sold on a discount basis. These securities have original maturities of 3 and 6 months, and 1 year.

Notes and Bonds

The Canadian government also issues, on an *as needed* basis, fixed-rate notes and bonds having original maturities somewhat longer than 2, 3, 5, 10 and 30 years. Coupon interest on such issues is payable semi-annually.

Method of Issuance

The government of Canada uses *primary distributors,* namely dealers and Canadian banks, to issue its *marketable* debt. Two techniques of issuance are used, allotments and auctions.

Under the *allotment system,* the primary distributors act as a selling group for a new issue. After consultation with these distributors, the Bank of Canada announces the amount, the coupon, and the issue price for each maturity tranche to be sold. The Bank of Canada, acting as fiscal agent for the Canadian government, pays to all distributors who sell new bonds a *commission* per bond sold.

The *auction system,* used by the Bank of Canada to distribute new notes and bonds resembles the auction system used by the U.S. Treasury to distribute similar securities. The Bank of Canada generally announces an auction of 2-year notes every two months; it announces auctions of 3-, 4-, 5- and 7-year notes at occasional intervals. One week prior to an auction, the Bank of Canada announces the maturity and size of the issue to be auctioned; and at that time, the new issue begins trading in a *when issued* (*wi*) market *on a yield basis.* On the auction date, primary distributors submit to the Bank of Canada competitive bids for the new issue; notes are allocated to the bidders bidding the lowest yield, but subject to the constraint that no more than 20% of a new issue may be allocated to one bidder.

Government of Canada bonds (*Canadas*) are issued at a price close to par with a fixed coupon. Denominations available range from C$1M to C$1MM.

Secondary Market Practices

Canadian government bonds are not listed on any stock exchange. The secondary market in such securities is, like the secondary market for U.S. Treasuries, an *OTC market* made by dealers.

The market for Canadas is the single largest sector of the Canadian bond market; and most Canadian government issues are actively traded in both the domestic and the international capital markets. Hence, most Canadian government issues have good liquidity.

Canadian government issues are traded actively by domestic and by overseas investors, and most Canadian dealers will make markets in all outstanding issues. Also, there is a growing repo market in Canada, one in which dealers can both finance and borrow Canadas. Consequently, Canadian government issues have good liquidity.

Price Quotes in the Secondary Market

Quotes for both bills, notes and bonds are decimal. Canadian T bills are quoted on a yield basis. Canadian government notes and bonds are traded with prices quoted as a percentage of face value carried to 3 decimal places. The normal bid-offer spread can be as wide as 5bp.

Applicable Conventions

Key conventions used in the trading of Canadian Treasury securities are as follows:

Settlement and Value Dates

The value date is the settlement date.

Interest-Payment Convention

Calculations for Canadian T bills are made using standard discount formulas. The day-count convention used is ACT/360.

Calculations for Canadian bonds are made using the ISMA bond equation. The day-count convention used is ACT/365.

Coupon-Payment Frequency and Date

Canadian notes and bonds pay coupon interest semi-annually.

Settlement of Trades

Canadian government bonds are available in either bearer or registered form.

For Canadian notes having a *remaining term-to-maturity* of less than 2 years, good delivery is T+1. For Canadian government bonds having a *remaining term-to-maturity* greater than 2 years, good delivery is T+3.

Price-Yield Calculations

Price-yield calculations are done according to the standard ISMA equations.

GLOSSARY: COMMON MONEY MARKET AND BOND MARKET TERMS

accretion (of a discount) In portfolio accounting, a straight-line accumulation of capital gains on discount bonds in anticipation of receipt of par at maturity.

accrued interest Interest due from issue or from the last coupon date to the present on an interest-bearing security. The buyer of the security pays the quoted dollar price plus accrued interest.

active A market in which trading volume is high.

ACT/360 A day-count convention according to which accrued interest equals the coupon times the face amount times a fraction equal to actual days since the last coupon date over 360, the number of days assumed to comprise one year.

ACT/ACT A day-count convention according to which accrued interest equals the coupon times the face amount times a fraction equal to actual days since the last coupon date over actual days in the current coupon period. U.S. Treasury notes and bonds accrue interest according to the ACT/ACT convention.

actuals The cash commodity as opposed to the futures contract.

ACUs *Asian currency units.* An expression for Eurodollars deposited in Far East centers.

add-on rate A specific rate of interest to be paid. Stands in contrast to the rate on a discount security (e.g., a Treasury bill, that pays *no* interest).

after-tax real rate of return Money after-tax rate of return minus the inflation rate.

agencies Federal agency securities. See also **agency bank.**

agency bank A form of organization commonly used by foreign banks to enter the U.S. market. An agency bank cannot accept deposits or extend loans in its own name; it acts as an agent for the parent bank. Term often used on the Street to refer to both a foreign bank's agencies and its branches.

agent A firm that executes orders for or otherwise acts on behalf of another (the principal) and is subject to its control and authority. The agent may receive a fee or commission.

all-in cost Total costs, explicit and other. Example: The all-in cost to a bank of CD money is the explicit rate of interest it pays on that deposit *plus* the FDIC premium it must pay on the deposit *plus* the hidden cost it incurs because it must hold some portion of that deposit in a noninterest-bearing reserve account at the Fed.

all or none (AON) Requirement that none of an order be executed unless all of it can be executed at the specified price.

American option An option that may be exercised at any time during the life of the option. U.S. option exchanges, such as the CBOE, trade American options only.

amortize In portfolio accounting, periodic charges made against interest income received from premium bonds bought at a premium in anticipation of receipt of (1) the call price at call or (2) par value at maturity.

arbitrage Strictly defined, buying something where it is cheap and selling it where it is dear; for example, a bank buys 3-month CD money in the U.S. market and sells 3-month money at a higher rate in the Eurodollar market. In the money market, often refers: (1) to a situation in which a trader buys one security and sells a similar security in the expectation that the spread in yields between the two instruments will narrow or widen to his profit, (2) to a swap between two similar issues based on an anticipated change in yield spreads, and (3) to situations where a higher return (or lower cost) can be achieved in the money market for one currency by utilizing another currency and swapping it on a fully hedged basis through the foreign-exchange market.

asked The price at which securities are offered.

at-the-money option An option selling at a price such that it has zero intrinsic value.

away A trade, quote, or market that does not originate with the dealer in question; for example, "The bid is 98–10 away [from me]."

back contracts Futures contracts farthest from expiration.

back-to-back loan An example of a back-to-back loan would be IBM agreeing to lend dollars to British Petroleum in exchange for the latter lending pounds to IBM. Such agreements are struck when exchange controls in one or more countries prevent normal capital flows.

back up (1) When yields rise and prices fall, the market is said to back up. (2) When an investor swaps out of one security into another of shorter current maturity (e.g., out of a 2-year note into an 18-month note), he is said to back up.

bank discount rate Rate at which banks make loans priced on a discount basis.

bankers' acceptance (BA) A draft or bill of exchange accepted by a bank or trust company. The accepting institution guarantees payment of the bill.

bank line Line of credit granted by a bank to a customer.

bank notes Unsecured notes issued by a bank in the form of an MTN. No FDIC premium is paid by the issuing bank.

bank wire A computer message system linking major banks. It is used not for effecting payments, but as a mechanism to advise the receiving bank of some action that has occurred, for example, the payment by a customer of funds into that bank's account.

BANs Bond anticipation notes are issued by states and municipalities to obtain interim financing for projects that will eventually be funded long term through the sale of a bond issue.

basis (1) Number of days in the coupon period. (2) In *commodities* jargon, basis is the spread between a futures price and some other price. A money market participant would talk about *spread* rather than basis.

basis point 1/100th of 1%; also known as an 01 (pronounced *ooh one*).

basis price Price expressed in terms of yield to maturity or annual rate of return.

basis swap See **interest rate swap.**

BBA British Bankers Association.

bearer security A security the owner of which is not registered on the books of the issuer. A bearer security is payable to the holder.

bear market A declining market or a period of pessimism when falling market prices are anticipated. (Remember: "Bear down.")

best-efforts basis Securities dealers do not underwrite a new issue, but sell it on the basis of what can be sold. In the money market, this usually refers to a firm order to buy or sell a given amount of securities or currency at the best price obtainable over a given time period; it can also refer to a flexible amount (up to a limit) at a given rate.

bid The price offered for securities.

blind broker A broker who acts as principal and does not give up names to either side of a brokered trade. Blind brokering of securities is common, whereas blind brokering of Fed funds and Euro time deposits would be infeasible, since the seller must know the name of the buyer in order to ensure that he [the seller] does not exceed his preset credit lines to that name.

block A large amount of securities, normally much more than what constitutes a round lot in the market in question.

bond equivalent yield Usually, yield calculated so as to be directly comparable to yield to maturity as calculated for a U.S. Treasury note or bond.

book-entry securities The Treasury and federal agencies have largely moved to a book-entry system under which the securities they issue are not represented by engraved certificates; instead, for each issue, the Fed maintains computerized records of *interests* held by member banks in the issue; member banks, in turn, maintain computerized records (1) of securities they own and (2) of the securities they hold for customers. In the United States, many other money and bond market securities have gone or are going book entry; for some such securities, paper certificates still exist, but, the latter rarely, in some cases never, move from seller to buyer; instead, they are kept in a central depository, such as DTC, or by another agent.

book value The value at which a debt security is shown on the holder's balance sheet. A security's book value is often acquisition cost ± amortization/accretion, a number that may differ markedly from the security's market value. It can be further defined as *tax, accreted,* or *amortized* book value.

bp Market abbreviation for basis points. Thus, 1bp stands for 1 basis point, 10bp for 10 basis points.

bridge financing Interim financing of one sort or another.

British clearers The large clearing banks that dominate deposit taking and short-term lending in the U.K. sterling market.

Broken date See **cock date.**

broker A broker brings buyers and sellers together for a commission paid by the initiator of the transaction or by both sides; he does *not* position. In the money market, brokers are active in interbank markets for funds and in interdealer markets for securities and derivatives.

bullet-barbell swap The *bullet* bond must have a duration whose value lies between that of a barbell comprising a short-duration bond and a long-duration bond. The swap may call for buying the bullet and selling the barbell or vice versa. Typically, the purpose of a bullet-barbell swap is to change the convexity of the portfolio while holding its duration constant; such a swap may also result in a pick up of yield.

bullet loan A bank term loan that calls for no amortization. The term is commonly used in the Euromarket.

bullet (loan or security) All principal is due at maturity.

bull market A period of optimism when rising market prices are anticipated. (Remember: "Bull ahead.")

Bunds German government securities.

buy a spread Buy a near futures contract and sell a far one.

buy-back Another term for a repurchase agreement.

calendar List of new bond issues scheduled to come to market.

call An option that gives the holder the right, but not the obligation, to buy the underlier at a specified price during a specified period.

callable bond A bond that the issuer has the right to redeem prior to maturity by paying some specified call price.

call money Interest-bearing bank deposits that may be withdrawn on 24-hours' notice. Many Eurodeposits take the form of call money.

Canadian agencies Agency banks established by Canadian banks in the United States.

cap A series of options in which the writer guarantees the buyer, a payer of floating, that he will pay the buyer whatever additional interest he must pay on his loan if the rate on that loan goes above an agreed rate, *X*.

cash commodity or security The actual commodity or security as opposed to a futures contract for it.

cash management bill Short bill issues that the Treasury occasionally sells because it needs to replenish its cash balances before its next new issue will settle.

cash market Traditionally, this term has been used to denote the market in which commodities were traded, for immediate delivery, against cash. Since the inception of financial futures, a distinction has been made between the cash markets in which these securities trade for immediate delivery and the futures markets in which they trade for future delivery.

cash price Price quote in the cash market.

cash settlement In the money market, a transaction is said to be made for cash settlement if the securities traded are delivered against payment in Fed funds on the same day the trade is made—settlement occurs on the trade date.

CBOE Chicago Board Options Exchange, an options exchange.

CBT Chicago Board of Trade, a futures exchange.

certificate of deposit (CD) A time deposit with a specific maturity evidenced by a certificate. Large-denomination CDs are typically negotiable.

cheap Said of a fixed-income security that trades, relative to comparable securities, at a rather low price (i.e., at a rather high yield).

CHIPS The computerized Clearing House Interbank Payments System run by New York Clearing House. Most Euro transactions are cleared and settled through CHIPS rather than over Fed wire.

circle Underwriters, actual or potential as the case may be, often seek out and "circle" retail interest in a new issue before final pricing. The customer circled has basically made a commitment to purchase the new issue, at least if it comes at or below a stipulated price. In the latter case, if the price is higher than that stipulated, the customer supposedly has first offer at the actual price.

clean price The clean price of an interest-bearing security, is the price paid for principal. The clean price excludes accrued interest, which is included in the *dirty* price of such a security.

clear A trade is settled by the seller delivering securities versus the buyer delivering funds, both in proper form. A trade that does not clear is said to *fail.*

cock date In the Euromarket, an off-the-run period, for example, 28 days. Also referred to as a broken date. A cock date contrasts with a fixed date, which is 30, 60, 90, and so on, days hence.

collar A cap plus a floor.

commercial paper An unsecured promissory note with a fixed maturity of no more than 270 days. Commercial paper is normally sold at a discount from face value.

committed facility A legal commitment undertaken by a bank to lend to a customer.

competitive bid (1) Bid tendered in a Treasury action for a specific amount of securities at a specific yield or price. (2) Issuers, municipal and public utilities, often sell new issues by asking for competitive bids from one or more syndicates.

compound yield The effective yield earned when a simple yield is compounded.

confirm Abbreviation, widely used in the money and bond markets, for a confirmation. See **confirmation.**

confirmation A memo sent to the other side of a trade describing all relevant data: On trade date X for settlement on date Y, you bought (sold) a given face amount of a given security for a specified dollar sum.

consortium bank A merchant banking subsidiary set up by several banks that may or may not be of the same nationality. Consortium banks are common in the Euromarket and are active in loan syndication.

convertible bond A bond containing a provision that permits conversion of that bond into the issuer's common stock at some fixed exchange ratio.

convexity The slope of the price-yield relationship for a fixed-income security. Also, the rate of change of a bond's duration as its yield to maturity changes. Convexity is normally positive but can be negative. The property of convexity is additive; thus, a manager of a portfolio of bonds can calculate the convexity of that portfolio.

convexity of a bond portfolio Equals the weighted sum of the convexities of all bonds in the portfolio, where the weight applied to each bond is the market value of that bond.

to corner a market To obtain control of a market by purchasing a large amount of total supply in the market. A Treasury issue may be cornered only if the dominant buyers of that issue refuse to lend the issue in the reverse market and thereby force the issue to trade *special* in this market. See **squeeze.**

corporate bond equivalent See **equivalent bond yield.**

corporate taxable equivalent Rate of return required on a par bond to produce the same after-tax yield to maturity that the premium or discount bond quoted would.

country risk See **sovereign risk.**

to coup an auction In the Treasury market, to gain control of a new issue by buying a dominant position in that issue at auction. Currently, the Treasury has rules in place designed to prevent any one bidder from obtaining, during the auction of a new issue, any more than 35% of that issue.

coupon (1) The rate of interest that the issuer of a bond promises to pay holders of that bond annually on face value. (2) A certificate attached to a bond evidencing interest due on a coupon date.

coupon-payment currency A multicurrency FRN that's denominated in one currency may pay coupon interest in another currency. If the *coupon-payment currency* differs from the *denomination currency,* then the issuer must specify the source of the *exchange rate* quote he will use to convert the coupon interest due on each coupon date from the denomination currency to the coupon-payment currency.

coupon swap See **interest rate swap.**

cover To eliminate a short position by buying and delivering out securities shorted.

covered call write Selling calls against securities owned by the call seller.

covered interest arbitrage Investing one currency, say, dollars in an instrument denominated in another currency and hedging the resulting foreign-exchange risk by selling the proceeds of the investment forward for dollars.

credit enhancement The backing of paper with collateral, a bank LOC, or some other device to achieve a higher credit rating for the paper.

credit risk The risk that an issuer of debt securities or a borrower may default on his obligations, or that payment may not be made on sale of a negotiable instrument. (See **overnight delivery risk.**)

cross-currency swap An interest-rate swap in which the interest payments due are denominated in different currencies.

cross hedge Hedging the risk in a cash-market position by buying/selling a futures contract for a similar but not identical instrument.

CRTs Abbreviation for machines using cathode-ray tubes to display market quotes.

current coupon A bond selling at or close to par; that is, a bond with a coupon close to the yield currently offered on new bonds of similar current maturity and credit risk.

current issue In Treasury bills, notes, and bonds, the most recently auctioned issue. Trading is more active in current issues than in off-the-run issues.

current maturity Current time to maturity of an outstanding note, bond, or other money market instrument; for example, one year after issue, a 5-year note has a current maturity of four years.

current yield Current yield on a bond is the bond's annual coupon in dollars divided by its clean price in dollars.

curve risk The risk that an investor's holding period will differ from the current maturity of the bond he buys.

curve trader A trader who does arbitrages along the yield curve.

cushion bonds High-coupon bonds that sell at only a moderate premium because they are callable at a price below that at which a comparable noncallable bond would sell. In a falling market, cushion bonds offer considerable downside protection.

CUSIP number CUSIP is an acronym for the Committee on Uniform Securities Identification Procedures. Treasury securities, most federal credit agencies (including mortgage banks), municipal bonds, corporate stocks, and corporate bonds all have identifying CUSIP numbers. These numbers are assigned, for a fee, by Standard & Poor's.

dated date The date on which a bond begins to accrue interest.

daylight overdraft Being overdrawn (*OD*) in a deposit account during some period of a business day. A foreign bank typically runs a daylight overdraft with its U.S. correspondent bank; big U.S. banks run daylight overdrafts with the Fed; banks worldwide run daylight overdrafts with CHIPS. A daylight overdraft exposes the institution that extends it to a credit risk.

day trading Intraday trading in securities for profit as opposed to investing for profit.

dealer A dealer, as opposed to a broker, acts as a principal in all transactions, buying and selling for his own account.

dealer loan Overnight, collateralized loan made to a dealer financing his position by borrowing from a money market bank, usually his clearing bank.

debenture A bond secured only by the general credit of the issuer.

debt leverage The amplification in the return earned (positive or negative) on equity funds when an investment is financed partly with borrowed funds.

debt securities IOUs created through loan-type transactions: commercial paper, bank CDs, bills, notes, bonds, and other instruments.

default Failure to make timely payment of interest or principal on a debt security or to otherwise comply with the provisions of a bond indenture.

delivery month A month in which a futures contract expires and delivery may be taken or made.

delta hedge of an option A hedge of an option with a position in the underlier where the hedge ratio is based on the option's delta.

delta of an option The rate of change of the value of an option with respect to the price of the underlier, evaluated at the current market price of the underlier.

demand line of credit A bank line of credit that enables a customer to borrow on a daily or an on-demand basis.

denomination currency The par value of a *multicurrency* FRN must be denominated in a particular currency. Typically, the *denomination currency* is the currency in which the note is *priced.*

deposit note An FDIC-insured, negotiable time deposit issued by a bank in the form of an MTN, always with a maturity at issue of 18 months or longer.

depository institution (DI) A commercial bank, a savings bank, an S&L, a credit union, or any other institution accepting deposits. A U.S regulatory term.

direct paper Commercial paper sold directly by the issuer to investors.

direct placement Selling a new issue not by offering it for sale publicly, but by placing it with one or several institutional investors.

dirty price Price (for principal) *plus* accrued interest, if any, on an interest-bearing security.

discount basis See **discount rate.**

discount bond A bond selling below par.

discount house British institution that uses call and overnight money obtained from banks to invest in and trade money market instruments.

discount paper See **discount securities.**

discount rate Yield basis on which short-term, noninterest-bearing money market securities are quoted. A rate quoted on a discount basis is therefore not directly comparable to the simple yield paid by a number of money market instruments.

***the* discount rate** The rate of interest charged by the Fed to member banks that borrow at the discount window. The discount rate, belying its name, is an add-on rate.

discount securities Noninterest-bearing money market instruments that are issued at a discount and redeemed at maturity for full face value; for example, U.S. Treasury bills.

discount window Facility provided by the Fed to enable member banks to borrow reserves against collateral in the form of governments or other acceptable paper.

disintermediation The investing of funds that would normally have been placed with a bank or other financial intermediary directly into debt securities issued by ultimate borrowers; for example, into bills or bonds.

dispersion of a bond Dispersion is a time-weighted average of a bond's discounted cash flows where the weights are squares of particular times to particular cash flows. Dispersion measures the sensitivity of a bond's duration to time.

distributed After a Treasury auction, there will be many newly auctioned securities in dealers' hands. As dealers sell those securities to retail, the issue is said to be distributed.

diversification Dividing investment funds among a variety of securities offering independent returns.

DM Deutsche (German) marks.

documented discount notes Commercial paper backed by normal bank lines plus a letter of credit from a bank stating that it will pay off the paper at maturity if the borrower fails to do so. Such paper is also referred to as **LOC** (letter of credit) **paper.**

dollar bonds Municipal revenue bonds for which quotes are given in dollar prices. Not to be confused with *U.S. Dollar* bonds, a term commonly used in the Eurobond market.

dollar duration of a bond The duration of a bond times its market value.

dollar price of a bond Percentage of face value at which a bond is quoted; its *clean* price.

don't know (DK, DKed) "Don't know the trade"—a Street expression used whenever one party lacks knowledge of a trade or receives conflicting instructions from the other party (for example, with respect to payment).

due bill An instrument evidencing the obligation of a seller to deliver securities sold to the buyer. Occasionally used in the T bill market.

dumbell swap See **bullet-barbell swap.**

duration See **effective duration** and **Macaulay duration.**

duration-contraction swap An investor does a bond swap in which the duration of the bond he buys is less than the duration of the bond he sells. If the investor doing such a swap imposes the constraint that the swap not shorten the duration of his bond portfolio, he will have to add cash to his proceeds from the sale of the longer-duration bond in order to fund the purchase of a sufficient amount of the shorter-duration bond.

duration-extension swap An investor does a bond swap in which the duration of the bond he buys exceeds the duration of the bond he sells. If the investor doing such a swap imposes the constraint that the swap not lengthen the duration of his bond portfolio, he will have to invest some of the proceeds from the sale of the shorter-duration bond in cash (i.e., in a money market instrument).

duration of a bond portfolio Equals the weighted sum of the durations of all bonds in the portfolio, where the weight applied to each bond is the market value of that bond.

Dutch auction Auction in which the lowest price necessary to sell an entire new issue becomes the price at which all the issue offered is sold. This technique is again being used in Treasury auctions.

Edge Act corporation A subsidiary of a U.S. bank set up to carry out international banking business. Most such "subs" are located within the United States.

effective duration An approximation for the change in a bond's price given a small change in its yield to maturity. Often referred to on the Street simply as duration. The property of duration is additive; thus, a portfolio manager may calculate the duration of bond portfolio.

either/or facility An agreement permitting a bank customer to borrow either domestic dollars from the bank's head office or Eurodollars from one of its foreign branches.

either-way market In the interbank Eurodollar deposit market, an either-way market is one in which the bid and asked rates are identical.

elbow The elbow of a negatively-sloped yield curve is the maturity range, if any, at which the curve steepens. The elbow, if one occurs, is considered to provide an attractive maturity range for certain short-term investments, for example, the maturity range in which it's most attractive to initiate a ride along the yield curve.

eligible bankers' acceptances In the BA market, an acceptance may be referred to as eligible because it is acceptable by the Fed as collateral at the discount window and/or because the accepting bank can sell it without incurring a reserve requirement.

equivalent taxable yield The yield on a taxable security that would leave the investor with the same after-tax return he would earn by holding a tax-exempt municipal; for example, for an investor taxed at a 50% marginal rate, equivalent taxable yield on a muni note issued at 3% would be 6%.

Eurobond A bond issued in the Euro market outside the confines of any national capital market. A Eurobond may or may not be denominated in the currency of the issuer.

Euro CDs CDs issued by a U.S. bank branch or foreign bank located outside the United States. Almost all Euro CDs are issued in London and are denominated in dollars.

Eurocurrency deposits Deposits made in a bank or bank branch that is not located in the country in whose currency the deposit is denominated. Dollars deposited in a London bank are Eurodollars; German marks deposited there are Euromarks.

Eurodollars U.S. dollars deposited in a U.S. bank branch or a foreign bank located outside the United States. Also includes dollars deposited in U.S. International Banking Facilities (IBFs).

Euro Feds Eurodollars transmitted over the Fed wire instead of through CHIPS. Normally, Euro Feds move from a foreign branch of one U.S. bank to a foreign branch of another U.S. bank, for example, from Citi Nassau to Morgan London. Foreign banks use CHIPS, not the Fed wire, to pay and receive Euros because they may not run daylight overdrafts at the Fed.

Euro lines Lines of credit granted by banks (foreign or foreign branches of U.S. banks) for Eurocurrencies.

Euro MTNs An MTN issued in the Euromarket. See **MTNs.**

European option An option that may be exercised only at expiration of the option.

event risk The risk that a corporate bond will be downgraded, perhaps severely, due to some unpredictable outside event, principally a leveraged buy-out.

excess reserves Balances held by a bank at the Fed in excess of those required.

exchange rate The price at which one currency trades for another.

Ex-dividend date (bonds) During the period from the last coupon date up to, but not including the ex-dividend date, a bond with an ex-dividend date trades with accrued interest or *cum-dividend.* However, starting with the ex-dividend date, such a security trades *without the coupon,* which means that the next coupon payment will be paid to the holder of record as of the ex-dividend date, *not* to the holder as of the coupon-payment date. This practice is similar to the practice prevailing in equities markets, since an equity (stock) *always* trades ex-dividend after its *record* (ex-dividend) date.

exempt securities Instruments exempt from the registration requirements of the Securities Act of 1933 or the margin requirements of the Securities and Exchange Act of 1934. Such securities include governments, agencies, municipal securities, commercial paper, and private placements. Munis and governments are now regulated under separate and much later acts.

exercise To invoke the right to buy or sell granted under terms of an options contract.

exercise price The price at which an option holder may buy or sell the underlier. Also called the striking price.

expensive Said of a fixed-income security that trades, relative to comparable securities, at a rather high price (i.e., at a rather low yield).

extension swap Extending maturity through a swap, for example, selling a 2-year note and buying one with a slightly longer current maturity.

fail A trade is said to fail if on the settlement date either the seller fails to deliver securities in proper form or the buyer fails to deliver funds in proper form.

federal credit agencies Agencies of the federal government set up to supply credit to various classes of institutions and individuals; for example, S&Ls, small business firms, students, farmers, farm cooperatives, and exporters.

Federal Deposit Insurance Corporation (FDIC) A federal institution that insures bank deposits, currently up to $100,000 per deposit.

Federal Financing Bank A federal institution that lends to an array of federal credit agencies' funds, which it obtains by borrowing from the U.S. Treasury.

Federal funds (Fed funds) (1) Noninterest-bearing deposits held by member banks at the Federal Reserve. (2) Also, "immediately available" funds (e.g., when an interdealer trade in governments is cleared, delivery of securities bought is made versus payment in Fed funds).

Federal funds (Fed funds) rate The rate of interest at which Fed funds are traded. This rate is currently pegged by the Federal Reserve through open market operations.

Federal Home Loan Banks (FHLB) The institutions that regulate and lend to savings and loan associations. The Federal Home Loan Banks play a role analogous to that played by the Federal Reserve Banks vis-à-vis member commercial banks.

Fed funds See **Federal funds.**

Fed wire A computer system linking member banks to the Fed, used for making interbank payments of Fed funds and for making deliveries of and payments for Treasury and agency securities.

figuring the tail Calculating the yield at which a future money market instrument (one available some period hence) is purchased when that future security is created by buying an existing instrument and financing an initial portion of its remaining time to maturity with a term repo.

firm Refers to an order to buy or sell that can be executed without confirmation for some fixed period.

fixed dates In the Euromarket, the standard periods for which Euros are traded (one month out to a year) are referred to as the fixed dates.

fixed-dollar security A non-negotiable debt security that can be redeemed at some fixed price or according to some schedule of fixed values (e.g., bank deposits and government savings bonds).

fixed-income security An interest-bearing security that pays a fixed rate of interest and is redeemed at maturity at par.

fixed-rate loan A loan on which the rate paid by the borrower is fixed for the life of the loan.

flat trades (1) A bond in default trades flat; that is, the price quoted covers both principal and unpaid, accrued interest. (2) Any security that trades without accrued interest or at a price that includes accrued interest is said to trade flat.

flex repo A repo for a variable (usually declining) sum done for some period, often several years.

float The difference between the credits given by the Fed to banks' reserve accounts on checks being cleared through the Fed and the debits made to banks' reserve accounts on the same checks. Float is always positive, because in the clearing of a check, the credit sometimes precedes the debit. Float adds to the money supply.

floating-rate debt See **floating-rate note.**

floating-rate note (FRN) A note on which the coupon automatically resets on predetermined dates in step with changes in the level of interest rates as measured by some predetermined, market-determined index—3-month LIBOR, the 1-month T bill rate, and so on. The holder may have the right to demand redemption at par on specified dates.

floating short Especially, in a new Treasury issue, where big short positions are common, a *floating short* is said to exist if the amounts of the issue sold short exceed the amount of the issue sold by the Treasury *minus* the amounts of the issue bought by lock-it-up investors who aren't going to sell or lend the issue any time soon. Whenever a floating short exists in an issue, short positions in that issue exceed the amounts of the issue that shorts are easily able either to buy or to reverse in; and the issue trades on *special*—at a reverse rate below the repo rate for general collateral.

flower bonds Government bonds that are acceptable at par in payment of federal estate taxes when owned by the decedent at the time of death.

footings A British expression for the bottom line of an institution's balance sheet; total assets, which equal total liabilities plus net worth.

foreign bond A bond issued by a nondomestic borrower in a domestic capital market.

foreign-exchange rate The price at which one currency trades for another.

foreign-exchange risk The risk that a long or short position in a foreign currency might, due to an adverse movement in the relevant exchange rate, have to be closed out at a loss. The long or short position may arise out of a financial or a commercial transaction.

forward contract In Eurocurrencies, a contract under which a deposit of fixed maturity is agreed to at a fixed price for future delivery.

forward Fed funds Fed funds traded for future delivery.

forward market A market in which participants agree to trade some commodity, security, or foreign exchange at a fixed price at some future date.

forward rate The rate at which forward transactions in some specific maturity are being made; for example, the dollar price at which DM can be bought for delivery three months hence.

FRABBA The rate at which a FRA is to settle as established by the British Bankers Association.

FRAs Under a FRA, one party agrees to pay another some fixed rate for some defined period on a Eurodeposit having an agreed notional sum. If the FRA were for the 4s 5s, the agreement would concern a one-month rate to be paid four months hence. A FRA is settled at maturity by a cash payment, the amount and direction of which depends, inter alia, on the difference between the agreed forward rate and the prevailing market rate at the time of settlement.

free reserves Excess reserves minus member bank borrowings at the Fed.

full-coupon bond A bond with a coupon equal to the going market rate and consequently selling at or near par.

futures market A market in which contracts for future delivery of a commodity or a security are bought and sold.

future value (of a present amount of principal) The value at a future date of principal invested today at either a simple or a compound rate of interest.

gamma of an option The rate of change of the option's delta with respect to a change in the price of the underlier. Gamma measures the sensitivity of a delta-hedged position in an option to changes in the price of the underlier.

gap Mismatch between the maturities of a bank's assets and liabilities.

gapping Mismatching the maturities of a bank's assets and liabilities, usually by borrowing short and lending long.

gap trade A market is said to gap trade when prices in it move discontinuously from range to range in response to announcements of economic numbers.

general obligation bonds (GOs) Municipal securities secured by the issuer's pledge of its full faith, credit, and taxing power.

Gilts British government securities.

give-up The loss in yield that occurs when a block of bonds is swapped for another block of lower-coupon bonds. Can also be referred to as "after-tax give-up" when the implications of the profit (loss) on taxes are considered.

Glass-Steagall Act A 1933 act in which Congress forbade commercial banks to own, underwrite, or deal in corporate stock and corporate bonds.

go-around When the Fed offers to buy securities, to sell securities, to do repo, or to do reverses, it solicits competitive bids or offers, as the case may be, from all primary dealers. This procedure is known as a go-around.

good delivery A delivery in which everything—endorsement, any necessary attached legal papers, and so on—is in order.

good funds A market expression for immediately available money, that is, Fed funds.

good trader A Treasury coupon issue that can readily be bought and sold in size. If a trader can short $10 or $20 million of an issue and sleep at night, that issue is said to be a good trader.

governments Negotiable U.S. Treasury securities.

gross spread The difference between the price that the issuer receives for its securities and the price that investors pay for them. This spread equals the selling concession plus the management and underwriting fees.

haircut Margin in a repo transaction; that is, the difference between the actual market value measured at the bid side of the market and the value used in a repo agreement.

handle The whole-dollar price of a bid or offer is referred to as the *handle.* For example, if a T bond is quoted 101-10 bid and 101-11 offered, 101 is the handle. Traders are assumed to know the handle, so a trader would quote this market to another trader by saying he was at 10-11. (The 10 and 11 refer to 32nds).

hedge To reduce risk, (1) by taking a position in futures equal and opposite to an existing or anticipated cash position, or (2) by shorting a security similar to one in which a long position has been established.

hedge fund A hedge fund get its name from the fact that such a fund may use any tool—futures, derivatives, options, shorts, leverage—both to make and to hedge whatever positions it takes (*bets* it makes), whether the position be in fixed-income securities, stocks, commodities, or foreign exchange. Hedge funds are limited partnerships that, to escape SEC registration, accept no more than 99 limited partners. Belying its name, a hedge fund often takes big risk positions, and some have a track record of earning extraordinary annual rates of return. A hedge-fund's general partner—superstars include Soros and Steinhardt—has virtually unlimited power to take whatever positions he chooses; typically, he takes a management fee of 1% of assets invested and a slice—as much as 20%—of profits earned.

hit A dealer who agrees to sell at the bid price quoted by another dealer is said to *hit* that bid.

holding period The period over which a trader or investor holds or intends to hold a position.

holding-period yield Yield earned by a trader or investor on a given position over a given holding period.

IBFs (International Banking Facilities) Shell branches that U.S. banks may form in a number of states to do limited types of Eurobusiness.

IMM International Monetary Market, a futures exchange.

the IMM swap A swap of 1-year fixed against 3-month LIBOR, where the 3-month rate floats. The start, end, and intermediate reset dates are set to coincide with the dates on four successive IMM contracts for 3-month Eurodollars.

indenture of a bond A legal statement spelling out the obligations of the bond issuer and the rights of the bondholder.

index-linked bond An index-linked bond is a specific type of *variable-rate* instrument; it pays a *constant coupon rate,* but its *face or redemption value is adjusted* over its life to reflect changes in some specified index, most typically, the consumer price index.

interest-payment convention The convention, of which there are many, according to which a given interest-bearing security accrues and pays coupon interest.

in the box This means that a dealer has a wire receipt for securities indicating that effective delivery on them has been made. This jargon is a holdover from the time when Treasuries took the form of physical securities and were stored in a rack.

in-the-money option An option selling at a price such that it has intrinsic value.

interbank When interbank refers to a rate, as in "Japanese BAs trade at a spread to *interbank,*" the rate referred to is the interbank rate on Euro time deposits.

interest-rate exposure Risk of gain or loss to which an institution is exposed due to possible changes in interest-rate levels.

interest-rate swap An exchange by borrowers or asset holders of interest-rate payments at two different rates (often one rate is fixed, the other floating). In a *basis swap,* both rates are floating.

investment banker A firm that engages in the origination, underwriting, and distribution of new issues.

ISDA International Swap Dealers Association.

JGBs Japanese government bonds.

joint account An agreement between two or more firms to share risk and financing responsibility in purchasing or underwriting securities.

junk bonds High-risk bonds that have low credit ratings or are in default.

key-rate duration Duration defined to measure the sensitivity of a portfolio of bonds to a change in the shape of the yield curve.

leverage See **debt leverage.**

leveraged lease The lessor provides only a minor portion of the cost of the leased equipment, borrowing the rest from another lender.

LIBID The London Interbank Bid rate for Eurodollar time deposits of a given tenor.

LIBOR The London Interbank Offered Rate on Eurodollar deposits traded between banks. There is a different LIBOR rate for each deposit maturity. Different banks may offer slightly different rates, so when LIBOR is used as a benchmark (e.g., in an interest rate swap agreement), the rate used is always an average of the offered rates posted, at a given hour, Greenwich mean time, by an agreed-upon set of reference banks.

LIFFE London International Financial Futures Exchange.

lifting a leg Closing one side of a long-short arbitrage before the other side is closed.

LIMEAN The average of LIBOR and LIBID for Eurodollar deposits of a given tenor.

line of credit An arrangement by which a bank agrees to lend to the line holder during some specified period any amount up to the full amount of the line.

liquidity A liquid asset is one that can be converted easily and rapidly into cash without a substantial loss of value. In the money market, a security is said to be liquid if the spread between bid and asked prices is narrow and reasonable size can be done at those quotes.

liquidity diversification Investing in a variety of maturities to reduce the price risk to which holding long bonds exposes the investor.

liquidity risk In banking, risk that moneys needed to fund assets may not be available in sufficient quantities at some future date. Implies an imbalance in committed maturities of assets and liabilities.

locked market A market is said to be locked if the bid price equals the asked price. This can occur, for example, if the market is brokered and brokerage is paid by one side only, the initiator of the transaction.

lockup CDs CDs that are issued with the tacit understanding that the buyer will not trade the CD. The issuing bank may insist that it safekeep the CD to ensure that the understanding is honored by the buyer.

long (1) Owning a debt security, stock, or other asset. (2) Owning more than one has contracted to deliver.

***the* long bond** In the United States, the most recently auctioned 30-year Treasury bond.

long bonds Bonds with a long current maturity.

long coupons (1) Bonds or notes with a long current maturity. (2) A bond on which one of the coupon periods, usually the first, is longer than the others or than standard.

long hedge *Purchase* of a *futures* contract to lock in the yield at which an anticipated cash inflow can be invested.

Macaulay duration The time-weighted average of the discounted cash flows thrown off by a bond where each weight is the actual time that an investor would have to wait to receive that cash flow.

make a market A dealer is said to make a market when he quotes bid and offered prices at which he stands ready to buy and sell.

margin (1) In a repo or a reverse repurchase transaction, the amount by which the market value of the securities collateralizing the transaction exceeds the amount lent. (2) In a securities lending transaction, the amount by which the funds lent exceed the value of the securities lent. (3) In futures markets, the money that a buyer or seller must put up to ensure performance on the contracts into which he has entered. (4) In options, similar meaning as in futures for buyers and sellers of put and call options.

marginal tax rate The tax rate that would have to be paid on an additional dollar of taxable income.

marketability A negotiable security is said to have good marketability if there is an active secondary market in which it can easily be resold.

market value The price at which a security is trading and could presumably be purchased or sold.

mark to market Price all positions (securities and derivatives, if any) in a portfolio at current market price.

matched book (1) A nonbank dealer commonly runs a large matched book in repo. His objective is to earn a spread profit by reversing in securities at one rate and repoing them out at a slightly lower rate. A dealer may attempt to enhance the profitability of its matched book by mismatching maturities—by gapping, which might be to borrow short and to lend long. (2) If the distribution of the maturities of a bank's liabilities equals that of its assets, it is said to be running a *matched book.* The term is commonly used in the Euromarket.

match fund A bank is said to match fund a loan or other asset when it does so by buying (taking) a deposit of the same maturity. The term is commonly used in the Euromarket.

medium-term notes (MTNs) Continuously offered notes, having any or all of the features of corporate bonds and ranging in maturity from nine months out to 30 years. Bank deposit notes are a form of MTN.

merchant bank A British term for a bank that specializes not in lending out its own funds, but in providing various financial services, such as accepting bills arising out of trade; underwriting new issues; and providing advice on acquisitions, mergers, foreign exchange, portfolio management, and so on.

mismatch A mismatch between the maturities of a bank's interest-bearing assets and liabilities. See also **book** and **unmatched book.**

MM Market abbreviation for million. Thus, $10MM means $10 million.

modified duration An expression for the change in a bond's price given a small change in its yield to maturity.

MOF Multioption facility. A type of Eurobank line.

money market The wholesale market in which short-term debt instruments (bills, commercial paper, bankers' acceptances, etc.), is issued and traded.

Generally, money market paper has a high credit quality, but *junk* commercial paper is sometimes sold.

money market (center) bank A bank that is one of the nation's largest and consequently plays an active and important role in every sector of the money market.

money market certificates (MMCs) Six-month certificates of deposit with a minimum denomination of $10,000 on which banks and thrifts may pay a maximum rate tied to the rate at which the U.S. Treasury has most recently auctioned 6-month bills.

money market fund Mutual fund that invests solely in money market instruments.

money market yield (1) Simple yield of any short-term, fixed income security, calculated on a 360-day-year basis. (2) Yield on a discount security calculated as a simple yield on a 360-day-year basis. (3) Holding-period yield calculated over the current coupon period for an FRN is referred to as its money market yield.

money rate of return Annual return as a percentage of asset value.

money supply definitions promulgated by the Fed in January 1983:

M–1 Currency in circulation plus demand deposits plus other checkable deposits including NOW accounts.

M–2 M–1 plus money market deposit accounts plus overnight repos and money market funds and savings and small (less than $100,000) time deposits at all depository institutions plus overnight repos at banks plus overnight Euros held by nonbank U.S. depositors in the Caribbean branches of U.S. banks plus balances at money funds (excluding institutions-only funds).

M–3 M–2 plus large (over $100,000) time deposits at all depository institutions, term repos at banks and S&Ls plus balances at institutions-only money funds.

L M–3 plus other liquid assets such as term Eurodollars held by nonbank U.S. residents, bankers' acceptances, commercial paper, Treasury bills, and other liquid governments, and U.S. savings bonds.

mortgage bond Bond secured by a lien on property, equipment, or other real assets.

MTNs See **medium-term notes.**

multicurrency clause Such a clause on a Euroloan permits the borrower to switch from one currency to another on a rollover date.

municipal (muni) notes Short-term notes issued by municipal bodies in anticipation of tax receipts, proceeds from a bond issue, or other revenues.

municipals Securities issued by state and local governments and their agencies.

naked option position An unhedged sale of a put or call option.

naked position An unhedged long or short position.

nearby contract For a given futures contract (e.g., the U.S. Treasury bond futures contract), the contract nearest to expiration.

negative carry The *net* cost (often expressed as a rate differential) incurred when the cost of carry exceeds the current yield on securities being financed or when the reverse rate earned is less than the current yield on securities borrowed to cover a short.

negotiable certificate of deposit A large-denomination (generally $1MM face) CD that is negotiable but cannot be redeemed by the issuer before maturity.

negotiated sale Situation in which the terms of an offering are determined by negotiation between the issuer and the underwriter rather than through competitive bidding by underwriting groups.

new-issues market The market in which a new issue of securities is first sold to investors.

new money In a Treasury refunding, the amount by which the par value of the issues offered exceeds that of maturing issues redeemed.

NIF Note issuance facility, a type of Euro bank line associated with the issuance of Euronotes and Euro commercial paper.

NOB Note-bond spread a trader puts on by using futures contracts.

noncompetitive bid In a Treasury auction, bidding for a specific amount of securities at a price, whatever it may be, equal to the average price of the accepted competitive bids.

note Coupon issues with a relatively short original maturity are often called *notes.* Muni notes, however, have maturities ranging from a month to a year and pay interest only at maturity. U.S. Treasury notes are coupon securities issued with an original maturity of 2 to 10 years.

NOW (negotiable order of withdrawal) accounts. These amount to checking accounts on which depository institutions (banks and thrifts) may pay a rate of interest subject to federal rate lids.

OATs Acronym for debt securities issued by the French national government; these are properly titled *Obligations Assimilable du Trésor.*

observation date The indenture of every FRN specifies a rule stating on precisely what dates the value of the reference index must be observed for the purpose of determining the next coupon-rate reset.

OCC Options Clearing Corporation, the issuer of all listed options trading on U.S. options exchanges.

odd lot Less than a round lot.

offer Price asked by a seller of securities.

off-the-run issue In Treasuries and agencies, an issue that is not included in dealer or broker runs. With bills and notes, normally only *wi, current, old,* and *old, old* issues are included in a run.

old In the U.S. Treasury market, refers to the-next-to-most-recently-auctioned issue (e.g., the old 10-year would be the next-to-last 10-year note auctioned by the Treasury).

old old In the U.S. Treasury market, refers to the issue that preceded the next-to-most-recently-auctioned issue (e.g., the old, old 10-year would be the 10-year note that was issued preceding the next-to-last 10-year note auctioned by the Treasury).

one-man picture The price quoted in the brokers' market is said to be a one-man picture if both the bid and ask come from the same source.

one-sided (one-way) market A market in which only one side, the bid or the asked, is quoted or firm.

open book See **unmatched book.**

open repo A repo with no definite term. The agreement is made on a day-to-day basis, and either the borrower or the lender may choose, on any day, to terminate the repo. The rate paid is higher than on overnight repo and is subject to adjustment if rates move.

opportunity cost The cost of pursuing one course of action measured in terms of the forgone return offered by the most attractive alternative.

option (1) **Call option** A contract sold for a price that gives the holder the right to buy from the writer of the option, over a specified period, a specified amount of securities at a specified price. (2) **Put option:** A contract sold for a price that gives the holder the right to sell to the writer of the contract, over a specified period, a specified amount of securities at a specified price.

original maturity Maturity at issue. For example, a 5-year note has an original maturity at issue of five years; one year later, it has a current maturity of four years.

out-of-the-money option An option selling at a price such that it has negative intrinsic value.

overnight delivery risk A risk brought about because differences in time zones between settlement centers require that one party to a trade make a payment or a delivery and not know, until the next day, whether his counterparty has deposited an appropriate amount of securities or funds in his account. Particularly apparent where delivery occurs in Europe for payment in dollars in New York.

over-the-counter (OTC) market A market created by dealer-to-dealer or dealer-to-customer trading as opposed to the auction market prevailing on an organized exchange. Many OTC markets are brokered.

paper Money market instruments: commercial paper and other securities.

paper gain (loss) Unrealized capital gain (loss) on securities held in portfolio, based on a comparison of current market price to original cost.

par (1) Price of 100%. (2) The principal amount at which the issuer of a debt security contracts to redeem that security at maturity, *face value.*

parallel loan An example of a parallel loan would be IBM agreeing to lend dollars to a sub of British Petroleum in exchange for the latter lending pounds to an IBM British sub. Such agreements are struck only when exchange controls in one or more countries prevent normal capital flows.

par bond A bond selling at par.

partial-payment-in-kind bond (partial-pay PIK) A partial-pay PIK has a *coupon,* but on a coupon date, it does *not* pay out the *full* coupon interest due. Instead, it pays *only part* of that amount. The *unpaid portion* of the coupon interest due *accumulates;* and the sum of that accumulated unpaid coupon interest is paid out when the partial-pay PIK matures.

pass-through A mortgage-backed security on which payment of interest and principal on the underlying mortgages are passed through to the security holder by an agent.

paydown In a Treasury refunding, the amount by which the par value of issues maturing exceeds that of new issues sold.

payment-in-kind bond (PIK) A PIK is a bond that carries a coupon but makes *no* periodic payments of coupon interest. Instead, unpaid coupon interest on a PIK *accumulates* and is paid in full when the PIK matures.

pay-up (1) The loss of cash resulting from a swap into higher-priced bonds. (2) The need (or willingness) of a bank or other borrower to pay a higher rate to get funds.

pickup The gain in yield that occurs when a block of bonds is swapped for another block of higher-coupon bonds.

picture The bid and asked prices quoted by a broker for a given security.

placement A bank depositing Eurodollars with (selling Eurodollars to) another bank is often said to be making a placement.

plus Dealers in governments often quote bids and offers in 32nds. To quote a bid or offer in 64ths, they use pluses; for example, a dealer who bids 4+ is bidding the handle plus 4⁄32 + 1⁄64, which equals the handle plus 9⁄64.

PNs Project notes are issued by municipalities to finance federally sponsored programs in urban renewal and housing. They are guaranteed by the U.S. Department of Housing and Urban Development.

point (1) 00bp = 1% = 1 point. (2) One percent of the face value of a note or bond. (3) In the foreign-exchange market, the lowest level at which the currency is priced. Example: "One point" is the difference between sterling quoted at $1.8080 and sterling quoted at $1.8081.

portfolio Collection of securities held by an investor.

position (1) To go long or short in a security. (2) The amount of securities owned (long position) or owed (short position).

positive carry The *net* gain earned when the cost of carry is less than the yield on the securities being financed.

premium (1) The amount by which the price at which an issue trades exceeds the issue's par value. (2) The amount in excess of par that an issuer must pay to call or to refund an issue before that issue matures. (3) In money market parlance, the fact that a particular bank's CDs trade at a rate higher than others of its class, or that a bank has to pay up to acquire funds.

premium bond A bond selling above par.

prepayment A payment made ahead of the scheduled payment date.

present value (of a future payment) The value today of a future payment discounted at an appropriate rate of interest.

presold issue An issue that is sold out before the coupon announcement.

price elasticity of a bond The ratio of a small percentage change in a bond's price to a small percentage change in its yield to maturity.

price risk The risk that a debt security's price may change due to a rise or fall in the going level of interest rates.

prime rate The rate at which banks lend to their best (prime) customers. The all-in cost of a bank loan to a prime credit equals the prime rate plus the cost of holding compensating balances if the latter are required.

principal (1) The face amount or par value of a debt security. (2) One who acts as a dealer (as opposed to an agent) and who buys and sells for his own account.

principal-payment currency A *multicurrency* FRN that's denominated in one currency may repay principal in some other currency. If the *principal-payment* currency *differs* from the *denomination currency,* then the issuer must specify the source of the *exchange-rate quote* he will use to convert the par value of the FRN stated in the denomination currency to the equivalent par value stated in principal-payment currency.

private placement An issue that is offered to a single or to a few investors as opposed to being publicly offered. Private placements do not have to be registered with the SEC.

prospectus A detailed statement prepared by an issuer and filed with the SEC prior to the sale of a new issue. The prospectus gives detailed information on the issue and on the issuer's condition and prospects.

put An option that gives the holder the right to sell the underlying security at a specified price during a fixed time period.

range markets Markets with lots of sidewise motion.

RANs (revenue anticipation notes) These notes are issued by states and municipalities to finance current expenditures in anticipation of the future receipt of nontax revenues.

rate risk (1) In general, the risk that the value of a position will be adversely affected by a rise or fall in interest rates. (2) In banking, the risk that profits may be adversely affected because a rise in interest rates raises the cost of funding fixed-rate loans or other fixed-rate assets.

ratings An evaluation given by Moody's, Standard & Poor's, Fitch, or other rating services of a security's creditworthiness.

real market The bid and offer prices at which a dealer could do size. Quotes in the brokers' market may reflect not the real market but pictures painted by dealers playing trading games.

"red" futures contract month A futures contract in a month more than 12 months away; for example, in November, the Dec (pronounced Dees) bond contract would mature 1 month later, the red Dec bond contract 13 months later.

red herring A preliminary prospectus for a new issue that contains all information required by the SEC except for the offering price and the coupon.

reference index Every FRN has a reference index upon which the calculation of each successive new coupon is based.

refunding Redemption of outstanding bonds funded by the sale of a new bond issue.

registered bond A bond whose owner is registered with the issuer.

regular (way) settlement In the U.S. money and bond markets, the *regular* way trades in governments and many other securities are settled is that delivery of the securities purchased is made against payment in Fed funds on the next business day following the transaction.

Regulation D Fed regulation that required member banks to hold reserves against their net borrowings from foreign offices of other banks over a seven-day averaging period. Reg D has been merged with Reg M.

Regulation Q Fed regulation imposing lids on the rates that banks may pay on savings and time deposits. Currently, time deposits with a denomination of $100,000 or more are exempt from Reg Q.

reinvestment rate (1) The rate at which coupon payments received by an investor from a debt security can be reinvested over the life of that security. (2) Also, the rate at which funds from a maturity or sale of a security can be reinvested. Often used in comparison to *give-up* yield.

reinvestment risk The risk that an investor will have to reinvest the successive coupons dropped by a bond he buys at yields less than the yield to maturity at which he bought his bond.

reopen an issue Occasionally, the Treasury, when it wants to sell additional securities, will sell more of an existing issue (reopen it) rather than offer a new issue.

repo See **repurchase agreement.**

repurchase agreement (repo or RP) A holder of securities sells these securities to an investor with an agreement to repurchase them at a fixed price on a fixed date. The security "buyer" in effect lends the "seller" money for the period of the agreement, and the terms of the agreement are structured to compensate the lender of money for this. Dealers use repo extensively to finance their positions. Exception: When the Fed is said to be doing repo, it is lending money to banks and dealers, which has the effect of increasing bank reserves.

reserve requirements The percentage of different types of deposits that depository institutions are required to hold on deposit at the Fed in noninterest-bearing reserve accounts.

reset frequency The indenture of every FRN incorporates a *reset-frequency* rule for determining the dates upon which the issue's coupon will be reset.

retail Individual and institutional customers as opposed to dealers and brokers.

revenue bond A municipal bond secured by revenue from tolls, user charges, or rents derived from the facility financed.

reverse See **reverse repurchase agreement.**

reverse repurchase agreement Most typically, a repurchase agreement initiated by the lender of funds. Reverses are used by dealers to borrow securities they have shorted. Exception: When the Fed is said to be doing reverses, it is borrowing money, that is, it is absorbing bank reserves.

revolver See **revolving line of credit.**

revolving line of credit A bank line of credit on which the customer pays a commitment fee and may take down and repay funds according to his needs. Normally, the line involves a firm commitment from the bank for a period of several years.

rho of an option The rate of change of the value of an option with respect to the risk-free rate of interest.

risk Degree of uncertainty of return on an asset or on any position in financial instruments.

roll over Reinvest funds received from a maturing security in a new issue of the same or a similar security.

rollover Most term loans in the Euromarket are made on a rollover basis, which means that the loan is periodically repriced at an agreed spread over the appropriate, currently prevailing LIBOR rate.

rollover yield Holding-period yield calculated over the current coupon period for an FRN is referred to as its rollover or money market yield.

round lot In the money market, round lot refers to the minimum amount for which dealers' quotes are good. This may range from $100,000 to $5MM, depending on the size and liquidity of the issue traded.

RP See **repurchase agreement.**

RUF A revolving underwritten facility. A type of Euro line associated with the issuance of Euro notes and of Euro commercial paper.

run A run consists of a series of bid and asked quotes for different securities or maturities. Dealers give runs and, in brokered markets, so too do brokers.

S&L See **savings and loan association.**

safekeep (1) For a fee, banks will safekeep (i.e., hold in their vault or in their book-entry account, collect coupons on, and present for payment at maturity) bonds and money market instruments; also, referred to as bank custody. (2) For customers, most dealers will safekeep, at their custody bank, for no fee any securities that that customer has bought from them; repo, combined with dealer safekeeping of the collateral, is the risk equivalent of an unsecured loan.

sale repurchase agreement See **repurchase agreement.**

savings and loan association (S&L) Federal- or state-chartered institution that accepts savings deposits and invests the bulk of the funds thus received in mortgages and other fixed-income securities.

savings deposit Interest-bearing deposit that is made at a depository institution and that has no specific maturity.

scale A bank that offers to pay different rates of interest on CDs of varying maturities is said to "post a scale." Commercial paper issuers also post scales.

scalper A speculator who actively trades a futures contract in the hope of making small profits off transitory upticks and downticks in price.

seasoned issue An issue that has been distributed well and that trades well in the secondary market.

secondary market The market in which previously issued securities are traded.

sector Refers to a group of securities that are similar with respect to maturity, type, rating, and/or coupon.

Securities and Exchange Commission (SEC) Agency created by Congress to protect investors in securities transactions by administering securities legislation.

sell a spread Sell a nearby futures contract and buy a far one.

serial bonds A bond issue in which maturities are staggered over a number of years.

settle See **clear.**

settlement date The date on which a trade is cleared by delivery of securities against funds. The settlement date may be the trade date or a later date.

shell branch A foreign bank branch—usually in a tax haven—which engages in Eurocurrency business but is run out of a head office.

shop In Street jargon, a money market or bond dealership.

shopping Seeking to obtain the best bid or offer available by calling a number of dealers and/or brokers.

short A market participant assumes a short position by selling securities he does not own. The seller makes delivery by borrowing the securities sold or reversing them in.

short bonds Bonds with a short current maturity.

short book See **Unmatched book.**

short coupons Bonds or notes with a short current maturity.

short hedge Sale of a futures contract to hedge, for example, a position in cash securities or an anticipated borrowing need.

short sale The sale of securities not owned by the seller (1) in the expectation, by the seller, that the price of the securities sold will fall or (2) as part of an arbitrage. A short seller must eventually *cover* his short sale by purchasing the securities he has shorted.

short squeeze A squeeze that's inimical to the interests of entities that have shorted a security. See **squeeze.**

short the board Sell T-bond or other financial futures contracts traded on the CBT.

SIMEX The Singapore futures exchange.

simple margin For an FRN, the yield measure, *simple margin, takes into account any required amortization of a premium or accretion of a discount over the FRN's remaining term to maturity.* The simple margin offered by an FRN is the sum of (1) the required amortization of a premium or accretion of a discount, measured in basis points, plus (2) the FRN's spread over the index rate, also measured in basis points.

simple yield Yield on an interest-bearing security figured with *no allowance for compounding.* Simple yield may be calculated on a discount security; in that case, it is the rate of discount converted to the equivalent simple interest rate.

simple yield to maturity An algebraic expression for calculating yield to maturity on a bond. Simple yield to maturity is easy to calculate, but it only *approximates* a bond's actual yield to maturity because it does not properly *discount* future cash flows.

sinking fund Indentures on corporate issues often require that the issuer make annual payments to a sinking fund, the proceeds of which are used to retire randomly selected bonds in the issue.

size Large in size, as in "size offering" or "in there for size." What constitutes size varies from one sector of the money market to another.

skip-day settlement The trade is settled one business day beyond what is normal.

sovereign bonds Bonds issued by the national government of a sovereign state.

sovereign risk The special risk, if any, that attaches to a security (or deposit or loan) because the borrower's country of residence differs from that of the investor's. Also referred to as **country risk.**

special issue An issue is said to be special or to go on special when, because it is much sought after by short sellers, it can be reversed in only at a reverse rate that lies below the repo rate for general collateral.

specific issues market The market in which dealers reverse in an issue they have shorted or want to short. Typically, the reverse rate on such an issue lies below the repo rate for general collateral.

spectail A dealer that does business with retail but concentrates more on acquiring and financing its own speculative position.

spot market Market for immediate as opposed to future delivery. In the spot market for foreign exchange, settlement occurs two business days after the trade date.

spot rate The price prevailing in the spot market.

spread (1) Difference between bid and asked prices on a security. (2) Difference between yields on or prices of two securities of differing sorts or differing maturities. (3) In underwriting, difference between price realized by the issuer and price paid by the investor. (4) Difference between two prices or two rates. (5) What a trader of commodities, spot and future, would refer to as the *basis*.

spreading In the futures market, buying one futures contract and selling another to profit from an anticipated narrowing or widening over time of the spread between prices of (or rates on) the two contracts.

spread to reference index Typically, an issuer of an FRN specifies that each new coupon paid by that issue will be set at a *spread* to the specified *reference index.*

squeeze In a Treasury issue, a squeeze is evidenced in two ways: (1) the issue typically trades *expensive* to the yield curve, and (2) the issue goes *on special* in the reverse market, so that a trader who must borrow the issue to cover a short receives on the funds he lends a rate significantly less than the repo rate on general collateral. A squeeze may occur naturally or may result from market manipulation.

stepped-coupon bond A bond that promises to pay the investor a coupon rate that will be increased by a fixed amount on one or more fixed dates.

stop-out price The lowest price (highest yield) accepted by the Treasury in an auction of a new issue.

striking price See **exercise price.**

STRIPs STRIP is an acronym for Separate Trading of Registered Interest Principal. Dealers create *zero-coupon* STRIPs by dividing Treasury bonds into pieces comprising each periodic coupon payment and one corpus (principal) payment. When an issue is stripped, the corpus is assigned a unique CUSIP number, and each coupon payment is assigned a *generic* CUSIP number that is applied to *all* coupon payments due, on a specified date, from *all* strippable bonds.

stub Refers to the *short* part of a *long* first coupon period.

subject Refers to a bid or offer than cannot be executed without confirmation from the customer.

subordinated debenture The claims of holders of this issue rank after those of holders of various other unsecured debts incurred by the issuer.

sub right Right of substitution—to change collateral—on a repo.

swap (1) In securities, selling one issue and buying another. (2) In foreign exchange, buying a currency spot and simultaneously selling it forward.

swap rate In the foreign-exchange market, the difference between the spot and forward rates at which a currency is trading.

swaption An option on an interest-rate swap.

swing line See **demand line of credit.**

Swissy Market jargon for Swiss francs.

switch British English for a swap.

TABs (tax anticipation bills) Special bills that the Treasury occasionally issues. These bills mature on corporate quarterly income tax dates and can be used at face value by corporations to pay their tax liabilities.

tail (1) The difference between the average price in a Treasury auction and the stop-out price. (2) A future money market instrument (one available some period hence) created by buying an existing instrument and financing the initial portion of its life with term repo.

take (1) A dealer or customer who agrees to buy at another dealer's offered price is said to take that offer. (2) Eurobankers speak of taking deposits rather than buying money.

take-out (1) A cash surplus generated by the sale of one block of securities and the purchase of another, for example, selling a block of bonds at 99 and buying another at 95. (2) A bid made to a seller of a security that is designed (and generally agreed) to take him out of the market.

taking a view A London expression for forming an opinion as to where interest rates are going and acting on it.

TANs Tax anticipation notes issued by states or municipalities to finance current operations in anticipation of future tax receipts.

technical condition of a market Demand and supply factors affecting price, in particular the net position—long or short—of dealers.

technicals (1) Supply and demand factors influencing the cash market. (2) Value or shape of technical indicators.

TED spread The spread between T-bill futures and Eurodollar futures.

tenor Maturity.

term bonds A bond issue in which all bonds mature at the same time.

term Fed funds Fed funds sold for a period longer than overnight.

term loan Loan extended by a bank for more than the normal 90-day period. A term loan might run five years or more.

term repo (RP) Repo borrowings for a period longer than overnight; may be 30, 60, or even 90 days.

term structure of interest rates The relationship for zero-coupon bonds between yield to maturity and term to maturity.

theta In options pricing, the rate at which the value of an option changes as time passes.

thin market A market in which trading volume is low and in which consequently bid and asked quotes are wide and the liquidity of the instrument traded is low.

TIBOR LIBOR as established in Tokyo.

tick Minimum price movement on a futures contract.

tight market In a tight, as opposed to a thin, market, trading is active; and the spread between the bid and offer is narrow.

time deposit Interest-bearing deposit made at a depository institution and having a specific maturity.

Tom next In the interbank market in Eurodollar deposits and in the foreign-exchange market, the value (delivery) date on a Tom next transaction is the next business day. (Refers to "tomorrow next.")

trade date The date on which a trade is done. The settlement date may be the trade date or a later date. Confirms always specify both the trade date and the settlement date.

to trade numbers To trade securities based on the release of a new *economic statistic* (*number*); for example, trading based on announcement of the latest number for the CPI, the U.S. trade deficit, and so on.

trade on top of Trade at a narrow or no spread in basis points to some other instrument.

to trade "tight" An issue that's being squeezed is said to "trade tight" in the cash market, to trade "special" in the finance market. See **squeeze.**

trading paper CDs purchased by accounts that are likely to resell them. The term is used in the Euromarket.

treasurer's check A check issued by a bank to make a payment. Treasurer's checks outstanding are counted as part of a bank's reservable deposits and as part of the money supply.

Treasury bill A noninterest-bearing discount security issued by the U.S. Treasury to finance the national debt. Most bills are issued to mature in 3 months, 6 months, or 1 year.

TT&L account Treasury tax and loan account at a bank.

turnaround Securities bought and sold for settlement on the same day.

turnaround time The time available or needed to effect a turnaround.

two-sided market A market in which both bid and asked prices, good for the standard unit of trading, are quoted.

two-way market A market in which both a bid and an asked price are quoted.

underlier The thingamabob against which an option is written. The underlier may be a stock, a bond, a futures contract, oil, land, whatever.

underwriter A dealer who purchases new issues from the issuer and distributes them to investors. Underwriting is one function of an investment banker.

unmatched book If the average maturity of a bank's liabilities is less than that of its assets, it is said to be running an unmatched book. The term is commonly used in the Euromarket. Equivalent expressions are **open book** and **short book.**

value date In the market for Eurodollar deposits and foreign exchange, value date refers to the delivery date of funds traded. Normally, on a spot transaction, the value date is two days after a transaction is agreed upon; on a forward transaction (e.g., in foreign exchange), the value date is the future date specified in the forward agreement.

variable-price security A security, such as stocks and bonds, that sells at a fluctuating, market-determined price.

variable-rate CDs Short-term CDs that pay interest periodically on *roll* dates; on each roll date, the coupon on the CD is adjusted to reflect current market rates.

variable-rate loan Loan made at an interest rate that fluctuates with the prime rate.

variable-rate notes Notes that pay a rate of interest pegged to some benchmark rate or price.

visible supply New muni bond issues scheduled to come to market within 30 days.

when-issued trades Typically, there is a lag between the time at which a new bond is announced and the time at which this new security is actually issued. During this interval, the security trades **wi,** "when, as, and if issued."

wi When, as, and if issued. See **when-issued trades.**

wi wi T bills trade on a wi basis between the day they are announced and the day they are settled. Late Tuesday and on Wednesday, two bills will trade wi, the bill just auctioned and the bill just announced. The latter used to be called the wi wi bill. However, now it is common for dealers to speak of the just auctioned bill as the 3-month bill and of the newly announced bill and the wi bill. This change in jargon resulted from a change in the way interdealer brokers of bills list bills on their screens. Cantor Fitzgerald still lists a new bill as the wi bill until it is settled.

without If 70 were bid in the market and there was no offer, the quote would be "70 bid without." The expression *without* indicates a one-way market.

write an option To sell an option.

Yankee bond A foreign bond issued in the U.S. market, payable in dollars, and registered with the SEC.

Yankee CD A CD issued in the domestic market (typically in New York) by a branch of a foreign bank.

yield curve A graph showing, for fixed-income securities that expose the investor to *no* credit risk, the relationship between current maturity and yield to maturity. Yield curves are typically drawn using yields on governments of varying current maturities.

yield-pickup swap A standard two-bond in which the investor buys one bond and sells another with the intention of increasing yield while holding duration constant.

yield to average life (1) On asset-backed securities, such as mortgage backs, refers to the yield that the investor would earn if the collateral underlying the security he owns is paid off according to some assumed schedule. (2) The average yield the investor can expect to earn on a bond, the indenture of which provides for scheduled redemptions.

yield to call Yield to maturity calculated on the assumption that a callable bond will be called on its first call date.

yield to maturity The rate of return yielded by a debt security held to maturity when both interest payments and the investor's capital gain/loss on the security are taken into account.

INDEX

D

E

F

G

H

I

J-L

M

N

O

P

R

S

V

W

Y

Z

Notation Used in This Book (All Rates Are in Decimal Form)

Symbol	*Variable Denoted*
y	Simple yield: the annual rate at which interest accrues
n	Compounding periods during one year
y_c	Effective yield with compounding on a money market instrument; also, current yield on a bond
y^*	Breakeven yield
y_{360}	Simple yield (360-day basis); also referred to as *money market yield*
y_{365}	Simple yield (365-day basis)
y_{be}	Bond equivalent yield
y_{tm}	Yield to maturity; also, internal rate of return; also, stated yield to maturity for a bond on a quote sheet
y_{hp}	Holding-period yield
y_w	Yield-to-maturity divided by the number of coupon periods per year: $y_w = y_{tm}/w$
y_s	Simple yield on a bond
r	Rate
r_{re}	Reinvestment rate; the rate at which all coupons on a bond are assumed to be reinvested
r_{rp}	Repurchase (*rp*) rate; also known as the repo rate
r_t	Term repo rate
r_{rv}	Reverse (*rv*) rate; also known as the resale (*rs*) rate, reverse repurchase rate, or simply reverse rate.
r^*	Breakeven rate
r^*_{rp}	Breakeven repo (*rp*) rate
r^*_{rv}	Breakeven reverse (*rv*) rate
r_{wh}	Rate of withholding tax
d	Rate of discount on a T bill or other discount security
d_1	Rate of discount at the beginning of a transaction
d_2	Rate of discount at the end of a transaction
d^*	Breakeven sale rate on a bill *tail*
d_p	Rate at which a discount security is bought
d_s	Rate at which a discount security is sold
c	Coupon rate
I	Dollar amount invested
D_p	Dollar amount of discount on a discount security
F	Face value of a security; also, for a bond, nominal value against which coupon interest is calculated; typically, $F = 100$
cF	Annual coupon on a note or bond in denomination currency
C	Periodic coupon payment, $C = cF/w$
C_n	Next coupon payment; value reflects long or short first or last coupon periods
R	Redemption value, which is the principal amount to be paid by the issuer or borrower at maturity; typically, $R = 100$
P	Price of a bond excluding accrued interest; referred to as *clean* price or *flat* price
AI	Accrued interest from last coupon-payment date to settlement date (as measured by the appropriate day-count convention)
B	Price of a bond including accrued interest, referred to as the *dirty* price of a bond: $B = P + AI$
B_h	Dirty price of a bond for a 1 basis point *decrease* in yield
B_l	Dirty price of a bond for a 1 basis point *increase* in yield
K	Number of dropped coupons
C_k	*k*th *periodic* coupon payment